A Light in the Darkness

Janusz Korczak, His Orphans, and the Holocaust

Albert Marrin

THE FERGUSON LIBRARY
ONE PUBLIC LIBRARY PLAZA
STAMFORD, CONNECTICUT 06904

Alfred A. Knopf

New York

THIS IS A BORZOI BOOK PUBLISHED BY ALFRED A. KNOPF

Text copyright © 2019 by Albert Marrin
Public domain: front cover photos and back cover group photo
Back cover: Korczak portrait © BPK Bildagentur/Art Resource, NY;
dormitory photo by Roman Wroblewski
Jacket art (clouds) used under license from Shutterstock.com

All rights reserved. Published in the United States by Alfred A. Knopf,
an imprint of Random House Children's Books, a division of
Penguin Random House LLC, New York.

Knopf, Borzoi Books, and the colophon are registered trademarks of
Penguin Random House LLC.

For picture credits, please see page 381.

Visit us on the Web! GetUnderlined.com

Educators and librarians, for a variety of teaching tools, visit us at
RHTeachersLibrarians.com

Library of Congress Cataloging-in-Publication Data is available upon request.

ISBN 978-1-5247-0120-8 (trade) — ISBN 978-1-5247-0121-5 (lib. bdg.) —
ISBN 978-1-5247-0122-2 (ebook)

The text of this book is set in 12.2-point Sabon MT Pro.

Printed in the United States of America
September 2019
10 9 8 7 6 5 4 3 2 1

First Edition

Random House Children's Books supports the First Amendment
and celebrates the right to read.

For the innocents.
May they never be forgotten.
May a better world grow out of their suffering.

I wanted to discuss the suffering of humanity in general, but perhaps we'd better confine ourselves to the sufferings of children.

—FYODOR DOSTOYEVSKY,
The Brothers Karamazov (1880)

CONTENTS

PROLOGUE

The Two Saddest Nations on Earth

Gone now are those little towns where the wind joined
Biblical songs with Polish tunes and Slavic rue,
Where old Jews in orchards in the shade of cherry trees
Lamented for the holy walls of Jerusalem.

Gone now are those little towns, though the poetic mists,
The moons, winds, ponds, and stars above them
Have recorded in the blood of centuries the tragic tales,
The histories of the two saddest nations on earth.

—Antoni Słonimski, "Elegy for the Little Jewish Towns" (1947)

If you want to visit that place from Warsaw, the capital of Poland, it is best to go by automobile. You can drive yourself or hire a car and a guide for about eighty dollars. With a little luck, the sixty-mile trip should take just over two hours.

Upon leaving Warsaw, located on both sides of the Vistula River, head northeast on the highway that parallels the Warsaw-Białystok railroad, which goes to the Russian border. About two miles after crossing a bridge over the River Bug, you must turn right at the village of Małkinia Junction. Here the road follows a branch line linking to the main rail line from the southeast. You are almost there. Another three and a half miles brings you to a

quiet village nestled beside the tracks. You can't miss it. The road sign says TREBLINKA.

Beginning in July 1942, engines towing boxcars crammed with Jewish people from Warsaw left the Treblinka station on a newly built two-mile-long sidetrack, or spur. Twice a day, every day, rain or shine, slow-moving trains passed through a damp, sandy plain dotted with marshes and pinewoods. After a while, iron wheels screeched to a halt at the gate of the Treblinka extermination camp.

During World War II (1939–1945), in which 47 million Europeans perished, over 60 percent of them civilians, Treblinka played a key role in the Holocaust—*Shoah* in Hebrew. Both terms refer to the effort by Nazi Germany, ruled by Adolf Hitler, to murder first Polish Jews, then all Jews in the countries German armies conquered. History records countless atrocities. Yet the

The railroad station at the Polish village of Treblinka, where transports stopped on the way to the Treblinka death camp. (Date unknown)

Holocaust is unique, because it is the only time a nation's leaders had the goal of systematically murdering every man, woman, and child of an ethnic or religious group. As British prime minister Winston Churchill said at the time: "There is no doubt that this is probably the greatest and most horrible crime ever committed in the whole history of the world."[1]

By the close of 1942, after only 155 days of operation, an astounding 713,555 people—an average of 4,600 a day, or almost 200 an hour—nearly all Jews, had died in Treblinka's gas chambers. Auschwitz, the best-known and most infamous camp, also killed Jews, about 1.2 million, plus a quarter of a million non-Jewish Poles and Gypsies. Besides being an extermination center, Auschwitz was a massive complex of factories served by tens of thousands of slave laborers. Treblinka was a factory, too, though designed to "manufacture" a single product—human corpses. In its time, it was the most lethal spot on planet Earth.[2]

Today, visitors to Treblinka park a short distance from the campsite. Then they walk along a line of concrete sleepers, symbols of the wooden rail ties that supported the tracks over which the death trains rolled. Unlike Auschwitz, whose buildings survive, nothing of the original camp remains. To hide their crimes, in 1943, as Soviet armies advanced, the Nazis bulldozed Treblinka. Now a visitors' center sells guidebooks, diagrams, and DVDs, but not T-shirts; few tourists would dream of wearing a garment bearing the name of such a place.

To enter the campsite is to enter a world of stone monuments. Stones are important in the Jewish tradition; Jews leave stones, rather than flowers, as signs of respect at gravesites. The main

monument at Treblinka is a massive stone structure, twenty-six feet in height. It is dedicated to the memory of the Jews murdered there, the vast majority of them Polish. No nation suffered as did Poland during World War II. The first victim of Nazi aggression, Poland had a prewar population of 33 million, and approximately one-tenth, or 3.3 million, of its people were Jewish. When the war ended, the Nazis had killed no fewer than 6 million Poles, of whom about half were Jewish.

A symbolic stone "cemetery" surrounds the main monument. It is symbolic, for Treblinka's victims have no graves. After people were gassed, the Nazis buried and later disinterred and burned their bodies. The cemetery consists of seventeen hundred jagged pieces of granite of various sizes set in concrete. Each piece represents a Polish community from which the Nazis sent Jews to Treblinka. The sizes are proportional to the number of Jews killed from a given place. Many of the smallest stones have no inscriptions at all. This indicates that those communities, tiny as they were, entirely disappeared. Not a soul survived.

One granite stone rises above the rest, and it bears a word in Polish: "Warszawa." This is as it should be, for what English speakers call Warsaw was the most Jewish of cities, its community second in size only to New York's. On the eve of World War II, 1.2 million people lived in Warsaw, of whom 375,000 were Jewish, a number equal to the entire Jewish population of France. A center of business, learning, and the arts, the city was, for Eastern European Jews, *the* place of opportunity. Jews who sought the chance to rise in the world went to Warsaw to study and work.[3]

Only a single stone at Treblinka bears a person's name. The English translation of the memorial inscription reads:

Janusz Korczak
(Henryk Goldszmit)
And the Children

Janusz Korczak was the pen name of Henryk Goldszmit—Henry Goldsmith in English. Korczak, the name by which he is best known, was a Polish Jewish physician, educator, humanitarian, and visionary. Admirers have compared him to Mother Teresa, Martin Luther King Jr., and the ancient Greek philosopher Socrates. He was also an internationally known author whose

The *Korczak Memorial Stone* at Treblinka. The Polish words *i dzieci* on the stone translate to "And the children." (2010)

books on child rearing, published nearly a century ago, are classics, as are his novels for children. Translations of Korczak's *King Matt the First* are still in print and enjoyed by youngsters the world over.[4]

Among the world's foremost champions of children's rights, Korczak worked his whole life for the benefit of children, especially the disadvantaged. Early in the last century, he gave up a thriving medical practice to become director of Dom Sierot, a Jewish orphanage in Warsaw. In doing so, he earned the nicknames "Stary Doktor" (Old Doctor), "Pan Doktor" (Mister Doctor), and "Father of Orphaned Children."

Korczak's ultimate goal was nothing less than reforming the world by changing adults' ideas about raising children. His philosophy, like a well-cut diamond, has many facets. Yet it boils down to this passage from his book *How to Love a Child*. "Children," he wrote, "are not the people of tomorrow, but people today. They are entitled to be taken seriously. They have a right to be treated by adults with tenderness and respect as equals. They should be allowed to grow into whatever they were meant to be. The unknown person inside each of them is the hope of the future."[5]

Janusz Korczak, c. 1930.

The Old Doctor understood that children depend on adults, because that is nature's way. Given this fact, the question was, How should adults use their power? Since every child is worthy of respect, it follows that every child is inherently precious, "a person born to be free." Thus, Korczak insisted, children do not exist to serve adults' national, political, economic, or religious aims. Children are people in their own right, not merely adults in the making. Adults must cherish them for themselves, not as living material to be sorted, shaped, molded, counted, cataloged, managed, regulated, regimented, bullied, programmed, trained, directed, commanded, worked, and indoctrinated.

Korczak never wavered in his beliefs. In 1940, the Nazis caged Polish Jews in ghettos, segregated walled-in sections of cities meant as the starting point on the road to extermination. When herded with his children into the Warsaw ghetto, the Old Doctor could have escaped with the help of gentile (non-Jewish) friends. Instead, duty overruled self-interest, even the impulse of self-preservation. The inscription on his memorial stone, "And the Children," refers to the orphanage children he accompanied into Treblinka's gas chambers.

An ancient Jewish belief holds that as long as "Thirty-Six Hidden Righteous Ones" are living on earth, God will allow humanity to continue. For their sake alone, it is said, the Almighty spares the too-wicked human race. Janusz Korczak supposedly belonged to this righteous group during his lifetime. Similarly, many Polish Catholics regard him as a holy man, "a saint, although not a Christian." Pope John Paul II, who was born and raised in Poland, called him "a symbol of true religion and true morality."[6]

Important as it is, the Old Doctor's story is also part of a far larger and more complex one, still relevant today. That other story raises profound questions. How could Germany—one of the modern world's most cultured and advanced nations—have murdered millions of innocents? Art, music, film, physics, chemistry, medicine, philosophy, engineering: Germany was a leader and innovator in all these fields. That such a nation was seduced by a man whose personal physician declared him "a devil" is still a matter of wonder. What made Adolf Hitler so fiendish? How was he able to corrupt Germany's young, turning them into tools of aggression?[7]

The "anti-Korczak" in every way, Hitler is among the most fascinating and most evil people who ever lived. "If Hitler isn't evil, who is?" asks his biographer Alan Bullock. "Hitler redefined the meaning of evil forever." He remains the gold standard of evil. But was he insane? If so, it might be a comfort, because we could easily dismiss him as "abnormal." Yet most psychiatrists who have studied him agree that Hitler was not crazy, at least not in the clinical sense. Though given to raging tantrums, he was a highly intelligent man with a first-class memory. Regardless, he was a madman of a special kind. Hitler was what we may call a "lunatic of one idea," an obsession that dominated his very being.[8]

Adolf Hitler's "one idea" was racism, the belief that a particular race is superior to all others. Yet he did not invent racism. Throughout history, people have often, perhaps usually, judged others not by the content of their character but by their appearance, ancestry, beliefs, and social position. Supposedly, a "superior" race is handsomer, smarter, braver, and more creative

and has "higher" moral values than its "inferiors." Such beliefs have satisfied "superior" people's egos and served their interests, justifying economic exploitation and the denial of civil rights—everything from segregation to slavery.

Today, social scientists consider racism the "witchcraft of our time," an outbreak of superstition with roots in ancient fears of people different from the majority or dominant group. Countless studies show that racism, like witchcraft, has no basis in scientific fact. According to a UNESCO Statement on Race, "mankind is one." All humans belong to the same species, *Homo sapiens,* descendants of ancestors who originated in East Africa some two million years ago. Humans share the same genetic heritage. Intelligence seems evenly distributed, each branch of the human family tree having roughly similar proportions of low-, average-, and high-intellect members. Color differences are literally skin-deep, the result of adaptations, over long periods, to extreme climate conditions. Thus, for example, light skin helps increase vitamin D exposure in areas with little sun, and dark skin helps protect against harmful ultraviolet rays in regions of intense sunlight, but skin color says nothing about one's character, intellect, abilities, or morals.[9]

Racism can be manifest in different ways and to different degrees. To give a revealing example: Since ancient times, slaveholders aimed to control their human "property" through violence and, when "necessary," murder. Nevertheless, they did not wish to destroy all slaves; that would have been economic insanity, for slaves cost money and created wealth for those who lived off their labor. Similarly, one can say, "I hate you. You deserve no civil rights."

However, that is a far cry from saying, "Because you are who you are, you and all like you, even your youngest, deserve to die."

Racism as an ideology, or worldview, is most sinister. As used in this book, the term *ideology* refers to a set of beliefs held as the master key to how human affairs work. Ideology makes every action fall into its proper place, like the splinters of a shattered mirror magically rejoined. An ideology explains all that has happened with people, is happening now, and will happen in the future. It is also a textbook on how to live, work, think, play, educate, and, yes, reproduce. For example, the ideologies of Communists and Marxists, followers of the nineteenth-century German economist Karl Marx, explain human activity in terms of how the economy operates and who controls it. In contrast, Adolf Hitler saw race as *the* force shaping human existence. "The racial question," he wrote, "gives the key not only to world history, but to all human culture."[10]

Martin Luther King Jr. understood the threat posed by racist ideology. The civil rights leader warned about it in his 1967 speech "The Other America," declaring that "in the final analysis, racism is evil because its ultimate logic is genocide"—the extermination of a racial, cultural, or religious group. When judged by scientific fact, Hitler's "one idea" is ridiculous. But that does not matter. Ideas have consequences. And even though an ideology may be ridiculous, if people believe it firmly, and if they are willing to act on their belief, the ideology is *effectively* true in its outcomes.[11]

This book is not a biography in the traditional sense of a detailed account of a person's life. Instead, I explore two themes as embodied in Janusz Korczak and Adolf Hitler, the humanitarian

and the racist fanatic. The first deals with their conflicting views of children: as valuable in themselves or as useful tools for achieving "higher" goals. Second, we must see how Hitler's racist ideology shaped his rule in Germany and conduct of World War II. What he began by attacking Poland in 1939 was no ordinary conflict. Nations have always fought over territory, resources, and prestige, but Hitler saw these as mere means to an end: world domination by the German "master race" and the extermination of the "racially inferior." As Hermann Göring, second only to Hitler as a leader of Nazi Germany, declared: "This is not the Second World War, but the Great Racial War."[12]

Children were central to Hitler's ideology. He valued children of the "master race" as instruments for achieving his goals— hideous child abuse masked as a high ideal. In Hitler's mental world, however, a Jewish child was identical to a disease that had to be eradicated. The numbers he destroyed are astounding. Only 11 percent of Jewish children aged sixteen and under survived in countries occupied by his armies. The Nazis were so thorough that in 1945 a Russian Jewish soldier wept when he came upon an eight-year-old girl in a Polish town. She was the first Jewish child he'd seen in an advance of more than a thousand miles.[13]

Obviously, the subject matter of history is not always pleasant, and this particular subject is immensely sad. "Truth hurts," my granny, a lady who saw a lot in her lifetime, used to say. As a historian, I strive to keep that bit of wisdom in mind. My duty is to try to understand, and help others understand, the truth about the past, warts and all. History matters to us today. It matters not because it offers lessons for dealing with similar situations. How

could it? After all, the past is past; having happened, an event can never repeat itself exactly. History matters because, as Pope John Paul II reminds us, "there is no future without memory." Knowing about the past is essential to shaping our future. History reminds us about the crimes humans are capable of while serving an ideology. And it also reminds us that history itself is not destiny. We see that even in the worst of times, humans have choices and are capable of decency, love, and mercy.[14]

The Old Doctor

I exist not to be loved and admired, but to love and act. It is not the duty of those around me to love me. Rather, it is my duty to be concerned about the world, about man.

—Janusz Korczak, *The Ghetto Years* (1942)

Starting Out

We have little information about Henryk Goldszmit's life story. Except for his diary, written in the three months before his death, all his personal papers were lost or destroyed during World War II. Much of what we know was recorded by friends and acquaintances, recalling what he had told them, or appears in his letters to them.

Even the exact date of his birth is uncertain. This we do know: The future champion of children's rights was born in Warsaw in July 1878 or 1879—probably 1878. The uncertainty is due to his father's failure to register his son's birth, as required by law, for several years. At the time of Henryk's birth, Poland was not an independent nation. In 1795, aggressive neighbors had banded together to overrun the country. Russia, Austria, and the German state of Prussia divided Poland among themselves. Russia took

the lion's share and declared Warsaw the capital of "Russian Poland." By falsifying his birthday, Henryk's father may have hoped to postpone, or even avoid, his son's being drafted into the army of the Russian czar. Other parents scrimped and saved to send their draft-age sons to America.[1]

Of Henryk's ancestors, we know nothing. His father, Józef Goldszmit, was an attorney specializing in divorce cases. Józef's own father, Hirsz Goldszmit, was a beloved country doctor who spoke German fluently and gave his five children Christian-sounding names like Maria and Magdalena. Józef's wife, Cecylia Gebicka, had an artisan background; her grandfather was a glazier, a person who puts glass in windows and mirrors. The couple had two children: Henryk and his younger sister, Anna. Anna's life and fate are a mystery to us.

Though not fabulously wealthy, the Goldszmit family was quite comfortable. Thanks to Józef's lucrative law practice, they lived in an elegantly furnished apartment in an upscale neighborhood. Servants earned low wages, so the family could easily afford a full-time cook and maid. A French governess saw to the children's education in a room set aside as a study, outfitted with bookcases, blackboards, and desks.

Young Henryk had no friends his own age and played alone with blocks and his sister's dolls. His snobbish mother thought other children, most of all poor children, were not good enough for her precious darling. Poor children, she insisted, were dirty and smelly, cursed, and fought like alley cats. Henryk's refuge from boredom was the kitchen, the domain of a wise peasant woman from the countryside. She would sit him on a high stool

as if he were "a human being and not a lapdog on a silk cushion." For hours, she told Polish folktales about dark forests inhabited by magicians and wizards, goblins and heroes. Her stories stirred the child's imagination, inspiring the master storyteller who'd endear himself to generations of children.[2]

Henryk's parents thought their son was too childish, too unfocused. His mother complained, "This boy has no ambition." He remembered how "my dad called me a gawk and a clod and, when he flew into a rage, even an idiot and an ass. . . . All I ever heard was—lazy, crybaby, idiot . . . and good-for-nothing."[3]

When Henryk turned seven, he attended a Russian elementary school. This grim place operated on the belief that the human mind was a muscle that would grow flabby if not toughened by exercise. Exercise, or "mental gymnastics," consisted of memorization and repetition, accepting approved "truths" without questioning. When called upon, pupils were expected to recite the correct answer word for word, like parrots.

Believing children were "untamed," teachers used strict discipline. Students had to sit still in class, at rigid attention, for long periods. "Why should they move their heads sideways," Henryk recalled a teacher asking, "when I am in front of them?" Rule breaking brought humiliating punishment. Years later, he cringed when remembering how a classmate was beaten for a harmless prank. A janitor spread out the offender on a desk while the teacher stood over him and hit him with a switch, a slender rod used as a whip. "I was terrified. It seemed to me that when they finished with him, I would be next. I was ashamed, too, because they beat him on his bare bottom. They unbuttoned everything—in

Janusz Korczak at age ten. (1888)

front of the whole class." The lesson: Adults did not respect children. Children were seen as tiny wheels in the great machine that was the adult world. They existed, Henryk decided, to live up to their elders' expectations and demands, not to be themselves in the here and now.[4]

The Goldszmit family's fortunes changed in the early 1890s. Normally a serious, self-controlled man, Józef began to act oddly. He would remain silent for hours, his eyes cast down, his face tense, and would then burst out incoherently. One day, in the courtroom, he stopped questioning a witness in mid-sentence. Arms flailing, he shouted: "They're here, they've come after me; go away. That's not my witness in the box, it's the devil come to mock me. Send him away, away." Doctors diagnosed a mental breakdown.[5]

Józef spent years in and out of mental hospitals. Family visits were an ordeal. Henryk heard screams and curses and saw wild-eyed people trussed in straitjackets, long-sleeved canvas garments used to bind the arms as a means of restraint. To calm patients, orderlies plunged them, straitjackets and all, into ice baths. "I was scared to death of the mental hospital to which my father was

taken several times," Henryk recalled years later. "I was the son of an insane man; it was an inheritance I had to live with." Henryk feared he might inherit his father's illness. Józef Goldszmit died in August 1896, possibly by his own hand. He was fifty-two years old.[6]

Józef had been the family breadwinner, so his illness and death caused a crisis. Savings vanished. Cecylia dismissed the servants. To make ends meet, she sold possessions—jewelry, silverware, carpets, and paintings—for a fraction of their value. Eventually, the Goldszmits left their luxurious apartment for a smaller, cheaper one in a run-down neighborhood.

Eighteen-year-old Henryk became the man of the house. At the end of the high school day, he earned a little money by tutoring children in mathematics, science, and Polish literature. He loved literature. At night, after finishing his homework, he wrote stories, plays, and poems. An untitled poem, dark and brooding, captures his mood at this time. Hoping a magazine editor would accept the poem for publication, Henryk read it to him with exaggerated emotion:

> *Ah, let me die!*
> *Don't let me live!*
> *Ah, let me descend into my dark grave!*

The editor cut him short. "I'll let you!" he told the budding poet. The effect on Henryk was like that of snow falling on delicate blossoms. He never wrote another poem.[7]

Around this time, the young man faced questions we must all

answer while growing up: Who am I? What is to become of me? What path should I take in life? How shall I earn a living? Henryk decided to become a doctor like his grandfather. Doctors earned a decent living and were respected. Besides, medicine seemed the best way to help others. "I am not going to be a writer but a doctor," he said. "Literature is words, medicine is deeds." So in 1898 the twenty-year-old enrolled in the medical school at the University of Warsaw.[8]

Yet Henryk never lost his enthusiasm for writing. In the same year he began his medical studies, he gained a new name. During odd moments, he wrote a play titled *Which Way?*, about the impact of mental illness on a family. When he heard about a literary competition sponsored by the famed Polish pianist Ignacy Paderewski, he submitted the play. Unknown as a writer, he thought he would have a better chance of winning the competition if he had a Polish-sounding pen name. He had come across *The Story of Janasz Korczak and the Swordbearer's Daughter* and decided to borrow the name of the novel's title character. However, the printer misspelled the first name and listed the playwright as "Janusz Korczak." Before long, Henryk adopted that name, by which the world knows him. We will use it here from now on.[9]

Though medical school was Korczak's main focus, he disliked the professors—aging men set in their ways and seemingly detached from the sufferings of the sick. Pompous know-it-alls, they drilled "dead facts from dull pages" into students' heads. Naturally, they resented the young man's outspoken criticisms. One

professor growled: "Hair will grow on the palm of my hand before you become a doctor."[10]

The professor was wrong. During his medical school years,
Korczak revealed an admirable quality—empathy, the capacity to
instinctively identify with another person and to share that person's feelings. Every big city had its slums, places "respectable"
folk steered clear of. New York had the Lower East Side, London
the East End. Warsaw had the Old Town, a district dating from
the Middle Ages, with grim tenements lining the Vistula River.
On nights off, Korczak and a friend, the poet Ludwik Licinski,
prowled Warsaw's mean streets. Licinski recalled: "Janusz knew
every nook and cranny; he knew the Old Town much better than
I did. . . . Together we were visiting brothels and taverns; at night
we were knocking about on the sandy beaches of the Vistula; we
were celebrating prostitutes' name days, and guzzling revolting,
rancid vodka with cutthroats." For the first time, Korczak saw
abandoned children, ragged, abused, homeless boys and girls begging for morsels of food.[11]

"Janusz," Licinski added, "played human hearts with incomparable mastery." He had a way of saying the right thing, at the
right time, in the right tone. A peacemaker, he broke up vicious
street fights, crying, "I beg you, good people! Why the blood?
We're all rascals. You . . . and you . . . and me. All of us. Don't
our heads get enough of a pounding as it is without us trying
to kill each other?" Sometimes he captivated hard men, capable
of murder, by telling a fairy tale in a calm, soothing voice. He
kissed street children on the forehead, and they flocked to him.

A little thief apologized, "Because you kissed me on the forehead. It made me sorry for what I did."

"Was it so strange to have someone kiss you?" the medical student asked.

"Yes, my mother is dead. I don't have anyone to kiss me anymore."[12]

It was no accident that Korczak's first book was a novel titled *Children of the Streets*. Published in 1901, it dealt with the ravages of poverty and neglect on society's most vulnerable.

Nor is it accidental that Korczak specialized in pediatrics, the branch of medicine dealing with the care of babies and children. After receiving his medical degree in March 1905, he began his residency in the Bersohn and Bauman Children's Hospital, which, though funded by Jewish charities, served all children. Korczak had barely settled into his position when he received a draft notice. Russia and Japan were at war, and he was called to serve as a doctor, with the rank of lieutenant, in the Russian Imperial Army. Little did he know that this would be the first of four wars in which he would serve.

The army sent Korczak to Manchuria, a region in northeastern China, aboard a hospital train on the Trans-Siberian Railway. Though the war was an important learning experience, he hated every minute of it. War revealed humanity at its worst, a carnival of waste and stupidity and cruelty. Korczak treated hideously wounded soldiers shrieking in pain and men driven mad by the sights and sounds of battle. He also worked in famine-stricken Chinese villages filled with dying children. "War is an abomination," he wrote in a magazine article. "Especially because no one

reports how many children are hungry, ill-treated, and left without protection." For the lieutenant, children always came first. "Before you go to war for any purpose," he told a group of rebellious Russian soldiers, "you should stop and think of the innocent children who will be injured, killed, or orphaned."[13]

In September 1905, a peace treaty brokered by U.S. president Theodore Roosevelt ended the Russo-Japanese War. When Korczak returned to Warsaw early the next year, a civilian again, he found that he had become a celebrity. Shortly before he'd left for the front, his second novel had hit the bookshops. Titled *Child of the Drawing Room,* it was based on his own experiences as a pampered, overprotected child. In his absence, the novel had become the talk of the town; everybody who was anybody read it, praised it, and longed to meet its author.

Thanks to that book, Korczak's medical practice thrived. The wealthy, Jew and gentile alike, boasted that he'd visited their homes to treat their children. At the slightest bellyache, they summoned him. Though he charged these parents high fees, he was often short-tempered with them. When, for example, a mother insisted her child should drink tea, he huffed: "If your child needed to drink tea, God would have given you milk in one breast, and tea in the other." However, when Korczak visited poor families, usually late at night, he was the soul of gentleness. To set a sick child at ease, he would sit beside her bed, pat her hands, and tell a story about each finger. He charged a minimal fee, if anything, and many times even left his own money to buy medicine.[14]

In 1909, Korczak received an invitation to a party to raise money for the Jewish Society for the Help of Orphans. The small

orphanage that the organization already funded occupied a ramshackle building and was run by a poorly trained staff. Rather than throw good money after bad, the society's directors decided to start over, and on a grand scale. They fired the old staff, hired a new one, and moved the orphanage to temporary quarters.

When Korczak arrived at the party, a guest introduced him to Stefania Wilczyńska. The daughter of a wealthy textile manufacturer, Wilczyńska was a thoroughly "modern woman." Well educated, a rarity for Jewish women at that time, she had recently graduated from the University of Liège in Belgium with a degree in natural science. The twenty-three-year-old was eight years younger than the doctor and several inches taller, at five feet eight inches. No beauty, Wilczyńska was heavyset, with dark, serious eyes. Her face, a woman who knew her recalled, was as "wide as a yeast cake, with warts sprinkled like raisins over it."[15]

Wilczyńska ran the temporary orphanage as a volunteer. During their conversation, she told Korczak about her work and how important it was, inviting him to visit. Whenever he had an hour or two to spare, he stopped by to play with the children, which he enjoyed as much as they did. Visits by the balding man with the thick eyeglasses and pointy goatee felt like holidays. He always seemed relaxed, and his pockets held endless treasures: candy, marbles, magic tricks. His fairy tales enchanted them, as they had the thugs he'd met during his ramblings in the Old Town.[16]

Gradually, something dawned on him: The only hope for humanity lay in bettering the lives of children. That insight brought him to a turning point. Janusz Korczak had become a successful pediatrician with a bright future. Should—or could—he abandon

that profession to pursue an ideal? While he struggled with the question, the society's directors, who saw great promise in him, made an offer. They would name him director of the new orphanage, with Wilczyńska as his chief assistant. Moreover, he would have the final say in designing the building and its program.

It was an offer Korczak could not refuse.

Stefania Wilczyńska. (Date unknown)

He explained: "I deserted medicine, I deserted the bodies of sick children, I abandoned the medical profession to become—of all things—a sculptor of the child's soul, to find myself floating in unknown waters! In so doing, I arrived at the world's greatest hurdle: guiding the future of the healthy child." That mission became his whole life. For reasons he never made clear, Korczak, the child's champion, decided not to marry or have children of his own.[17]

Dom Sierot, the Children's Home

Korczak's ideas became iron and wood, glass and brick, in 1912. Everything about the new building was different, including its name: Dom Sierot, which means "orphans' home" in Polish. Note: *home,* not *orphanage.* The director's choice of this name was deliberate, meant to highlight a break with the past. Orphanages had a bad reputation. Traditionally, they were warehouses for castaways, children without parents or those sent there by parents unable to care for them. Orphanages were often gloomy, crowded, unsanitary places ruled by fear and brutality. A child might resort to a life of crime rather than stay in such a so-called Bastille, a reference to the old Paris fort that doubled as a prison.

Located at 92 Krochmalna Street, in a run-down Catholic neighborhood, Dom Sierot was a spacious four-story building. Korczak lived in the attic. His room had a bed, a few chairs, a bookcase, and a huge desk that had belonged to his father, and he shared it with a mouse who ran about freely. The director fed his four-footed guest breadcrumbs, and it stayed close to home, never leaving the attic to explore the rest of the building. Wilczyńska, Korczak's assistant, had a room on the second floor. Sparsely furnished, it had, she wrote a friend, "a narrow, Spartan bed, as if no one had ever slept in it. A table—a small one . . . a chest of drawers, [and] a nice, old-fashioned wash-basin in a corner by the door." Though tiny, the room was enough for her.[18]

Dom Sierot had all the modern conveniences: electric lights, tiled bathrooms, flush toilets, faucets for hot and cold water, and a well-stocked library. Boys and girls slept in separate dormito-

Dom Sierot before World War II. Korczak's room is at the top. (c. 1939)

ries in rows of beds set two feet apart. Residents ranged in age from seven to fourteen. Korczak admitted any needy Jewish child if there was an opening. But he made certain exceptions to "avoid weeds that will choke the flowers"—that is, children who would demand so much attention as to prevent the others from developing as they should.[19]

In the summer of 1914, barely two years after Dom Sierot opened its doors, World War I exploded. Russia joined the Allies (Great Britain, Canada, Australia, Belgium, Italy, Japan, and, in 1917, the United States to fight Germany, Austria-Hungary, Bulgaria, and the Ottoman Empire, modern-day Turkey). Again, Korczak received a draft notice to report for duty in the czar's army. This was his second war, and his duties in a divisional field

hospital only deepened his hatred of war. This terrible conflict, this "orgy of devils," had submerged "all the world . . . in blood and fire, in tears and mourning."[20]

The director's departure left "Madame Stefa," as Wilczyńska now liked people to call her, to run the children's home by herself. She rose to the challenge. Visitors likened her to a Swiss watch— always prompt, organized, efficient. "I am," she said, "neither an accomplished speaker nor a prolific writer. I can only work hard, though slowly and cautiously." When the German Army occu- pied Warsaw in August 1915, high-ranking officers visited Dom Sierot, having heard of its innovations. Impressed by what they saw, they tried to question Madame Stefa about the place and her life there. "I have no personal matters," she said, brushing past them. "Everything concerns the children."[21]

Despite its early victories, Germany lacked the population and resources to defeat the Allies even after a revolution toppled the czar, forcing Russia to make peace on German terms. America's declaration of war in April 1917 was the last straw, ending any chance of a German victory. In November 1918, Germany sued for peace. According to the terms of the armistice, or cease-fire, Germany would immediately withdraw from all occupied terri- tory. Thus, after 123 years of foreign rule, Poland regained its in- dependence. By separate agreements, Russian and Austrian forces left Poland as well.

Upon returning to the orphans' home, Korczak described what had happened in terms a young child could understand. "It is nice to have your own drawer or closet, for then it is absolutely your own, and a place where no one else has a right to poke about

without your permission. . . . But, unfortunately, someone stronger . . . takes away your things, and dirties the room, and will not listen to you." Poland had been like a room taken over by stronger nations. Now it was independent.[22]

Korczak had barely hung up his uniform when he received a summons to his third war, this time in the army of the Polish Republic. The Russian Revolution had ignited a civil war, ending in victory for the Bolsheviks, another name for Communists. As a result, imperial Russia became the Soviet Union, an immense nation the Bolsheviks ruled with an iron hand. In 1920, Vladimir Lenin, the Soviet dictator, invaded Poland, the gateway to Western Europe, as the first step in a world revolution. "The road to worldwide conflagration will run over the corpse of Poland," he declared.[23]

Though Lenin's Red Army outnumbered Poland's army by five to one, Poles had no intention of submitting to the despised Russians. In the Battle of Warsaw (August 12–25, 1920), they performed what many called a miracle. Not only did they smash the invader, they saved Western Europe from Bolshevik invasion. Major Korczak was thrilled. "Warsaw is mine, and I am hers," he wrote. "We are one. Together with her, I have rejoiced and I have grieved. . . . Warsaw has been my workshop; here are my landmarks and my graves."[24]

Proud Varsovians—residents of Warsaw—declared their home "a city of the future," a symbol of modernity. The government spent lavishly on the capital, building roads, bridges, and airports. Theaters, art galleries, and film companies sprang up like mushrooms after a rainstorm. Warsaw became a center for the study of

mathematics and the sciences—biology, chemistry, and physics. Marie Curie, discoverer of the radioactive elements radium and polonium, opened her Radium Institute, a research facility and hospital, in Warsaw. She was the first woman awarded a Nobel Prize, and she was the first person to receive two Nobels, one in physics and one in chemistry.

Dom Sierot flourished, too, under its director and guiding spirit, though Korczak wasn't always recognizable as such to those meeting him for the first time. Once, for instance, a would-be donor came upon a man in a threadbare green smock puttering around in the front yard. Mistaking him for the janitor, he asked where he could find the doctor. The "janitor" shrugged, went inside, put on his jacket, returned, and introduced himself. The visitor was so startled that he left without saying a word.[25]

The children could not get enough of Korczak. Whenever he came downstairs, a former resident recalled, "children would rush around him from all sides and not leave him alone." The moment he sat down, children piled onto his lap, so many that he resembled "a tree with many small birds on it." He would slide down the main banister, laughing all the way. His sense of humor was legendary. For example, one night at nine, a little boy let out a thunderous fart, which was followed by a gale of laughter in the dormitory. The next night, at nine sharp, Korczak poked his head in and cried: "Chaim, it is 9 o'clock, you can do it again."[26]

Yet Korczak was no softie. It was all but impossible to fool him. A master disciplinarian, he was like a human lie detector, a machine that records blood pressure variations in a person being asked questions. While questioning a child suspected of stealing,

the doctor would hold his wrist, checking his pulse without his knowledge. A suddenly faster pulse was a sure giveaway![27]

If a child did something that really displeased Korczak, he did not lose his temper. The doctor had what he called "a jar of strong scolding expressions." When he reached into the jar, out came a handful of colorful expressions. Always keen to preserve the culprit's self-respect, he would say: "You torpedo! You hurricane! You lamp! You table! You bagpipe!" He hurled no wounding insults, as his father had hurled at him. Instead, he stared hard at the offender and said, "I'm angry at you till lunchtime or supper." This way, the child understood that he was being scolded, but that the scolding would not last long and he would be forgiven.[28]

Korczak considered violent punishments such as whipping and withholding food—common in orphanages at the time— "monstrous, sinful, criminal." He also felt that instilling fear was equally harmful. As a leading pediatrician, he lectured medical students on his specialty. To illustrate a lecture titled "The Child's Heart," Korczak had the class gather in a lab with a fluoroscope, a machine that produces an X-ray image of body organs as they work in real time. When the students were seated, he led a four-year-old boy into the darkened room. Removing the boy's shirt, he placed the child behind the machine and switched it on. The darkness, the strangers he could barely make out, and the whirring of the machine were terrifying. While the students watched the boy's heart race, Korczak said softly: "The next time you are about to yell at a child or punish him because you have lost patience, the next time you are even tempted to strike him . . . think of this child and this heart that you see fluttering here. Think of it

and stop." Enough said! Class dismissed! Korczak headed for the door with the boy's hand in his.[29]

Dom Sierot operated according to a set of principles. In the midst of his duties in an army field hospital, Korczak somehow found time to write his most important book. *How to Love a Child,* published in 1919, is a basic text in the literature of child rearing.

According to the author, children are not miniature adults; they are unique beings, as different from adults as caterpillars are from butterflies. "Every moment in the child's life exists *now,* already, *not* in the future," Korczak declared. "Every event makes a lasting impression; every moment counts." It follows that children have certain rights simply because they *are* children. Chief among these are "the right to live for today" and "the right to be oneself." Korczak insisted that adults must not try to mold children according to their own desires. Instead, they must see that each day "is full of happy efforts, child-like, carefree without the responsibility that exceeds [a child's] age and powers." Children also need their own identity, "an identity that is chosen by the child, not for the child." In other words, children alone have the right to decide who they are; adults can only try to help them discover their true selves.[30]

A key aspect of self-discovery involved taking on responsibility. Korczak expected Dom Sierot's children to contribute in various ways. Even the youngest had to take turns in the kitchen, peeling potatoes, setting the tables in the dining room, and cleaning up after each meal. However, no job was so lowly that the director himself would not do it. In an essay titled "Why Do I Collect the

Dishes?," Korczak explained that he aimed to instill, by example, the attitude that all honest work is honorable. "I have fought that there should be no elite work and crude work, no clever and stupid, no clean and dirty. Work for nice young ladies and for the mob." A job well done earned credits toward a special reward: a postcard picturing a scene with colorful flowers, animals, and landscapes signed by the director. Some residents kept their postcards for the rest of their lives.[31]

Together, Korczak and the children worked out a constitution for Dom Sierot. The constitution made the home a democratic "children's republic" under the rule of law. Korczak taught that respect for the law is the basis of society, separating civilized humans from wild beasts. The home's basic law embodied

Children peeling potatoes outside Dom Sierot. (Date unknown)

a principle at the heart of all healthy human relations: respect. "Respect," the doctor wrote, "implies that I as a person have my rights, e.g. to be who I am, but not at the expense of the other, who also has rights. So the law protects me by granting me my rights and thereby gives me freedom, but at the same time limits this freedom by granting the same rights to others."[32]

Its Children's Parliament won praise for Dom Sierot as "the most democratic [republic] in Europe." The parliament passed a code of laws, a thousand articles covering every imaginable offense and its consequences. It also set the home's calendar. Suggestions for holidays included:

- *June 22nd. There is a slogan: "Not worth getting out of bed." Whoever likes may stay up all night. Should the weather be fair, a night march across the city will be arranged.*
- *Dirty Children's Day. Slogan: "No washing allowed." Anyone wishing to wash on that day [must] pay a fine to be fixed by the Parliament.*
- *Untidy Day. Whoever is voted as caring the least for his clothes will receive a garment so that he may not look untidy on festive days.*

We cannot say if the Children's Parliament adopted any of these suggestions, but they received a hearing, and a vote, as did all of the children's ideas.[33]

The Court of Peers administered justice. It consisted of five judges, elected weekly to enable every child to have a chance to

serve, and a prosecutor, a defense lawyer, and a secretary. The court's main objective was not to punish but to teach respect for the law and people's rights. Korczak wrote in *How to Love a Child:*

> *If anyone has done something bad, it is best to forgive. . . .*
>
> *But the Court must defend the timid that they may not be bothered by the strong. The Court must defend the conscientious and hard-working that they should not be annoyed by the careless and idle. The Court must see that there is order because disorder does the most harm to the good, the quiet and the conscientious.*
>
> *The Court is not justice, but it should try for justice. The Court is not the truth, but it wants the truth.*[34]

Any child could sue anyone, including staff members, for violations of the code. Punishments varied with the severity of the offense. If a child was found guilty on a minor charge, like messing up someone's bed, the judges dismissed the case, provided the defendant promised never to do it again. More serious offenses—rudeness, cursing, cutting school—brought a stern warning. Repeat offenders, and thieves and bullies, were expelled. However, an expelled child could reapply for admission after three months. Meanwhile, the child lived with relatives or survived as best he or she could. No more than two children were permanently expelled during the home's thirty-year existence.[35]

Children hauled Korczak into court five times, only to see him acquitted four times. The fifth time, a seven-year-old girl accused

him of being too playful. Without warning, he'd lifted her off the ground, set her on a tree branch, and laughed when she begged him to take her down. The court found the director guilty and accepted his apology. Satisfied that justice had been done, the girl burst into tears, threw herself into Korczak's arms, and hugged him tight. Justice had been served, and that was all she wanted.[36]

Most children spent seven years in Dom Sierot. When they reached age fourteen, Madame Stefa invited the most promising to stay on as junior staff members. In bidding goodbye to departing children, Korczak offered only the hope for a better life. He used to say:

We do not give you a God, for you must find Him, by solitary effort, in your own souls.

We do not give you a Motherland, for you must find her in your own hearts and thoughts.

We do not give you love of man, for there is no love without forgiveness, and forgiving is a labor and toil everyone must undertake for himself.

We give you one thing only: a yearning for a better life, a life of truth and justice, which we cannot have now, but which maybe will come tomorrow.

Perhaps that yearning will lead you to God, Motherland and Love.[37]

Whenever possible, Korczak arranged apprenticeships for boys as barbers, tailors, shoemakers, and carpenters. Other boys found jobs themselves, as messengers, porters, and shop clerks. Girls

Stefania Wilczyńska (far right) and Dr. Korczak (three people to the left of Madame Stefa) with the staff and children at Dom Sierot. (Date unknown)

might work as housecleaners, maids, and babysitters. Otherwise, "graduates" were on their own. None, evidently, went on to attend college.[38]

Nevertheless, the director had reason to be proud. Dom Sierot changed lives. Korczak hated no one, and he taught his children not to hate, either. A man in his eighties remembered the impact of Korczak's teaching. "If not for the home," he said, "I wouldn't know that there are honest people in the world who never steal. I wouldn't know that one could speak the truth. I wouldn't know that there are just laws in the world." Another man idolized the director "because he was a father to me, at a time when I desperately needed one." A woman reminisced about how, on her first day in the home, she received the first dress, undershirt, and underpants she'd ever owned. During Saturday visits to relatives, she

kept lifting up her skirt as she walked down the street—that way, "everyone, even the boys, could see my beautiful underpants." Of the 455 children who left the home over the twenty-year period from 1912 to 1932, nearly all were better human beings for the experience. Only two became beggars, two prostitutes, and three thieves.[39]

During those two decades, Korczak's name became a household word in Poland. Officials at Warsaw Radio gave him a program of his own. For fifteen minutes on Thursday afternoons, the "Old Doctor," as Korczak called himself, told funny stories with imitations of animal sounds, interviewed street children, and gave parents child-rearing advice. The program had wide appeal; both children and adults looked forward to it. "The Old Doctor proved to me for the first time in my life," a child listener said years later, "that an adult could enter easily and naturally into our world. He not only understood our point of view, but deeply respected and appreciated it." Notice the key words: *understood, respected,* and *appreciated.*[40]

Korczak also spent one day a week in Warsaw's juvenile court as an expert adviser on children's matters. Dom Sierot's director believed in the innate goodness of children and in their ability to improve if given a chance and the proper guidance. It followed that juvenile delinquency was not just the child's fault, but also the fault of society, which had turned the child in the wrong direction. "The delinquent child is still a child," Korczak reminded judges. "He is a child who has not given up yet, but does not know who he is. A punitive sentence would adversely influence his future sense of self and his behavior. Because it is society that has

failed him and made him behave this way, the Court should not condemn the criminal but the social structure." Thanks to Korczak, some judges gave delinquents a second chance, provided they sought help and improved.[41]

In 1923, Korczak published *King Matt the First*, his first children's book. Its hero is an eleven-year-old prince who becomes king after the death of his parents. King Matt's first decrees ordered chocolate and merry-go-rounds for all the kingdom's children. However, Matt soon realizes that adults treat children as second-class citizens. To remind adults of the injustices they commit, Matt commands them to go to school, while children go to work. Unfortunately, children are not prepared to do adults' work. In the chaos that follows, foreign invaders overthrow the boy-king, bind him with golden chains, and exile him to a desert island. "Reformers come to a bad end," Matt realizes. "Only after their death do people see that they were right and erect monuments to their memory."

The author might also have said the same about himself, because for him, as a man and as a Jew, things were about to change for the worse.

Neighbors and Strangers

Dom Sierot was not built on a desert island. It lay in the midst of a wider society—a society alien to most Polish Jews.

The history of their alienation goes back a very long time. Jews had lived in the "Holy Land" (roughly the land between the Jordan

River and the Mediterranean Sea) ever since Moses freed the Israelites from Egyptian bondage and led them there some three
thousand years ago. Eventually, Roman conquerors renamed the
area Palaestina, Latin for "the Land of the Philistines," a seafar-
ing people who had once lived there; Palestine is the modern term
for Palaestina. The Romans were harsh masters, and the Jews re-
belled several times. After finally crushing resistance in AD 135,
Roman legions slaughtered much of the population and banished
most of the survivors to lands across the Middle East and Europe.
Jews call that event the Diaspora, or scattering.

In the centuries following the Diaspora, Jews in western Europe often faced persecution or even expulsion for their religious
beliefs. Moving eastward, large groups of German Jews first arrived in Poland in the 1330s, invited by King Casimir the Great.
His Majesty believed, correctly, that their experience in trade
would contribute to the kingdom's economic development. In return, Jews enjoyed official protection and the freedom to practice
their religion, unique in Europe at that time. Small wonder they
called their new home Polin, which means "here you shall dwell"
in Hebrew. Jews had come "by the grace of God," they said, to
"a second Palestine," or the "Jew's Paradise." There they became
royal tax collectors, also serving the landed nobility by managing
their estates and lending them money.[42]

The Catholic Church was the first Polish institution to react
against the Jewish presence. The clergy feared that a prosperous
non-Christian minority would interfere with the church's growth.
As a result, bishops ordered the faithful not to mingle with Jews
unless absolutely necessary, and then for only the briefest time.

For identification, Jewish men had to wear tall, pointed hats, shaped like dunce caps. Worse, preachers accused Jews of horrible crimes. Isaac Bashevis Singer, a Polish-born author who received the 1978 Nobel Prize for literature, describes what it must have been like back then. The bishop in his novel *The King of the Fields* thunders, "The Jews killed Christ. They hung him on a cross. . . . They are cursed here on earth and they will never inherit the kingdom of heaven." It was said that Jews were children of Satan, demons who poisoned wells and spread plague. Supposedly, Jews were also vampires, using the blood of murdered Christian children when making *matzo,* the flat bread eaten during Passover, the festival celebrating the Israelites' flight from Egyptian slavery. To this very day, the "blood libel" persists in some parts of Europe and the Middle East.[43]

In times of trouble—crop failures, droughts, floods, plagues—people blamed the Jews for their hardships. Mass hysteria ignited pogroms, organized assaults against a defenseless group of people. Before the rise of Adolf Hitler, the worst anti-Jewish pogrom occurred in 1648–1649, when mobs massacred more than a hundred thousand Jews in Poland and neighboring Ukraine.

In reaction, Jewish survivors, often segregated from the wider community, turned inward for safety and to preserve their identity. According to historian Richard C. Lukas, by the time Poland regained its independence after World War I, the gulf between Jew and gentile had become a chasm. There were "two communities—Poles and Jews—who had lived together for centuries in the same country, the same city, the same village, but maintained, for the most part, separate existences, lifestyles, and value systems."

Religious Jews, especially, refused to assimilate, to integrate into society by adopting its language, customs, and attitudes. In effect, one recalled, "we lived in a self-imposed ghetto without walls."[44]

Most Polish Jews lived in a *shtetl,* a small town where they usually outnumbered gentiles. A traveler described a typical shtetl as "a jumble of wooden houses clustered higgledy-piggledy about a marketplace . . . with its shops, booths, tables, stands, butchers' blocks." On market days, hundreds of peasants parked their wagons in the town square, where Jews would buy their grain and cattle. Then, with money in their pockets, the peasants would buy from Jews the things they could not produce for themselves: matches, tobacco, sugar, lamp oil, nails, needles, thread, pots, pans, pants, shirts, and dresses, to list just a few. These items were made by shtetl artisans or were brought by Jewish merchants from distant factories.[45]

Shtetl life revolved around a synagogue, or prayer house, led by a rabbi, an expert on Jewish religious teaching, ceremony, and law. Young boys attended *heder,* an elementary school for Jewish children, and older boys attended *yeshiva,* a Jewish school of higher education. Both types of schools taught only religious subjects. "Modern" subjects—geometry, algebra, chemistry, biology, geography, Polish history—had no place in them. Girls and young women lacked formal education, but learned to read and write at home. Pious Jews, particularly the ultra-Orthodox called Hasidim, were easily identified. Men wore a black *caftan,* a long-sleeved, ankle-length tunic, over their trousers, and a black skull-cap called a *yarmulke* under a broad-brimmed hat. Religious men did not shave; long beards and side curls twisted behind their ears

signified piety. Religious women dressed modestly, in clothes that covered their bare arms and legs. Married women cut their hair short. Hair was their "crowning glory"; except in the presence of their husbands, married women wore kerchiefs or wigs.[46]

The vast majority of Polish Jews knew two languages. Hebrew was the language of the Bible and prayer. Yiddish, or "Jewish German," was the language of everyday life. When Jews first came to Poland from Germany, they spoke German. Over time, their German borrowed many Polish and Russian words, as well as Hebrew ones, and Yiddish emerged as a distinct language. Yiddish is written in Hebrew characters from right to left, and is read the same way. It is a highly expressive language, able to convey deep emotion and cutting humor.

Polish was another matter. Isaac Bashevis Singer wrote only in Yiddish. In 1944, at the height of World War II, Singer recalled: "Rarely did a Jew think it necessary to learn Polish; rarely was a Jew interested in Polish history or Polish politics. . . . Even in the last few years it was still a rare occurrence that a Jew would speak Polish well. Out of the three million Jews living in Poland, two-and-a-half million were not able to write a simple letter in Polish. . . . [My] father did not know more than two words in Polish. And it never occurred to him that there was something amiss in that." During the 1931 census, 81 percent of Polish Jews declared Yiddish their mother tongue. Nor could many Jews recognize the Polish flag![47]

Many traditional Jews held stereotypical views of the Poles—that is, opinions that were overly simplified and prejudiced. Thus, on the basis of limited experience, traditional Jews might make

unfair, negative generalizations about Poles as a group. The Yiddish word *goy* (plural *goyim*), for example, meant more than "a gentile person." It implied ignorance, coarseness, and sinfulness. "What do they know, these goyim?" a Hasid asked. "A goy knows nothing, a goy does not think, the only thing he knows how to do is beat up Jews." A young male goy, called a *sheygetz,* was allegedly a brute who thought with his fists. This mythical Pole guzzled vodka until he became so *shiker* (drunk) that he lost his senses. A Yiddish folk song put it this way: "*Shiker iz a goy—Shiker iz er—trinken miz er—vayl er iz a goy*" ("A goy is a drunkard—but drink he must—because he is a goy"). Similarly, the term *shikse* meant more than "a young gentile woman"; it also implied immodesty and sexual "looseness."[48]

Apart from the belief in one God, traditional Jews saw nothing in common between their religion and Christianity. To them, Christianity mimicked paganism, worshipping "idols"—statues and paintings of God, Jesus, the Virgin Mary, and the saints. In their view, the Holy Spirit, the Trinity, and the Resurrection were mere "superstitions."

Traditional Jews showed their disdain in various ways. For example, at many rural crossroads in Poland, travelers would see a crucifix—a cross with the figure of the crucified Christ on it—signifying divine protection. Jews refused to look at this "graven image." Author Elie Wiesel, recipient of the Nobel Peace Prize in 1986, was born in Romania, but his attitudes mirrored those of Polish Jews. "[Christian] rituals," Wiesel recalled, "had no interest for me; quite the contrary. I turned away from them. Whenever I met a priest . . . I would avert my gaze and think of something

else. Rather than walk in front of a church with its pointed and threatening belfry, I would cross the street. . . . Christians were more present in my imagination than in my life. What did a Christian do when he was alone? What were his dreams made of? How did he use his time when he was not plotting against me?"[49]

For many traditional Jews, marrying a Christian amounted to a betrayal of everything Jewish. The scandal stained the entire family in its own eyes and in the eyes of the community. Traditional Jews disowned the offending daughter or son. Parents tore their clothes in shame and despair, as if mourning the death of a family member. When, for instance, the daughter of a rabbi converted to Catholicism and married a Polish policeman, her parents could not contain their grief. "[They] followed the carriage, crying and screaming and beating their heads to a bloody pulp

Jewish men reading from their holy books on the Sabbath. (1941)

on the sides of the wagon pleading with their daughter. . . . After this shameful tragedy, the [bride's] . . . three sisters never married, neither did their cousins in the nearby town. No one would marry them."[50]

Such behavior troubled Isaac Bashevis Singer. A character in his novel *The Manor* asks: "How can anyone move into someone else's home, live there in total isolation, and expect not to suffer by it? When you despise your host's god as a tin image, shun his wine as forbidden, condemn his daughter as unclean, aren't you asking to be treated as an unwelcome outsider? It is as simple as that."[51]

Yet not all Polish Jews saw themselves as outsiders. Though still deeply religious, perhaps a third of the total number adapted to Polish society as best they could. These people spoke Polish, read Polish, and worked beside Poles. Though born Jewish, about a tenth of them considered themselves "Poles of Jewish faith," true Poles in every way. Both groups were virtually all city folk, living in Łódź, Lublin, Białystok, and, of course, Warsaw. Assimilated Jews formed an important part of Poland's economic and professional elite. They were factory owners, bankers, scientists, doctors, and lawyers.[52]

Korczak and Madame Stefa were born into assimilated families. Though we cannot be certain about Stefa, we do know that religion was not part of Korczak's upbringing. To be sure, he had no idea that he was Jewish until the age of five. When his beloved canary died, he decided to bury it. The janitor's son, seeing him digging in the courtyard, asked what he was doing. Giving the bird a proper funeral, complete with flowers and a cross over its

grave, he said. The older boy replied that the little bird, like the little boy, was Jewish. And since only Christians went to heaven, when a Jew died, the best he could expect was a very dark place, though not hell. The younger boy thought this was "certainly something to consider."[53]

Korczak may have decided that religion—Jewish, Christian, or another—was not for him. We have no record of his attending synagogue, let alone praying. Nor do his writings show any trace of Jewish consciousness. The Old Doctor knew no Hebrew or Yiddish; he thought, spoke, wrote, and likely dreamed in Polish. He considered himself a Polish citizen and patriot who had served his country in wartime. A former aide at Dom Sierot had reason to call him "the greatest assimilationist that I met in my life."[54]

Similarly, Korczak's children did not attend heder. They walked to neighborhood public schools, where instruction was entirely in Polish. As noted by Itzchak Belfer, a former resident of the orphans' home, Dom Sierot "was run along secular lines." Everyone had to speak Polish, though the home offered language courses, and one could choose to study Hebrew and Yiddish. On Friday nights, the main table in the dining hall had a *challah,* a special braided bread eaten in Jewish homes on the Sabbath, and Sabbath candles. After the meal came the *Oneg Shabbat* (literally "joy of the Sabbath"), which included stories, songs, and discussions.[55]

Deepening Crisis

By the 1930s, Polish Jews, whatever their beliefs, faced a deepening crisis. The collapse of the American stock market in October 1929 plunged the developed world into the Great Depression, the worst economic downturn in modern times. Banks shut their doors, and the life savings of millions of everyday people vanished into thin air. Stocks and bonds became worthless paper. Industrial production all but stopped, causing mass unemployment and misery.

The Great Depression also fueled anti-Semitism, the dislike and suspicion of Jews, in Europe and America. Poland was no exception. Unable to control events, frightened people sought scapegoats to blame for the crisis. As a result, old myths about Jews, never entirely forgotten, were revived and took on new strength. Catholic journalists, one historian observed, held that "the Jewish minority in Poland posed a threat to . . . the Polish nation." The Catholic press endlessly repeated charges that Jews killed Christ, used the blood of murdered Christian children in their rituals, and stole jobs from Catholics.[56]

In 1936, Cardinal August Hlond, head of the Catholic Church in Poland, issued a pastoral letter titled "On Catholic Moral Principles." In it, His Eminence accused Jews of multiple misdeeds, ranging from cheating in business to spreading pornography. Therefore, he said, Catholics should shun Jews and boycott their businesses. However, he added a note of caution: To be fair, Catholics must remember that not all Jews are bad. There are "very many Jewish faithful who are honest, just, compassionate, and

charitable." The cardinal warned, "It is not permissible to hate anyone. Not even the Jews. . . . You may not attack Jews, beat them, hurt them, slander them. In a Jew you should respect and love a human being as thy neighbor." Yet, be wary.[57]

The "Jewish problem" infected Polish politics. The National Democrats, the party in power during the 1930s, was intensely anti-Semitic. "The Jews," its official platform declared, "represent the source of all evil and the source of all misfortune for Poland." It called for stripping Jews of the right to vote and expelling them from Poland's cultural life: the press, theater, films, literature. It demanded full-scale economic war against the Jews, boycotting their shops, seizing their businesses, and preventing them from competing with Poles.[58]

Poland's Jews felt prejudice in many ways. Medical and legal societies, strongholds of the assimilated, barred new Jewish members and expelled old ones. Universities made anti-Semitism official policy. Rules set quotas on the number of Jewish students admitted each year, regardless of an individual's ability. Catholic students heckled, cursed, and beat up Jewish classmates, and "many," noted an official report, "come to school armed with clubs, knives and sticks." During lectures, Jews could only use the "ghetto benches," segregated seating at the back of the hall, each bearing a metal tag reading HERE SITS A JEW. In protest, many stood against the walls rather than take what they called "seats of shame."[59]

Government policies hurt Jews even more. Legislators imposed crippling taxes on Jews and prohibited them from working at government plants that produced chemicals, tobacco, matches, salt,

and alcohol. Though the wealthy could weather the storm, ordinary folk could not. Under the pressure of official "Buy Polish" campaigns, hundreds of small Jewish-owned businesses closed each month, leaving employees jobless. Poverty became the norm in many communities, as Jewish workers' and artisans' standard of living fell to the point where families of eight lived in one-room tenement "apartments." Such grinding poverty shocked Jewish visitors from abroad. London's *Jewish Chronicle* described Polish Jews as "a helpless minority sunk in squalid poverty and misery." Sholem Asch, an eminent Jewish writer based in New York, was appalled. Polish Jews were being slowly "buried alive," Asch noted. "Every second person was undernourished, skeletons of skin and bones, crippled, candidates for the grave." A British visitor called Jewish Warsaw "a teeming city of wretchedness."[60]

What to do?

The Promised Land

Anti-Semites thought they had the answer. The only way to solve Poland's "Jewish problem," they urged, was for Jews to leave the country. Graffiti appeared on walls saying, "Jews, back to Palestine!" Zionists agreed.[61]

Zionism is the belief that Jews need a country of their own. Politically, Zionists wished to "reclaim" Palestine, also called the "Land of Israel." For over thirteen hundred years, however, Muslim Arabs had occupied Palestine. During the 1400s, the area had fallen under Ottoman Turkish rule. Though a small Jewish com-

munity remained, chiefly in Jerusalem, Muslims were the overwhelming majority. However, in the 1880s, the Turks allowed Zionists to set up their first *kibbutz,* or farming settlement. Then, as now, all property belonged to the kibbutz. In return for their labor, settlers received food, housing, education, and childcare instead of wages. In 1909, Zionists began building Tel Aviv on the sand dunes along the Mediterranean Sea.

A Zionist poster promoting Jewish settlement in Palestine, written in both Romanian and Hungarian. (1930s)

During World War I, British leaders aimed to take Palestine away from Turkey. In British hands, Palestine would serve as a base, safeguarding access to Middle Eastern oil. However, rather than bear the costs of a full-scale occupation, leaders decided that a Zionist-dominated Palestine, friendly to Britain, would protect its economic interests. So in November 1917, British foreign secretary Arthur James Balfour issued a statement. Known as the Balfour Declaration, it said that the British government favored the creation of a "national home for the Jewish people" in Palestine. It added that nothing should threaten the rights of the "existing non-Jewish communities"—namely, the Arabs.

However, the Balfour Declaration failed to answer key

questions: What, exactly, was a "national home"? A refuge for oppressed European Jews? A Jewish state in the Middle East? What right did Britain have to declare a national home for another people without consulting the Arab majority? Could Britain give away land it did not own, land that still legally belonged to the Ottoman Empire? Thus, without intending to, Britain planted the seeds of a conflict between Muslims and Jews that would run through the history of the modern Middle East like a scarlet thread.

Arabs objected to the British plan—strongly. A leading professor at Al-Azhar, the great center of Muslim learning in Cairo, Egypt, explained the Arab position. Allah—God—had allowed the faithful to conquer Palestine, he said. The land belonged to them by divine right, and taking it from them would be, in effect, taking it from Allah. "We will again place our trust in our swords and in the justice of the One God. We shall be masters of our ancient home even if it becomes a graveyard."[62]

Trouble soon began. Arab mobs shouted "Death to the Jews," "We will push the Zionists into the sea," and "This country will become a river of blood." And blood did flow. Throughout the 1920s and 1930s, riots erupted in the cities and had to be suppressed by British troops. In the countryside, Arab gangs staged hit-and-run raids on Jewish settlements. Despite all this, Polish Zionists saw a better future in Palestine than in the land of their birth. "The Jewish youth is dominated by a Palestine mania," a nineteen-year-old wrote in his diary. Zionist training camps sprang up to prepare city folk for kibbutz life. To speed them along, the Polish government gave some Zionist groups money.[63]

It so happened that Madame Stefa had a dear friend in Pales-

tine. Once a favorite of hers at the orphans' home, Feiga Lipshitz had married, become a mother, and moved to Ein Harod (Well of Harod), a kibbutz in northern Palestine. Depressed and overworked, Madame Stefa needed a change. So in 1932, she took a leave of absence to join the Lipshitz family. Despite the primitive living conditions, she easily fell into the rhythm of settler life. She learned modern Hebrew quickly and got along with everyone. For three months, she worked in the children's houses, where kibbutz members cared for the young while their parents worked in the fields. She returned to Warsaw tanned, refreshed, and energetic as ever.[64]

Initially, the Old Doctor opposed Zionism. As an assimilated Jew, he thought his Polish brethren belonged in Poland, not struggling to adapt to so alien a place as Palestine. Madame Stefa's experience, however, aroused his curiosity. Like her, after years of putting in seven-day workweeks, he needed a change of scene. By the summer of 1934, he had scraped together enough money and was ready to leave for a six-week visit. Madame Stefa paved his way with a letter to Ein Harod: "Please consider having Dr. Korczak stay with you for a few weeks. . . . He wants to learn about kibbutz life, and all that he asks in return is a bed, a table, and a chair. He is even willing to wash floors."[65]

Korczak's ship docked at Haifa on July 24, 1934. Upon arriving at the kibbutz, he still wore a jacket, a shirt with a starched collar, and a tie. Why, he asked, was everyone wearing shorts and not protecting their legs from the sun? When told that he'd better do the same if he wished to survive in the scorching heat, he joked: "But if I take them off, what will remain of Korczak?" Still,

he removed his jacket and tie, opened his shirt collar, and rolled up his pants. But no shorts for him![66]

To earn his keep, the educator peeled potatoes in the kitchen. He made friends with the children, using the few Hebrew phrases he'd learned. As he watched the older children helping in the fields, they struck him as so different from his orphans in Warsaw. These youngsters were strong and lean, growing up with "the heat of the sun in their soul" and "the burning wind in their blood." At night, speaking through an interpreter, Korczak discussed his five commandments of parenting: "Love *the child,* not just your own. Observe the child. Do not pressure the child. Be honest with yourself in order to be honest with the child. Know yourself so that you do not take advantage of a defenseless child."[67]

The Old Doctor's six weeks passed quickly—too quickly. As he prepared to leave, he asked a new friend, "What do you think I should tell everyone in Warsaw about Palestine?" The man replied: "Tell the Poles that this country is by no means a hell for those Jews told [by anti-Semites] 'Go to Palestine!' And tell the Jews that a new world is being built here, that it's worthwhile for them to take the risk."[68]

Meanwhile, back home, each day seemed worse than the day before. On the way to and from school, Korczak's children heard taunts: "Dirty Jews!" and "Hit the Jews! Hit them!" Upset, he placed newspaper notices begging attackers' parents, "Please, leave my children alone." Korczak himself felt the sting of anti-Semitism. One day, while he was riding in a crowded streetcar, a fellow passenger pointed to a vacant seat. "Would the old Jew

like to sit down?" he asked sarcastically. Korczak shot back: "The army major cannot sit down because he has a boil on his ass." Having insulted so august a personage as a major in the Polish Army, the man hurriedly got off at the next stop.[69]

Yet Korczak could not conceal his pain when hearing anti-Semites rail, "No Jew can be in charge of our juvenile offenders." The authorities followed through, dismissing him from his job with Warsaw's juvenile court. That same year, 1936, despite its popularity, Warsaw Radio canceled his weekly program.[70]

Dejected and angry, Korczak took a time-out with another six-week visit to Ein Harod. However, his second stay was troubling. He worried that, as work on Tel Aviv neared completion, Arabs would lose their jobs at the port of Jaffa nearby. "But what about the Arab children?" he asked. "Would they go hungry if the Jaffa port were closed?" He also found the kibbutz on high alert. Arab gangs had recently set fire to its crops and taken potshots at settlers. At night, armed men had to stand watch while everyone else slept. The fifty-eight-year-old Korczak volunteered for guard duty. "Don't you know that I'm a Polish officer who has served in three wars?" he asked his hosts. They knew but didn't want to put their guest at risk. Though disappointed, he urged them to let the older boys and girls join the adults on guard duty. "You shouldn't wrap children in cotton," he advised. "The struggle to create life here is their destiny." Despite the danger, he hoped to return in 1937 for a longer stay. If all went well, he planned to learn Hebrew and retire, spending his remaining years in Palestine, but this was not to be.[71]

Toward the Brink

With the onset of the Great Depression, the Old Doctor sensed that not only Poland but the entire world was hurtling toward disaster. He could not give that disaster a name or a date, because its true nature was unknowable, at least for the time being.

Korczak expressed his fears in a 1931 play titled *The Senate of Madmen,* which he called "a black farce." To be sure, its mood was so dark that the play closed after only a few performances. The action takes place in an insane asylum, the type of place the playwright knew all too well from his father's illness. But this is no ordinary asylum. It represents a world increasingly run by lunatics. Lurking inside each inmate is "a powerful brute" called "homo-rapax"—man as a raptor, a predator, a beast of prey. The demons of the past are returning, an old inmate tells a boy named Janek: "Barbaric sports, pagan dances and lewd songs are here again. . . . The times [are] bad, my boy: Sadness, crime, premonitions of things to come." The child is humanity's only hope, he says, because "when God abandons the human race and goes back to heaven, He returns in a rain of pearls that falls right into the hearts of children."[72]

Two years later, the Old Doctor was more pessimistic, fearing that none in Dom Sierot would ever see a rain of pearls. "I'm afraid that we're simply witnessing the meaningless destruction of everything honest and kindly, the massacre of the sheep by the wolves." For on January 30, 1933, the most ravenous "wolf" of modern times took power in Germany. Everything that the Old

Doctor was—humane, gentle, modest, peace-loving—Adolf Hitler was not. We cannot understand the tragedy that befell millions of innocents without understanding this man, who, ironically, liked the nickname "Wolf." We must leave the great educator for a while to tell this hater's story.[73]

The Hater

You love hatred and want to measure the world against it.
You throw food to the beast in man . . .

—Erich Kästner, "Marching Song" (1945)

The Führer

Adolf Hitler was born on April 20, 1889, in Braunau am Inn, Austria, near the German border. His father, Alois, was a customs inspector, and his mother, Klara, from a poor farming family. A high-strung child, Adolf received good marks in elementary school, but did poorly in high school, because he had no interest in "dull" subjects like mathematics. His low grades outraged his father, a foul-tempered man given to shouting and freely using his hands on his wife and son. Alois wanted Adolf to become a civil servant like himself, but the youngster had a grander vision. He imagined himself an artistic genius whom the world would recognize, honor, and reward.

Two years after his father's death in 1903, Adolf persuaded his mother to allow him to quit school and study at home. But instead of buckling down as he'd promised, the teenager idled

Adolf Hitler as a baby. (Date unknown)

away his time, daydreaming, reading whatever caught his interest, and drawing. In 1907, Hitler went to Vienna, the Austrian capital, to study art. But he was not the genius he thought, flunking the entrance examination of the Academy of Fine Arts. After his mother died of breast cancer later that year, he became a drifter, sleeping in flophouses, eating in soup kitchens, and selling his drawings to picture framers. Disgusted with Vienna, in 1913 he moved to Munich, a city in southern Germany. When World War I began in the summer of 1914, he enlisted in the German Army at once.

In key ways, Private Hitler was a product of the war. That great school of killing taught the young man that human life is cheap, a commodity to be used in achieving desired objectives. For him, as for all frontline troops, death became a familiar sight, a normal part of existence; on average, over six thousand soldiers, in all the armies, died each day for more than four years. At least twice as many were wounded each day, often dreadfully disfigured, their faces torn by bullets and explosions.[1]

Private Hitler was an oddball; members of his company remembered him as "a man resolutely alone." He had no friends

and seemed not to want any. "Always deadly serious, he never laughed or joked," a comrade recalled. Yet he was a good soldier, fighting in the most brutal battles on the Western Front. Promoted to corporal, he received the Iron Cross, First Class, an award usually reserved for officers, for courage under fire. He was wounded twice; the second time was by poison gas, and he had never felt such pain. "A few hours later, my eyes had turned to burning coals; it had grown black around me," he wrote in *Mein Kampf* (*My Struggle*), published in 1925, his blend of autobiography, ideology, and plan for action.[2]

In November 1918, Corporal Hitler lay in bed in a military hospital, his eyes bandaged, slowly recovering from temporary blindness. One day, a chaplain brought awful news: The war was over, and Germany had lost. In his despair, Hitler asked himself how this could have happened. German forces still held vast areas of Eastern Europe, Belgium, and France. So, like many other fighting men, he decided that traitors must have stabbed Germany in the back. "In these nights hatred grew in me, hatred for those responsible for this deed," he wrote. Then, like a flash of lightning, it dawned on him: God had spared him for a reason. He was the Chosen One, destined to punish the traitors and restore Germany's honor. At last, his life had a purpose, a direction, a mission: "I, for my part, decided to go into politics."[3]

After recovering his vision, Hitler returned to Munich but remained in the army until he was discharged in March 1920. Meanwhile, in the autumn of 1919, he began attending meetings of the German Workers' Party—though "party" was too grand a title for this band of seven misfits and malcontents. It wanted the

same things as Hitler. First, it demanded punishment of the "November criminals" who'd betrayed Germany. Next, it called for canceling the Treaty of Versailles, which gave parts of German-held western Poland, an area inhabited by many people of German ancestry, to the reborn Polish nation. The treaty also reduced the size of the German Army to a hundred thousand men, turning it into little more than a national police force without airplanes, warships, and heavy weapons. Finally, the party aimed to overthrow the democratic Weimar Republic, which had replaced the German monarchy.

During party meetings, Hitler discovered something he had not known about himself: "I could 'speak.'" He had a way with words, an inborn ability to electrify audiences. From then on, he

lost no opportunity to speak in public. Hitler spoke in grubby taverns that reeked of stale beer, their floors covered in sawdust, spit, and vomit. He spoke on street corners and at parks—anywhere people passed in large numbers—and in all weather. An early photo shows him, hatless

An election poster of Adolf Hitler based on a photo by Heinrich Hoffmann. (1932)

and wearing a raincoat, haranguing passersby while snow fell. His speeches attracted ever-larger audiences, and people began to join the German Workers' Party just to hear the thirty-year-old speak.[4]

Hitler's influence grew as the party grew. The failed artist took charge of its propaganda, hiring artists to design posters with short, snappy messages portraying him as Germany's savior: "Only Hitler!" "Hitler, Our Last Hope!" "We Are for Adolf Hitler." The most striking poster had just his last name and his face set against a black background.

Hitler also realized that the party needed a distinct symbol to set it apart from other groups. In a propaganda masterstroke, he adopted the hooked cross, or swastika, as its insignia. An ancient sign of good luck and prosperity, the swastika appears in the art of many peoples. Native Americans used it, as did the ancient Irish, Persians, and Greeks. In early-twentieth-century America, Coca-Cola used the design in its advertising, as did the Boy Scouts;

An example of Coca-Cola using the swastika design in its advertising. (Date unknown)

the Girl Scouts called their magazine *Swastika*. U.S. Army aircraft bore it as an insignia. Bold and eye-catching, the swastika could easily be chalked on sidewalks and depicted on flags, banners, lapel buttons, tiepins, and signet rings. Hitler would make this good-luck sign the most dreaded symbol of all time.[5]

By 1921, Hitler had taken

A U.S. Army aircraft with the swastika insignia. (1930)

charge of the party. He immediately changed its name to the National Socialist German Workers' Party, or the Nazi Party, an abbreviation of its name in German. To encourage party unity, he had members wear military-style uniforms with swastika armbands. Hitler also gave himself a title, *der Führer*—the Leader. To show their loyalty, Nazis had to salute him in the correct manner: by throwing the right arm high, with the hand extended, and shouting *"Heil Hitler!"*—"Hail Hitler!" Saluting became a ritual, like a sacred rite. Normally, Germans used the word *Heil* for relations between man and the divine. *Heilige Vater* means "Holy Father," and *Heilige Mütter,* "Holy Mary, Mother of God." In effect, the Nazi salute equated the Führer with God.

Yet you would not have given Hitler a second look if you had

passed him on the street. The Führer was not a striking figure—far from it. Dorothy Thompson, an American journalist, interviewed him for *Cosmopolitan,* a popular American magazine, in the winter of 1932. What a disappointment! She wrote that it took her less than a minute "to measure the startling insignificance of the man who has set the world agog. . . . He is the very prototype of the Little Man." Standing five feet nine inches tall, weighing about 180 pounds, he had pale skin, dark brown hair, and a "toothbrush" mustache to take attention away from his broad nose. Deeply offended by the piece, the Nazi leader had Thompson hustled out of Germany within a few days of his taking power early the next year.[6]

Hitler's eyes were his one outstanding feature. What eyes— bright blue in color! People found them stunning and unforgettable. American journalist William L. Shirer found them "hypnotic. Piercing. Penetrating. . . . What hit you at once was their power. They stared at you. They stared through you. They seemed to immobilize the person at whom they were directed, frightening some and fascinating others . . . but dominating them in any case." When Hitler stared at a person really hard, it felt as if his eyes pierced their very soul, reading their secret thoughts. To show his dominance, he would lock eyes with someone, refusing to "let go" until they turned away.[7]

Hitler lacked, for want of a better term, humanity. Even those closest to the Führer found him aloof and secretive. "He simply could not let anyone approach his inner being because that core was lifeless. Empty," wrote Albert Speer, a close adviser. Magda Goebbels, wife of propaganda minister Joseph Goebbels, often

visited him on social occasions. He was always polite and enjoyed playing with her children. However, close as they were, she could never get over the fact that "in certain ways Hitler simply isn't human."[8]

He had weird habits. For fun, Hitler would have an aide stand by with a stopwatch, timing how fast he could dress and undress. Death and decay fascinated him. Hitler often spoke of severed heads, and he enjoyed visiting graveyards at night. Contradictorily, at dinner parties, if a guest ordered a meat dish, Hitler, a vegetarian, looked nauseated. "I don't understand why you want it," he'd sneer. "I don't think you want to devour a corpse . . . the flesh of dead animals. Cadavers!" Easily upset, he threw temper tantrums. A Nazi official recalled: "He scolded in high, shrill tones, stamped his feet, and banged his fists on tables and walls. He foamed at the mouth, panting and stammering in uncontrollable fury. . . . He was an alarming sight, his hair disheveled, his eyes fixed, and his face distorted and purple. I feared he would collapse, or have an apo-

Hitler aide and propaganda minister, Joseph Goebbels. (Date unknown)

plectic fit." Of course, the public never saw this side of his personality.[9]

Nevertheless, Hitler's speeches struck a chord with millions of Germans. Already angry about losing the war, and resentful of the "dictated" Treaty of Versailles that cost their country so much territory, millions became impoverished in its aftermath. To pay its bills, the Weimar government printed vast amounts of money, triggering runaway inflation. When World War I began, 4.2 marks, the German monetary unit, equaled one American dollar. By November 1923, it took 200 *billion* marks to buy the equivalent of a dollar's worth of goods. An egg cost a million marks. Women wheeled baby carriages full of money to buy a loaf of bread. There was so much money around, and it was worth so little, that artists used the colorful bills to make papier-mâché sculptures. Worse, the life savings of millions of thrifty people, accumulated over decades, became worthless, leaving them with nothing for their old age. This was dangerous, for when money loses its value, people lose respect for the government. However, Hitler promised to "make Germany great again" (his phrase) by creating the Third Reich (Third Empire), which he said was destined to last a thousand years.[10]

Hitler's speeches attracted a trio of men who would later hold top positions in the Third Reich. We may call them smart fools, men of high intelligence but lacking wisdom, character, and integrity. Smart as they were, they literally gave themselves to their Führer. None doubted that he was master, and they his faithful servants, bound to him body, mind, and soul.

Decorated World War I fighter pilot and Hitler aide, Hermann Göring. (1932)

Hermann Göring, a decorated World War I fighter pilot, worshipped Hitler, springing to attention—all three-hundred-plus pounds of him—whenever he called on the telephone. "Every time I face him my heart falls into my stomach," said Göring. He believed the Führer, "sent to us by God to save Germany," was "simply infallible," incapable of error. Hitler was Göring's moral guide, for, as he acknowledged, "I have no conscience; my conscience is Adolf Hitler." Under the Third Reich, the brutal, greedy, luxury-loving Göring became Hitler's second-in-command and chief of Germany's air force, the Luftwaffe. When Göring gave an order, it was as if it came from Hitler himself.[11]

Heinrich Himmler became Hitler's enforcer. A soft-spoken man, this former chicken farmer was a fiend; some who knew him called him, behind his back, "a dirty little bit of vermin." Himmler led the SS (short for Schutzstaffel, or "Security Detail"), which Hitler had created in 1925 for his personal protection. In 1929, Himmler became its director and transformed it into both an all-powerful secret police force and a Nazi army (the Waffen-SS) sep-

arate from the Wehrmacht, Germany's regular military forces consisting of the army, navy, and air force. As with Göring, Hitler was his conscience, because he had "the greatest brain of all times." To drive home the point, Himmler declared: "If Hitler were to say I should shoot my mother, I would do it and be proud of his confidence." Himmler also had weird tastes. During World War II, he had tables and chairs made

SS chief Heinrich Himmler in 1938.

from human bones, and he treasured a copy of *Mein Kampf* bound in tanned human skin.[12]

Joseph Goebbels held a doctorate in German literature. Short and wiry, "the little doctor" became infatuated with Hitler at their first meeting. Afterward, Goebbels could not contain his joy. He wrote, "Adolf Hitler, I love you, because you are great and simple at the same time. You are what's called a genius." At other times, Goebbels called Hitler "my master . . . my father"; his master even convinced him that "he is Christ." Goebbels confessed, "I feel bound to him to my last breath." A master of modern propaganda methods, Goebbels became "Reich Minister of Popular Enlightenment and Propaganda." Despite the grand title, he

practiced the "big lie," believing that if you lied loud and often, you could make people believe anything.[13]

A Man of Words

The strength of Hitler's appeal remained his gift for words. Words rule our lives, because they are how we communicate. Words convey ideas and feelings to others, shaping, in turn, our thoughts, emotions, and actions. Read today, Hitler's speeches seem long, repetitive, and boring. This is because he meant them to be heard by crowds, not read, and surely not studied with a critical mind. Perhaps, as the saying goes, the pen is mightier than the sword. If so, then, as Hitler declared, "the magic power of the spoken word" is mightiest yet. Spoken words, he declared, were hammer blows "opening the gates to a people's heart." And words could kill.[14]

Hitler's way of delivering a speech was as important as the words he used. A speech, for him, was a theatrical performance, requiring just the right setting and body language. Days before a scheduled speech, he began to rehearse his facial expressions and gestures in front of a mirror. Like a professional actor, he experimented with his image, studying photos of himself striking various poses.

On the appointed day, the audience would gather in a meeting hall hours before Hitler arrived. He made sure never to be on time. For waiting built excitement, as did the gigantic banners and the band playing stirring marches. Elated, people spontaneously burst into Nazi slogans such as "We Want a New Order

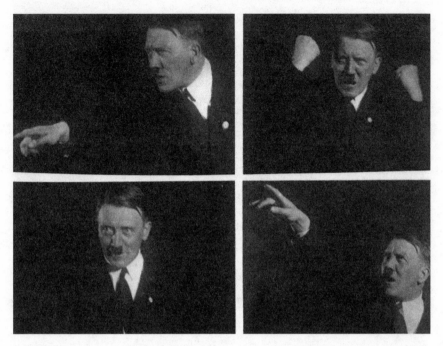

Adolf Hitler in 1930. The photos here were taken so that he might see how he appeared to audiences while striking different poses.

Under Adolf Hitler." Fight songs whipped up hatred of the Weimar Republic:

> *Throw grenades into the parliaments.*
> *Blood must flow, a whole lot of it.*[15]

Without warning, trumpets blared, drums rolled, and men with swastika flags appeared. Hitler entered. American journalist Louis P. Lochner, a careful observer, described a typical scene. Instantly, audience members sprang to their feet, their right arms outstretched, their cries of *"Heil Hitler!"* echoing off the walls. "A searchlight plays upon his lone figure as he slowly walks through the hall, never looking to the right or left, his right hand raised in

salute, his left hand at the buckle of his belt. He never smiles—it is a religious rite, this procession of the modern Messiah incarnate."[16]

When Hitler reached the podium, the crowd fell silent. He never read from a prepared text; that would have been too set, too formal, too constraining. Instead, he had key words and phrases jotted on a sheet of paper. The words came haltingly at first; after a few sentences, he might fall silent for a minute or two, as if dazed. Yet this hesitation was like an insect's feeling about with its antennae. Similarly, Hitler was getting the "feel" of his audience. Otto Strasser, a Nazi who later broke with him, analyzed his method:

I have been asked many times what is the secret of Hitler's extraordinary power as a speaker. I can only attribute it to his uncanny intuition, which infallibly diagnoses the ills from which his audience is suffering. . . . Adolf Hitler enters a hall. He snuffs the air. For a minute he gropes, feels his way, senses the atmosphere. Suddenly he bursts forth. . . . His words go like an arrow to their target, he touches each private wound on the raw, liberating the mass unconscious, expressing its innermost aspirations, telling it what it most wants to hear.[17]

Once the Führer connected with his audience, he became what one listener called "this thundering demon." He whipped himself into a frenzy, transformed into "a man hypnotized" by his own words. He struck dramatic poses, his arms flailing, his hands slicing through the air. He used combinations of unifying and fight-

ing words, all chosen for the desired emotional impact. He spoke of honor, loyalty, family, sacrifice, and the *Vaterland*—the Fatherland. He turned words into weapons. *Fight, break, crush, smash,* and *revenge* burst from his mouth. Hitler put all his energy into a speech. He sweated so profusely that the color of his uniform, he said, "invariably stained my underclothes." A speech, which might last two hours, was so strenuous that he lost up to six pounds. He made up the weight by gorging on chocolate and cake.[18]

Above all, Hitler was a hater, and he strove to ignite hatred in his listeners. "Hatred, burning hatred—this is what we want to pour into the souls of our millions of fellow Germans, until the flame of rage ignites in Germany and avenges the corruptors of our nation," he cried. Hatred is contagious, and his raw emotion brought the audience to a fever pitch. As the "fever" spread, something dreadful happened. Grown men lost control of themselves, trembling, sobbing, howling, wailing, rolling on the floor. Women collapsed in hysterics. An observer recalled: "The women turned out the whites of their eyes and fell down like wet rags. They lay there like slaughtered calves, sighing heavily. Joy and fulfillment!"[19]

Men and women surrendered their individuality and "gave" themselves to the Führer. "I belonged no more to myself, but to the movement," a man recalled. Decades later, Melita Maschmann realized how, as a fifteen-year-old, she'd shed her individuality, becoming part of what she called "the Whole." While she was attending a Nazi rally, an inner voice told her, "Well, for yourself you are now dead. . . . Everything that was *I* had been absorbed into the *Whole*!" In this way, Melita and countless others succumbed to Hitler's ideology.[20]

Nazi Ideology

During Hitler's youth, a revolution in scientific thought swept the Western world. In 1859, English naturalist Charles Darwin published *On the Origin of Species by Means of Natural Selection, or the Preservation of Favoured Races in the Struggle for Life*. In this work, usually called simply *The Origin of Species*, Darwin argued that all living beings had developed gradually, or evolved. Over millions of years, they had evolved through continuous small changes inherited from species that had come before. Those species best adapted to the environment survived through "natural selection," passing their traits to their offspring. In this way, the "struggle for existence," or the elimination of the weak, promoted the "survival of the fittest," producing the "most favored races." By "races," Darwin did not mean human races but "superior" strains within a given species better adapted to the environment.[21]

Darwin's theory had a huge impact on the way people thought. Before long, popular writers simplified it for ordinary readers. This, in turn, led to social Darwinism—the application of the laws of the struggle for existence and the survival of the fittest to human affairs. The Industrial Revolution was in full swing at this time, enabling the shrewd, the ruthless, and the lucky to make fortunes. The lords of industry, though not above using crooked means, argued that inequality was the "law of nature." Since they were "fitter" than the "common herd" of humanity, it followed that they deserved their wealth, power, and luxurious lifestyle. And since the poor were naturally "unfit," they deserved their lot: low wages, long hours, wretched living conditions.

ON

THE ORIGIN OF SPECIES

BY MEANS OF NATURAL SELECTION,

OR THE

PRESERVATION OF FAVOURED RACES IN THE STRUGGLE
FOR LIFE.

By CHARLES DARWIN, M.A.,

FELLOW OF THE ROYAL, GEOLOGICAL, LINNÆAN, ETC., SOCIETIES;
AUTHOR OF 'JOURNAL OF RESEARCHES DURING H. M. S. BEAGLE'S VOYAGE
ROUND THE WORLD.'

LONDON:
JOHN MURRAY, ALBEMARLE STREET.
1859.

The right of Translation is reserved.

The title page of Charles Darwin's *On the Origin of Species.* (1859)

We have no proof that Hitler read *The Origin of Species*. Most likely, he did not; nor did he need to. During his time in Vienna, newsstands sold cheap pamphlets explaining Darwin's theory in simple layman's terms. We cannot be sure if he read any of these or, if he did, which ones. Nevertheless, the theory captivated him, no matter how he came by it. What is more, he interpreted it in three ominous ways: natural law, racism, and anti-Semitism. The result was a witches' brew that turned every humane value, every tenet of morality, upside down.

Hitler's ideology rested on the idea that nature is all; nothing exists, or can exist, outside it. In his view, humans are not special beings created, as the great religions teach, in God's image, any more than are germs and worms. The Nazi leader's idea of paradise was not a peaceful garden, flowing with milk and honey. His perfect world, his Garden of Eden, was a jungle ruled by the law of struggle—the law of brute force. Though he did not use the

term, Janusz Korczak's "homo rapax," the human predator, was his ideal man.

All living beings devour each other, Hitler declared. "One creature drinks the blood of another. The death of one nourishes the other." Thus, might makes right—for that is how the world works. "Those who want to live, let them fight, and those who do not want to fight in this world of eternal struggle do not deserve to live." In Hitler's view, war was the highest form of struggle, the very essence of life. "War is the most natural, the most everyday matter," he declared. "War is eternal, war is universal. There is no beginning and there is no peace. War is life. . . . War is the origin of all things." Moreover, since the space on our planet is fixed and unchangeable, wars over territory and resources are inevitable and necessary.[22]

Hitler went further, marrying the idea of the struggle for existence to racism. To his mind, the idea of race embraced more than traditional justifications of bigotry, oppression, and slavery. The Führer insisted there is no "human family" to which we all belong. He held that races differed as much as flies from butterflies. Though both insects have wings, they differ in countless other ways. Similarly, races are not the same but are arranged in a sort of pyramid, with the "superior" at the top. Though the various races have human form, Hitler believed some were less evolved— less developed—than others. For example, he thought blacks closer to apes than to humans. At the peak of the pyramid stood the Aryan, or Nordic, race, represented by the Germans. Hitler and other racists cherished this myth. The Aryan race, however, does not exist. Properly used, the term *Aryan* refers to a family of

related languages spoken by half the world's people and has nothing to do with one's physical, mental, or moral qualities.[23]

Hitler also held that members of each race share a common "blood," which carries the "race-soul," or the race's unique qualities, from generation to generation. It followed that "blood-mixing" with "lesser" races amounted to "blood-poisoning," undermining racial "purity" and thus the ability to survive in the struggle for existence. "If a people no longer wants to respect the Nature-given qualities of its being rooted in its blood," he wrote, "it has no further right to complain over the loss of its earthly existence."[24]

These notions defy scientific fact. Blood is blood, the "river of life" that flows through our bodies—nothing less and nothing more. Blood carries oxygen, without which we cannot live, to every body cell, while carrying away carbon dioxide and other cellular waste materials. Blood has nothing to do with the genes, which are the parts of cells that determine which qualities living beings inherit from their parents. Terms like *Aryan blood, superior blood,* and *inferior blood* are biologically meaningless. But Hitler believed otherwise. And, for him, "Jewish blood" was the most dangerous substance in the universe.

"Jewish Blood"

Adolf Hitler hated Jewish people. Just hearing the word *Jew* caused physical changes in him. His face would darken, his mouth twisting into a grimace of disgust. Albert Speer, who met

with him regularly, thought Jew-hatred "an obsession central to his being, and finally the core and driving force of his pathology." Anti-Semitism in Poland was religious and economic, as we've seen. Hitler's hatred, in contrast, knew no bounds. Though dislike of Jews had been widespread in Germany for centuries, he blended it with the ideas of struggle for existence and racism. By doing so, he sharpened existing attitudes, creating a deadly mixture.[25]

The Nazi leader denied that Jews belonged to a religious and cultural community. Instead, he put them in a separate category—an alien species belonging neither to humanity nor even to the natural order. It is almost as if he imagined them as aliens in a science fiction novel. "The Jew is the anti-man, the creation of another god," Hitler declared. "He is a creature outside nature and alien to nature." Worse, Hitler accused Jews of being "the most diabolic creatures in existence." They could not help themselves, could not be otherwise, for having just one drop of "Jewish blood" made them enemies of humanity.[26]

Jews, Hitler believed, were the cause of all the evil in the world. He accused them of hatching a secret plot that took different forms at different times but had the common goal of world conquest. The Nazi leader claimed Jews, "the personification of the Devil," planned to destroy the Aryans, the "best" people who'd ever existed. Their method: intermarriage, or interbreeding, the gradual "corruption" of the Aryans' blood. Though Jews controlled business and banking, he claimed, they also created Communism and ignited the Russian Revolution. Democracy, too, was a "Jewish plot," for it empowered the common folk, not "supe-

rior" persons like the Nazis. The Weimar Republic was merely the "Jew republic," Hitler told audiences.[27]

In the 1980s, Polish-born Pope John Paul II said all Christians are spiritually Jews. "Whoever meets Jesus Christ meets Judaism. . . . The spiritual legacy of Israel [is] a living legacy that must be understood and treasured in its profundity and its richness." True enough, but this is exactly why Adolf Hitler despised the Christian religion.[28]

Though born to Catholic parents and baptized by a Catholic priest, the Nazi leader branded Christianity "an invention of sick brains"—that is, a Jewish invention. In after-dinner conversations, he referred to it in vile terms: "the drug of Christianity," "the pox of Christianity," "the disease of Christianity."[29]

His main charge was that Judaism had "infected" Christianity with the notions of humility, conscience, and pity, all qualities generally regarded as essential aspects of our humanity. Humility, as Jesus taught in the Sermon on the Mount (Matthew 5–7)—"Blessed are the meek, for they shall inherit the earth"— disgusted Hitler. So did conscience, the inner voice that tells us to do unto others as we would wish them to do unto us. As for pity, he blasted Christianity's preaching "the Jewish Christ-creed with its effeminate pity-ethics."[30]

These notions, Hitler snarled, were evil, because they went against nature's iron laws of struggle for existence and the survival of the fittest. Followed to their logical conclusion, they meant the end of the only paradise that existed for Hitler: the jungle. Unless races fought and the weak died, the human species would lose its vitality, he believed. "Darkness will again descend

on the earth, human culture will pass, and the world will turn to a desert." What is more, the Nazi leader convinced himself that he was "acting in accordance with the will of the Almighty Creator." Thus, by fighting the Jews and their evil influences, he said, *"I am fighting for the work of the Lord."*[31]

For Hitler, fighting meant killing, mass murder— extermination. Not that he preached this in public. After all, the raving fanatic was also a practical politician; he needed support and did not want to scare war-weary German voters. But in private letters and conversations, he described his real goal. In a letter dated September 16, 1919, the very first document of his political career, Hitler branded Jews a plague, a disease, "a racial tuberculosis." To fight this infection, he called for "the uncompromising removal of the Jew altogether."[32]

"Removal" was a vague term; it could mean simply exile from Germany. But early in 1922, Hitler made himself frighteningly clear. He gave an interview to journalist Josef Hell, a retired major in the German Army. Hell asked what he intended to do if he were ever free to act against the Jews. The question had the effect of a red-hot needle thrust into his flesh. Until then, Hitler had been relaxed, speaking calmly. Now the word *Jew* set him going. He stared wildly, clenched his fists, and began shouting. "Once I am really in power, my first and foremost task will be the annihilation of the Jews. As soon as I have the power to do so, I will have gallows built in rows. . . . Then the Jews will be hanged . . . and they will remain hanging until they stink."[33]

Nothing could change Hitler's mind; his ideas were fixed, as if set in concrete. Contrary ideas were, for him, simply part of

a "Jewish plot" to muddle understanding. Given the chance, he would kill every Jew on the planet. If he succeeded, he believed, the world would automatically return to its "natural" state. Races would fight each other, slaughter each other, and take each other's lands—as nature intended they should. Yet Hitler was also a patient man. Though the motive was there, the opportunity was not. He would bide his time, waiting for the right moment to turn his ideas into deeds.[34]

Hitler in Power

Hitler preached his hate messages throughout the 1920s. Since the government had tamed inflation, thanks largely to American loans, the Nazi Party could not score a breakthrough by electing enough members to control the Reichstag, Germany's parliament. However, the Great Depression was an unexpected stroke of good luck for Hitler. With unemployment soaring, millions yearned for a savior, someone to explain the cause of their troubles and make things better. Hitler's blaming the Jews for the calamity and his promises to put people back to work and make Germany great again translated into victories at the polls. In 1933, the Nazis became the largest party in the Reichstag. On January 30, their leader took office as chancellor, or head of the government.

Germans had mixed feelings about Hitler's victory. Millions thought it miraculous, a heaven-sent blessing. In one family, typical of many, the husband drank wine and shouted *"Sieg Heil!"*— "Hail victory!"—until drunk and hoarse. His wife wept for joy,

saying, "To think that I should live to see this! Now everything will be all right." Others were appalled. The Nazis, moaned a Berliner, "will destroy everything, law, order, civilization, everything we value." He was right.[35]

Chancellor Hitler used his office to dismantle the Weimar Republic from within, replacing it with a totalitarian system. Totalitarianism is a special form of dictatorship. A "normal" dictator is like the boss of a criminal gang. The boss uses violence for self-protection, for material gain, and to enrich his followers, thus keeping their loyalty. He cares nothing about how ordinary people live their lives, as long as they do not challenge him. A totalitarian dictator is more demanding. He has an ideology, and he aims to shape the world according to it. However, to succeed, he needs to exert absolute control over people's lives. Private life cannot exist, for he tells his subjects what they can and cannot do, say, think, feel, and believe. Under Hitler, the state claimed citizens' bodies and also their minds.

Hitler set out to create a "racial state," a nation devoted to racism and anti-Semitism. For starters, he made the Nazi Party Germany's official, and only, political party. All other parties— Communist, Social Democrat, Nationalist—were abolished, and thousands of their members were sent to Dachau, a concentration camp near Munich, the first of hundreds that would dot the German landscape. For their inmates, these places were the end of the world. One commander made this utterly clear, barking at new arrivals: "Forget your wives, children and families; here you will die like dogs." Many did. During Hitler's twelve-year rule (1933–1945), no fewer than thirty thousand Germans were executed in

Mass meeting: Adolf Hitler at the Bückeberg Harvest Festival. (1934)

these camps for opposing the regime. Dachau was not secret, and knowledge about it was meant to instill fear. "Shut up," people told one another, "or you'll go to Dachau."[36]

Meanwhile, Hitler ordered all private organizations dissolved and forced their members to join similar organizations run by the Nazi Party. These included social clubs, choirs, athletic leagues, youth groups, chess and checkers clubs, stamp collectors' clubs, bowling leagues, model airplane builders' clubs, trade associations, labor unions, teachers' organizations, and engineering and medical societies. Hans Frank took charge of Germany's legal profession. Hitler's personal lawyer and faithful flunky, Frank ranked his master alongside God. "Hitler is lonely. So is God. Hitler is like God," Frank famously said.[37]

Nazification meant putting all means of communication under Nazi control: radio stations, telephone and telegraph companies, newspapers, magazines, and films. The propaganda minister, Joseph Goebbels, who was nicknamed "Hitler's Mickey Mouse," banned "degenerate art." This label was applied to any painting, drawing, etching, or sculpture that failed to depict the superiority of the "Aryan" race. Modern art became taboo; Hitler declared it the "mental excrement of diseased brains." So, among the sixty-five hundred paintings that vanished from museums were those of the giants of modern art: Pablo Picasso, Vincent van Gogh, Henri Matisse, Paul Gauguin, and Paul Klee, to name a few. The German classics, works by Ludwig van Beethoven and Johannes Brahms, dominated the music scene. But Germans could not listen to jazz, at least in public performances. Nazis damned jazz as the music of savages. A vile poster titled "Degenerate Music" shows a black man wearing a Star of David playing jazz on a saxophone. Such displays of hatred encouraged the Ku Klux Klan, a group of violent American racists, to establish a chapter in Germany.[38]

The Nazis classified certain books as "mental excrement," pure filth. In May 1933, thugs "cleansed" libraries of "un-Aryan books." The economic works of Karl Marx, the novels of Thomas Mann, and the psychoanalytic writings of Sigmund Freud wound up in bonfires encircled by cheering Nazis. Some onlookers grimaced as they hurried past. They may have recalled a saying of the German Jewish poet Heinrich Heine: "There where they burn books, in the end they will also burn people." However, Hitler's *Mein Kampf* became a bestseller. Schools gave it as prizes, and newlyweds received it as a gift. Prudent people displayed it promi-

nently in their homes; there was no telling when the police might barge in, and *Mein Kampf* served as proof of one's loyalty. Royalties from its sales and the use of his image on postage stamps made Hitler a millionaire.[39]

A totalitarian state is also a police state, where the rulers keep order through terror. SS chief Heinrich Himmler was Nazi Germany's top terrorist. Himmler oversaw a network of police agencies, spies, and informers. His agents were in every city, town, railroad station, and restaurant—wherever Germans got together. Constant surveillance made many people yearn for privacy. Even in bed, said a young man, "unviolated private life is no longer possible . . . because dreaming is of course forbidden." Another man felt watched while sitting on the toilet, "because I didn't trust my backside any more."[40]

Himmler's deputy, Reinhard Heydrich, took charge of everyday business. Heydrich was an amazing person. A talented violinist, a daring pilot, and a champion athlete, he'd earned awards for skiing and fencing. He also had several nicknames, including "the Blond Beast" and "the Hangman." Like a block of iron, Heydrich was cold and hard; Hitler called him "the Man with the Iron Heart." These qualities served him well

SS chief Heinrich Himmler's deputy, Reinhard Heydrich, dubbed "the Hangman." (c. 1941)

as "SS Chief of Reich Security." Utterly ruthless, Heydrich ran the Gestapo (the name is a shortening of the German for "Secret State Police"). Unlike the police in a democracy, who are bound by the law, the Gestapo was a law unto itself, bound only by the will of Hitler. The Gestapo could do anything, to anyone, at any time, for any reason—or for no reason at all. Its agents could arrest people without a warrant, keep them in secret prisons, torture them, and execute them without a trial. Families knew nothing of their loved ones' fate; they simply vanished into unmarked graves.[41]

German Jews

In 1933, about 525,000 Jews lived in Germany; they accounted for less than 1 percent of a total population of 66 million. Jews lived almost entirely in cities, notably Berlin. Unlike the majority of their Polish cousins, German Jews strove for acceptance. Assimilated Jews played major roles in the professions, sciences, arts, and business; Jews owned Berlin's largest department stores and served as directors of its largest banks. Some Jewish families were fabulously wealthy, living in mansions and catered to by servants.

Nearly all German Jews saw themselves as "Germans of Jewish faith." German was their native language. The Ostjuden—Eastern European Jews—spoke Yiddish, considered by the Germans a "coarse" tongue, the language of "common" folk. Proud and patriotic, more than 18,000 Jewish men earned the Iron Cross in World War I, the same medal awarded to Hitler. When

Hitler took power, many German Jews thought the responsibility of governing would soften his anti-Semitism. After all, he seemed a practical man, a realist, a man of the world. A few wealthy Jews even contributed to the Nazi Party, hoping to have influence if the Nazis gained control of the government. They were wrong. The Nazi leader was racist to his fingertips. Nothing could change that fact, as Jews learned to their horror.

Hitler lost no time in moving against Germany's Jews. In April 1933, storm troopers, Nazi bruisers in brown shirts and jackboots, went on a rampage. Their "wild actions" culminated in boycotts and vandalism against Jewish businesses. Their slogan was *"Kauf nicht bei Juden"*—"Don't buy from Jews." Storm troopers stood outside Jewish-owned shops, chanting a bloodcurdling verse:

> When Jewish blood spurts from the knife,
> Then things will be twice as good.

Shouting "The Jews are our misfortune!" and "Germans, defend yourselves!" they smashed windows and beat up shoppers.[42]

A few days after the boycott ended, Leo Baeck, Berlin's leading rabbi, saw the handwriting on the wall. And what he "read" shook him to the depths of his soul. "The thousand-year history of the German Jews has come to an end," he declared. Baeck had reason for pessimism, yet even he never imagined the Nazis would threaten Jews' very lives.[43]

The screws steadily tightened, as Hitler made his ideology official German state policy. Eventually, more than two thousand anti-Semitic laws, decrees, orders, ordinances, edicts, rulings,

Propaganda from the 1933 boycott that states, "The Jews are our misfortune."
Der Stürmer, or "The Stormer," was a virulently anti-Semitic Nazi newspaper.

rules, and regulations would fill a four-hundred-page book printed in small type. These aimed at bringing "social death"— that is, denigrating, dominating, and segregating a minority so that it is no longer seen as human. Dehumanizing "the Other" lowers moral barriers, making it acceptable to oppress, and even destroy, them.[44]

The Nazis struck in every direction. Jews could no longer practice their professions: medicine, dentistry, law, engineering, university teaching. Towns posted signs warning JEWS KEEP OUT, JEWS NOT WANTED HERE, and JEWS ENTER THIS PLACE AT YOUR OWN RISK. Persons having "Jewish blood" were barred from health spas, resorts, theaters, concert halls, nightclubs, museums,

libraries, movie houses, skating rinks, and swimming pools. Hotels and restaurants displayed JEWS UNDESIRED signs in their windows. Tin labels marked park benches as ARYAN and JEW. If Jews used streetcars and other public transportation, they could not sit unless all "Aryans" had seats—just as African Americans in Southern states had to sit at the back of the bus. Nor could Jews buy, own, use, or borrow a host of common items. A short list included coffee, cake, white bread, vacuum cleaners, electric toasters, cars, motorcycles, bicycles, binoculars, baby carriages, phonographs, ice skates, hiking equipment, pets, flowers, fruit, typewriters, cameras, and radios.[45]

Jewish government employees lost their jobs and pensions. In 1935, the so-called Nuremberg Laws on Citizenship and Race

A woman hiding her face from passersby as she sits on a "for Jews only" bench. (1938)

deprived Jews of their German citizenship and civil rights, including the right to their own names. They had to take on new middle names: Israel for men and Sarah for women. And just as several of the American states banned interracial marriage, in Germany no Jew could have sexual relations with an "Aryan," let alone marry one.

On the night of November 9, 1938, the Nazis unleashed a wave of mob violence unlike any in modern German history. Nationwide, storm troopers and bands of Nazi sympathizers destroyed seventy-five hundred Jewish-owned stores and torched 276 synagogues. Bellowing *"Juda verrecke!"*—"Perish the Jews!"—thugs held defenseless people captive in synagogues; those who needed to relieve themselves had to go against the walls. Jews were humiliated, made to crawl on all fours covered with spittle and filth. Storm troopers hauled off thousands of Jewish men to concentration camps. Others invaded Jewish homes, trashing them and beating their residents, throwing some from third-floor windows. Ninety-one Jews lost their lives that night. Looters had a field day, taking whatever they wished. Police and firefighters stood by; they had orders to do nothing unless "Aryan" property was endangered. Germans called this pogrom Kristallnacht (Night of Broken Glass) after the shards of glass from broken windows littering the streets.[46]

Like their parents, German Jewish children experienced violence. Screaming mobs invaded orphanages. In one small town, for instance, Nazis sent children, ages six to sixteen, fleeing. The night was cold, and the children hadn't had time to put on their coats. Shivering and crying, they ran down the street, following

Shopkeepers and their helpers cleaning glass from the streets after Kristallnacht. (1938)

the director, to the town hall to ask for police protection. "We do not give protection to Jews," snarled the police chief, drawing his pistol. "Get out with those children or I'll shoot." The next morning, they returned to the orphanage, hungry and exhausted, only to find it wrecked.[47] Such an outrage Janusz Korczak never worried about; that was beyond the pale, even for Polish anti-Semites.

The only synagogue in Siegen, Germany, burning during Kristallnacht. (1938)

Many ordinary Germans reacted with shock and shame. Powerless to halt the violence, they stood by as storm troopers rampaged. Afterward, Christabel Bielenberg, an Englishwoman married to a German lawyer, recalled: "No one to whom I spoke rejoiced in the shambles; on the contrary [people] . . . stood around the newspaper kiosks registering puzzlement, even disgust, or else hurried past the hastily boarded up windows . . . with their gaze fixed firmly on their boots." Others murmured that one could not burn *Gotteshäuser* (houses of God) without divine retribution. "This fire will return!" said a man as a synagogue burned. "It will take a long curve and come back to us."[48]

A heroic few spoke out. Appalled, Bernhard Lichtenberg,

dean of St. Hedwig's Roman Catholic cathedral in Berlin, took to his pulpit. The priest, later killed by the Nazis, told the congregation a simple truth: "Outside the synagogue is burning. It is also a house of God." Another Berliner, an elderly man and a "pure Aryan," watched as children carried bags of candy from a Jewish-owned shop. A crowd of adults stood by, including several of the looters' parents and a smirking storm trooper. Incensed, the old-timer cried: "You think you are hurting the Jew. You do not know what you are doing. You are teaching your children to steal." Then he walked away. Yet his words had found their mark. Parents broke from the crowd, knocked the candy from their children's hands, and dragged them home.[49]

Following Kristallnacht, the entire Jewish community was fined one billion marks to pay for the damage the Nazis caused! All insurance payments for damages went to the government. Worse, Jews' bank accounts were frozen, and Jewish businesses were "Aryanized"—that is, owners were forced to sell to "Aryans" at knockdown prices. From then on, Jews had to survive on any cash they might have stashed away from selling their possessions or on the dwindling resources of Jewish charitable groups.

The loss of their ability to earn a living convinced many Jews that they had no future in Germany. Those who dreaded Hitler's next moves, and still had some money, fled. Of these, most went to England, France, Belgium, and the Netherlands. American public opinion was dead set against admitting Jewish refugees. Opponents said the newcomers would take American jobs and would threaten national security because the Nazis recruited Jews as spies. President Franklin D. Roosevelt, who should have

known better, repeated this rubbish. "It is rather a horrible story," he said, "but in some of the other countries that refugees out of Germany have gone to, especially Jewish refugees, they found a number of definitely proven spies." He did not name the "other countries." Nevertheless, the United States took in nearly two hundred thousand Jewish refugees between 1933 and 1939, more than any other country. One of these was Albert Einstein, a mathematics genius who worked out the theory for the atomic bomb. Had Hitler gotten this "ultimate weapon," he would surely have used it to realize his dream of world conquest.[50]

Jews who remained in Germany often had to make a heart-wrenching decision. Shocked by the violence of Kristallnacht, English charities organized Kindertransport (Children's Transport), a program to bring unaccompanied children, mostly Jewish, out of Germany and Austria, which Hitler had recently taken over. Beginning on December 2, 1938, some 10,000 Jewish children under the age of seventeen were taken to England and placed with foster families. In the United States, however, in February 1939, three months after Kristallnacht, Congress rejected a bill to allow 20,000 Jewish children into the country. Foes claimed that "twenty thousand charming children would all too soon grow into twenty thousand ugly adults."[51]

Saying goodbye was a painful experience. Hedy Epstein was fourteen when she left Germany. She recalled the scene at the railroad station in Freiburg, her hometown:

As the train started to pull out of the station, my parents ran alongside the train on the platform, and I remember sort of

Children of the Kindertransport arriving in London from Nazi Germany. (1939)

in my head, I heard the refrain, "You're leaving. You're leaving." I watched their faces, and tears were streaming down their cheeks. And I knew then: these people really loved me. That is why they're sending me away. Many years later I realized that by sending me away, my parents gave me the gift of life a second time.[52]

Parents often found the emotional strain of parting too much to bear. On December 11, 1938, the *New York Times* reported, "One mother died of a heart attack after kissing her 5-year-old goodbye. The child was not told. Seven mothers fainted as the children marched to the train." Few children ever saw their parents again.[53]

Little Nazis

Janusz Korczak once said, "It is really children who are the princes of feelings, the poets and thinkers. We should respect with humility the white, bright, holiness of childhood." That belief, as we have seen, led him to devote his life to helping children develop to their full potential as human beings.[54]

Adolf Hitler would have considered the Old Doctor's ideas squishy, naive, and absurd. For if the Third Reich were to last a thousand years, as he vowed it would, he had to instill Nazi ideology into future generations. Ultimately, everything depended on the young, for, as Hitler said, "who has the youth, has the future."[55]

It followed that the Führer needed to take complete charge of the physical, emotional, and mental development of German youth. Hitler believed the young were not precious in themselves, but were raw material, objects to be molded to serve his ideology. And the way to do this was to capture them during their formative years. The Nazi leader saw young minds as "blank slates" easily "inscribed" with the Nazi version of reality. He would cut them off from every source of doubt and, at the same time, discourage independent thinking. Because the young were naturally idealistic, and did not know enough to question Nazi ideology, they were more easily influenced than adults.

Hitler set out to immerse Germany's young people in an all-Nazi environment until, he declared, they "become ours, body and soul." Parents could complain all they wished. No matter;

Young Nazi supporters waving swastika flags. (1934)

they were yesterday's people, with yesterday's ideas, while Nazis were the shapers of tomorrow. When he finished with their children, Hitler bragged, he would own them, and they "will not be free again for the rest of their lives."[56]

The Führer wanted a German youth that would live by his

A young boy displays the Nazi flag on his scooter. (c. 1935)

ideal of brute force: "A youth will grow up before which the world will shrink back. A violently active, dominating, intrepid, brutal youth—that is what I am after. Youth must be all these things. It must be indifferent to pain. There must be no weakness or tenderness in it. I want to see once more in its eyes the gleam of pride . . . of the beast of prey. . . . I shall eradicate the thousands of years of human domestication. Then I shall have in front of me the pure and noble natural material. With that I can create the new order." The youth of Nazi Germany would conquer the world for their Führer.[57]

The success of Hitler's new order rested on giving the young the right education. The process began in kindergarten and continued through elementary school, high school, and university.

Classrooms became Nazi temples. As children entered, the teacher, invariably a Nazi wearing a swastika lapel pin, stood at the door. No more *"Guten Morgen, meine Kinder"*—"Good morning, my children." Together, they faced Hitler's portrait, extended their right arms, and cried, *"Heil Hitler!"* Everyone had to use the official "German greeting" for every interaction. *"Heil Hitler!"* cried the postman, garbage collector, shop clerk, and train conductor. When children came home for lunch, *Mutti*—Mommy—was supposed to greet them with *"Heil Hitler!"* If she did not, and a nosy neighbor found out, the Gestapo would ask why. Erika Mann, novelist Thomas Mann's daughter and a staunch anti-Nazi, estimated that children gave the salute from 50 to 150 times a day! She added: "Your evening prayers must close with *'Heil Hitler!'* if you take your devotions seriously." If you were a really devout Nazi, you also had a "Hitler corner" in your living room, a shrine adorned with his portrait, *Mein Kampf,* and fresh flowers. (Soviet households had similar "Stalin corners.")[58]

Kindergartners gave thanks to the Almighty for sending "our Führer"

A young German girl arranges a "Hitler corner," a shrine to the Führer. (1938)

during Germany's time of need. We get a sense of the devotion they were taught in this Nazified version of the Lord's Prayer:

> *Führer, my Führer, bequeathed to me by the Lord,*
> *Protect and preserve me as long as I live!*
> *Thou hast rescued Germany from deepest distress,*
> *I thank thee today for my daily bread.*
> *Abideth thou long with me, forsaketh me not,*
> *Führer, my Führer, my faith and my light!*
> *Heil mein Führer!*[59]

A Nazi hymn expressed the nobility of dying for Hitler:

> *We love our Führer*
> *We honor our Führer*
> *We follow our Führer*
> *Until we are men;*
>
> *We believe in our Führer*
> *We live for our Führer*
> *We die for our Führer*
> *Until we are heroes.*[60]

Racism and anti-Semitism were basic subjects, required of all schoolchildren. Committees of "race-experts" issued new textbooks with titles such as *People and Race*, *Race Science of the German People*, *Heredity and Racial Biology for Students*, and *Can You Think Racially?* The purpose of these books was to fos-

ter "race-consciousness," awareness of "Aryan" superiority and of the absolute need for "blood purity." They reminded readers that "your body does not belong to you; it belongs to the *Volk* [people]." Small children recited this ditty:

> *Keep your Blood pure,*
> *it is not yours alone,*
> *it comes from far away,*
> *it flows into the distance*
> *laden with thousands of ancestors*
> *and it holds the entire future!*
> *It is your eternal life.*[61]

Scientific advances and great music, art, and poetry: all, according to the Nazis, sprang from the "Aryan soul" and were "Aryan spiritual property." Likewise, mathematics—arithmetic, algebra, calculus, geometry, trigonometry—supposedly had "Aryan" roots. Nazi math dealt with practical military matters. A standard textbook, *National Political Practice in Arithmetic Lessons*, asked middle school pupils to solve this problem:

> *A bombing plane can be loaded with one explosive bomb of 35 kilograms, three bombs of 100 kilograms, four [poison] gas bombs of 150 kilograms, and 200 incendiary bombs of one kilogram.*
> *A. What is the load capacity?*
> *B. What is the percentage of each type of bomb?*[62]

Biology lessons illustrated the physical perfection of the "Aryan" race. Pure "Aryans" were said to be blond, blue-eyed, fair-skinned, tall, and slender. Many of the Nazi leaders, however, appeared to be total opposites of what they preached as the Nazi ideal. This discrepancy prompted skeptics to ask: "What does the ideal Aryan look like?" One pragmatic response was: "As tall as Goebbels, as slim as Göring, as blond as Hitler." Nevertheless, racists insisted that Aryan features were the animal kingdom's standard of excellence. That "birds can talk better than other animals," said Nazi race theorist Hermann Gauch, "is explained

Nazi youth salute at a rally. (1938)

by the fact that their mouths are Nordic in structure." This would be funny if it were not so asinine. Nevertheless, it shows that even university-trained people can make themselves believe almost anything, especially if doing so advances their careers.[63]

Every age group learned about the "evil," "unnatural," and "subhuman" Jews. Nazi authors churned out "hate-books" for use in elementary schools throughout Germany. For example, *The Poisonous Mushroom* was a basic reader for young children. It begins innocently enough by describing a favorite German activity. Franz and his mother walk through a forest, collecting mushrooms. Carefully, she points out the difference between edible mushrooms and deadly toadstools. Good mushrooms, she says, are like good people, and bad mushrooms are like Jews. In the story "What Hans and Elsa Experienced with a Stranger," two children meet an ugly man with thick lips and a big nose who offers them candy. The story ends with their mother having them memorize this:

> *A devil goes through the land,*
> *It's the Jew, well-known to us*
> *as a murderer of peoples*
> *a race defiler, a children's horror in all lands!* . . .
> *Stay away from every Jew,*
> *and happiness will come to you!*[64]

Erika Mann learned how ingrained hatred could become. In *School for Barbarians: Education Under the Nazis* (1938), she related a shocking incident. An ambulance had rushed a little boy to a hospital with a burst appendix. In the operating room,

he was given anesthesia, which put him into a deep sleep, and a surgeon worked to save his life. But the child began to scream— a scream that came from his unconscious mind. "Down with the Jews! Kill the Jews, we have to get rid of them!" When told about the incident, the surgeon's wife could not get over those words: "It drives me mad to think that my son might ever be able to turn to death and murder in his sleep, because he had been taught to do so, and because I had no right to stop that teaching."[65]

Jewish children faced hatred every day. Suddenly, boys and girls they'd always known and liked turned against them. "German girls I was friends with," one child said, "they call me 'dirty Jew.' My friends, the friends I grew up with!" Lore Gang-Salheimer, eleven years old in 1933, recalled, "It began to happen that non-Jewish children would say, 'No, I can't walk home from school with you anymore. I can't be seen with you anymore.'"[66]

Going to school became a daily ordeal. It started with the teachers. Traditionally regarded as positive role models for the young, teachers now used boorish insults like *Judenlümmel* (Jewish lout) and *Judensau* (Jewish pig). When, for example, a Jewish student entered the classroom, her teacher pointed at her and said, "Go to the back of the class. You are not one of us anymore"; the back of the room was called Israel. If a Jew raised his hand to answer a question, the teacher might say, "Put your hand down. Jews have no business in a German class." When children lined up in the lunchroom, the teacher in charge might cry, "Run along, Jew! Next, please!" Classmates followed their teacher's example, shunning the Jewish children, making nasty remarks, even

assaulting them. These humiliations continued until Jews were banned from public schools after Kristallnacht.[67]

The Hitler Youth

Before the rise of Hitler, German boys and girls had belonged to thousands of youth groups, which specialized in activities ranging from hiking, camping, sports, and singing to stamp collecting and model-airplane building. Upon taking power, the Nazis abolished all of these groups. Instead, boys had to enroll in the Hitler Youth (Hitlerjugend), and girls in the League of German Maidens (Bund Deutscher Mädel).

Besides racist and anti-Semitic indoctrination, both girls and boys received massive doses of anti-Christian propaganda to reinforce classroom learning. Nazis dubbed Christianity a "Jewish conspiracy" to "corrupt" the "Aryan" race and "poison" its blood. Hitler intended to abolish all forms of Christianity. Germans, said Joseph Goebbels, did not need the traditional religion, not when they had the Führer. "Hitler is a new, a greater, a more powerful Jesus Christ," the propaganda minister cried. "Our God, our Pope, is Adolf Hitler."[68] At meetings, lectures, and outings, speakers denounced Jesus Christ as "this swine," this son of a "Jewish tramp." They sang:

We are the merry Hitler Youth,
We need no Christian virtue,

For our leader, Adolf Hitler,
Is our redeemer. . . .
No evil priest can stop us
From feeling we are Hitler's children.
We follow not Christ. . . .
Singing we follow Hitler's banners.[69]

The Hitler Youth was the Führer's pride and joy; Hitler believed that from its ranks would come future generations of Nazi warriors and party officials. The youngest boys, ages six through nine, were called *Pimpfe,* or "squirts." Each carried a "book of deeds," a detailed record of his achievements and failures. Group leaders noted every boy's leadership potential, physical prowess,

Hitler Youth at a Nazi rally. (1936)

and knowledge of Nazi ideology. As a boy's tenth birthday drew near, he had to pass a test of courage. He might, for instance, have to jump from a second-story window with a heavy backpack or leap over burning logs. Only then would he receive his Hitler Youth dagger, its blade inscribed with the motto "Blood and Honor." The dagger symbolically bound him closer to Hitler than to his parents.[70]

When the squirt turned ten, he entered the German Young Folks (Deutsches Jungvolk), for boys through the age of fourteen. Members boxed, camped overnight in forests, and bathed in icy streams. These outings toughened them, satisfied their thirst for adventure and camaraderie, and created a sense of group solidarity, as in an army platoon. "We really had to freeze and swelter, we had to get soaked in our tents," one boy recalled. "But then there was the feeling of being in a group, going on hikes, the exertion. In the evening we all sat around the fire. And then we sang together. It was dark. The stars above me. It was very moving, something one never forgets."[71] From ages fifteen to eighteen, boys belonged to the Hitler Youth proper. All members of the Hitler Youth, regardless of their age, went on long marches with heavy backpacks, rain or shine, heat or cold. To keep up the pace, they sang constantly. A favorite song appealed to their sense of destiny:

> We shall march on
> When everything lies in ruins!
> For today Germany is ours,
> And tomorrow the whole world!

Finally, in a solemn ceremony, "the holiest hour of our lives," they swore an oath to "devote all my energies, all my strength to the savior of our country, Adolf Hitler."[72]

Hitler's future soldiers learned to handle pistols, rifles, machine guns, and explosives. Military-style training consisted of setting ambushes and crawling under barbed-wire entanglements while live machine-gun bullets snapped inches above their heads. These young men were considered state property. "Your body belongs to your country, as it is to your country that you owe your existence," proclaimed a slogan posted in meeting rooms. Death in battle was glorified at every turn. On a hillside opposite one training camp, American journalist Dorothy Thompson saw an enormous white banner that had a swastika and seven immense black words painted on it: "You Were Born to Die for Germany!"[73]

To bolster its claim to absolute power, Nazism sought to weaken the bonds between parents and children. Thus, the ideal Nazi child was also a spy. German parents had to watch what they said in front of their children. If they criticized Hitler or the Nazis, a boy was honor-bound to report the incident to his Hitler Youth group leader, who then reported it to the Gestapo, perhaps with fatal results for the parents.

When a young man left the Hitler Youth at age nineteen, he entered the Reichsarbeitdienst (Reich Labor Service). For six months, he "voluntarily" worked, without pay, in a factory or was kept busy bringing in harvests or replanting forests. Then he did a two-year stint in the Wehrmacht. Officers encouraged the toughest and most fanatical young men to apply for the military arm of the SS. Led by Heinrich Himmler, the Waffen-SS had the most

rigorous training of any armed force in the world. Not even the U.S. Marines trained as hard as its members.

To qualify for this force, an applicant had to prove his "pure" Aryan ancestry going back to the year 1750. Instructors drilled Waffen-SS values into the head of every recruit. Each was expected to be hard, pitiless, and brutal. Instructors constantly tested a recruit's obedience in various ways. After he became attached to a puppy he'd been ordered to raise, an instructor would tell him to shoot the animal or kill it with a knife. If the recruit dropped a bullet on the ground, an instructor would order him to pick it up with his teeth. The recruit had to learn to ignore pain. For example,

if he had an ingrown toenail, he was expected to sit still, tight-lipped, while a medic removed it without anesthetic.[74]

Training could easily become lethal. Combat veteran Peter Neumann recalled that recruits stood, stripped to the waist, as instructors set fierce German shepherds on them. They had to fight off the dogs with their bare hands—or

A Nazi recruitment poster for the Waffen-SS. (c. 1939)

die trying. At other times, they had to dig foxholes as armored cars bore down on them. If they dug too slowly, they died under the wheels. If a recruit tried to run away, an instructor shot him. Higher-ups called such deaths "wastage," a routine part of training.[75]

Waffen-SS men wore jet-black uniforms with a forked lightning insignia on the jacket lapel, high black boots, and a black cap with a skull-and-crossbones badge. Friedrich Reck-Malleczewen, a German nobleman who saw an off-duty group in a Berlin nightclub, said they sent chills up his spine. Years of indoctrination had turned them into obedient robots, men without pity or conscience. Had the nobleman known about Janusz Korczak's play *The Senate of Madmen,* he might have thought he'd seen the lunatics in the flesh.

> *Woe to Europe. . . . These young men would . . . not hesitate to send cathedrals tumbling into the air. . . . Oh, they will perpetrate still worse things, and worst, most dreadful of all, they will be totally incapable of even sensing the deep degradation of their existence.*[76]

Prophetic words.

Eugenics and Euthanasia

Sir Francis Galton, Charles Darwin's cousin, coined the word *eugenics* in 1883, defining it as "the science of the improvement of the human race by better breeding"—"genetic engineering" for short. Eugenics seemed to make sense. For thousands of years, stockmen had bred cattle to yield more meat and milk, and farmers bred hardier strains of corn and wheat. Logically, it followed that selective breeding could yield healthier, stronger, more intelligent human beings. However, that which is "logical" need not be true, because humans are not cattle or plants.[77]

Nevertheless, Galton's idea caught on quickly. By 1900, eugenics societies and publications flourished in Europe and the United States, backed by men like steel baron Andrew Carnegie and oil tycoon John D. Rockefeller. "Eugenists," as they called themselves, divided their field into two branches: "positive" and "negative." "Positive" eugenics encouraged the breeding of people with "superior" traits—traits not only physical and mental but also moral. "Positive" eugenics held that humans inherited qualities like decency, honesty, and self-discipline, a theory now discredited in favor of environmental influences. In contrast, "negative" eugenics discouraged the reproduction of people with "inferior" physical, intellectual, and moral traits.

Adolf Hitler believed in eugenics; it fit so neatly into his racist and totalitarian ideology. Through "positive" eugenics, he meant to use state power to create what he called "the god-man," the *Herrenvolk,* or "master race" of "Aryan supermen." Through

"negative" eugenics, he aimed to get rid of those deemed *Untermenschen,* or "subhumans."[78]

Women were essential to the success of the Nazi eugenics program. Hitler had a mistress, Eva Braun, whom he liked because she was so simple and unthreatening. The Führer thought women inferior to men. They were, he declared, "by nature" creatures of emotion and thus incapable of thinking logically. For that reason, he banned them from being judges and lawyers. Hitler described the ideal woman as "a cute, cuddly, naive little thing—tender, sweet, and stupid." A woman's world was, he said, "her husband, her family, her children, and her house." He liked his women plain. Female "race-comrades" should not paint their fingernails, pluck their eyebrows, or wear lipstick. "Do you know what lipstick is made of?" Hitler asked dinner guests. "Lipsticks are made of the fat skimmed off sewage."[79]

The education of women, as Hitler saw it, was unfeminine and a waste of time. So the Nazis limited the enrollment of women at universities to 10 percent of the student body. At age ten, girls had to join the Young Maidens' League (Jungmädelbund); at age fourteen, they moved on to the League of German Maidens. Both groups focused on building healthy bodies through hiking, sports, and calisthenics. Since nature created women as "breeding machines," healthy bodies meant healthy babies. To make sure that women kept breeding to the utmost, the government closed birth control clinics and outlawed abortion as a "crime against the race." Nazi judges punished anyone who performed abortions with heavy fines and up to fifteen years of hard labor in prison.[80]

Hitler urged Germans of "good stock" to marry early and

Members of the League of German Maidens. (Date unknown)

have as many children as possible. In response, Goebbels's propagandists created a "cult of motherhood." An official slogan announced: "Every woman must present a child to her beloved Führer." A deluge of paintings, sculptures, and posters depicted blond, blue-eyed mothers happily breastfeeding adorable blond, blue-eyed babies. To help newlyweds get started, the government offered interest-free loans. And when babies arrived, the state provided health care for mother and child free of charge.[81]

Hitler compared childbearing to warfare. He declared: "Every child that a woman brings into the world is a battle, a battle waged for the existence of her people." And like brave soldiers, German mothers won medals according to the number of children they bore. The Honor Cross of the German Mother became no less

prestigious than the warrior's Iron Cross. Mothers received the Bronze Cross for having four or five children, the Silver Cross for six or seven, and the Gold Cross for eight or more. Heroines who had twelve or more children received the Gold Cross with Diamonds. With these medals came special privileges. "I have donated a child to the Führer" became magical passwords. They allowed a woman to go to the head of any line and get a seat in a packed streetcar. Hitler Youth had to salute them, help them cross the street, and carry their packages. Mother's Day, an idea borrowed from the United States, became a major Nazi holiday.[82]

The SS chief demanded baby boys—lots of them. War was coming, Himmler knew, and he expected the Waffen-SS to take heavy losses. To ensure the future of the SS, he ordered his men to father as many children as possible. It did not matter if they already had wives; their duty to the race outweighed any marriage vows. To encourage baby production, Himmler created the breeding program Lebensborn (Spring of Life). In several secluded Lebensborn homes, SS men, married or not, would sire children with young women, married or not. Himmler asked only that the women be "racially sound."[83]

Group leaders urged members of the League of German Maidens to serve Hitler with their wombs. As the slogan went: "You can't all get a husband, but you can all be mothers." Some young women, seduced by propaganda, took the bait. Teenagers ran away from home without telling their parents of their plan to donate a child to the Führer. One girl, "with blazing eyes," announced to fellow train passengers: "I am going . . . to have myself impregnated."[84]

A propaganda poster for the League of German Maidens. The caption reads, "Build youth hostels and homes." (c. 1938)

The experience of seventeen-year-old Hildegard Koch was typical. When her group leader told her, "What Germany needs more than anything is racially valuable stock," Hildegard volunteered. Upon arriving at a Lebensborn facility, she found "about 40 girls all about my own age. No one knew anyone else's name, and no one knew where we came from. All you needed to be accepted there was a certificate of Aryan ancestry as far back as your great grandparents."[85]

Following an examination by an SS doctor, Hildegard was introduced to several eligible SS men, and she was given a week to choose a mating partner. She chose "a sweet boy" who "was actually a little stupid" but had "smashing looks." Neither knew the other's name. "He slept with me for three evenings in one week. The other nights he had to do his duty with another girl." Hildegard became pregnant. When her child was born, the SS held a naming ceremony in a chapel adorned with portraits of Hitler

An SS Lebensborn birthing facility. (1935)

and swastika emblems. An officer welcomed the infant into the SS's "racial brotherhood" with this blessing:

> *We believe in the god of all things*
> *And in the mission of our German blood,*
> *Which grows ever young from German soil.*
> *We believe in the race, carrier of the blood,*
> *And in the Führer, chosen for us by God.*

Afterward, a birth mother could leave with her new daughter or son or give the child to the SS, which would put the baby up for adoption by childless Nazi couples. Hildegard, like most of the Lebensborn mothers, never saw her child, a son, or his father again. Historians estimate that twenty thousand babies were born this way during the Hitler years.[86]

If "positive" eugenics aimed at bringing "race-comrades" into the world, "negative" eugenics aimed at preventing the birth of "defectives" or destroying them after birth. As the Nazis put it: "Not every being with a human face is human." In other words, Nazis considered entire categories of humans the equivalents of social parasites, "useless eaters" unworthy of respect and life itself.[87]

Hitler's "negative" eugenics program developed in two stages, one known by the German public, the other secret. The first stage involved sterilization, a surgical procedure to prevent a male from siring, and a female from conceiving, a new life. Sterilization by government order was not new in the 1930s, and it did not originate in Nazi Germany. Before Hitler came to power, the United States led the world in the sterilization of "defectives."

The procedure had the blessing of prominent people on both sides of the Atlantic. In 1913, former U.S. president Theodore Roosevelt declared that "society has no business to permit degenerates to reproduce their kind. . . . Some day we will realize that the prime duty . . . of the good citizen of the right type is to leave his or her blood behind him in the world, and that we have no business to [aid] perpetuation of citizens of the wrong type." Two years later, Helen Keller, blind and deaf from childhood, said much the same: "Our puny sentimentalism has caused us to forget that

A Nazi Party election poster that celebrates the importance of Aryan families. Only certain kinds of people were encouraged to procreate. (1936)

a human life is sacred only when it may be of some use to itself and to the world."[88]

Sterilization also had the blessing of the U.S. Supreme Court. In 1927, in *Buck v. Bell*, Associate Justice Oliver Wendell Holmes Jr. wrote the majority opinion. If, for the public good, America's "best citizens" could be sacrificed in war, he argued, "mental defectives" should be sterilized for the same reason. "It would be strange if we could not call upon those who already sap the strength of the state for these lesser sacrifices. . . . It is better for all the world, if instead of waiting to execute degenerate offspring for crime, or to let them starve for their imbecility, society can prevent those who are manifestly unfit from continuing their kind."[89]

Eventually, thirty states passed sterilization laws. California led the pack, sterilizing 20,108 people, chiefly women too poor to hire lawyers to fight for them in court. Eugenics experts deemed many of them "bad girls" who were "passionate," "oversexed,"

or "sexually wayward"—whatever those terms meant. From 1907 to 1964, some 63,643 Americans were legally sterilized. In Europe, Sweden, Denmark, Norway, and Finland forcibly sterilized hundreds of their citizens each year.[90]

Nazi Germany's Law for the Prevention of Hereditarily Diseased Offspring took effect on July 14, 1933. Known as the "Sterilization Law," it set up two hundred eugenics courts to rule on cases submitted by hospitals, social service agencies, and private physicians. Alcoholics, epileptics, people born with physical deformities, those with hereditary blindness and deafness, the intellectually disabled: all were to be sterilized. Their fate was public knowledge; Germans called the operation *Hitlerschnitt*—"Hitler's cut."[91]

The Gestapo also hunted gay men, whom Hitler called "disgusting apes." Himmler agreed with his Führer, saying, "The homosexual is a traitor to his own people and must be rooted out." The SS chief meant every word; he ordered the "liquidation" of his own nephew, SS lieutenant Hans Himmler, a gay man. As a rule, gay men wound up in concentration camps, where they had to wear a pink "triangle of shame" on their clothes and were forcibly sterilized. Officially known as "neutered beings," sterilized people did not have the right to marry. Within six years of the law's passage, four hundred thousand German men and women were sterilized in the name of "racial purity."[92]

The Nazis soon took the next step: murder. Not that they used such a graphic term. They called their secret killing *euthanasia,* a gentle-sounding word for "good death" or "mercy killing." The Nazis' euthanasia program was their first large-scale effort

to exterminate a group of innocent people—in this case, ill or handicapped Germans deemed undeserving of life.

Like sterilization, the practice of euthanasia originated outside Germany. It was first used by groups such as the Royal Society for the Prevention of Cruelty to Animals (RSPCA) in Britain and the ASPCA in America. In the late 1800s, cities were swarming with stray dogs. They carried rabies, a deadly disease, and would attack people. To reduce their numbers, local authorities hired "pest-killers," who went about their grisly job with poison, clubs, and hatchets. Appalled by the brutality of their methods, humanitarians urged that unwanted pets be "put to sleep" in "lethal chambers"—tiny rooms filled with carbonic acid gas.[93]

The idea of treating "defective" humans like stray dogs caught on. Eminent people like English science fiction writer H. G. Wells, a self-declared "genius," pontificated about "lethal chambers for the insane," saying the "swarms of black, brown, and dirty-white and yellow people . . . have to go." Irish playwright and music critic George Bernard Shaw, a keen racist, urged wholesale murder. In 1910, Shaw called for "an extensive use of the lethal chamber," since "a great many people would have to be put out of existence simply because it wastes other people's time to look after them." In 1915, as World War I raged, Virginia Woolf, England's foremost female author, saw residents of a mental hospital on an outing in a park. "It was perfectly horrible," Woolf wrote in disgust. "They should certainly be killed." Other non-German celebrities referred to the handicapped as "our social trash" and "human vermin."[94]

Hitler's Germany was unique: it alone created a secret euthanasia program. This would have been impossible without the active cooperation of the medical profession. Historians estimate
that 45 percent of German physicians were members of the Nazi
Party, a higher percentage than in any other professional group.
These were no Janusz Korczaks. Calling themselves "biological
soldiers," these individuals thought it was their duty to rid Germany of "life unworthy of life." No one made them turn killer;
they volunteered out of their belief in racism and eugenics, and
also out of a desire to advance their own careers. By doing so,
they violated the two-thousand-year-old Hippocratic oath taken
by all physicians to safeguard human life. In *The Nazi Doctors:
Medical Killing and the Psychology of Genocide* (1986), psychiatrist Robert Jay Lifton explained the gravity of their crime:
"Psychologically speaking, nothing is darker or more menacing,
or harder to accept, than the participation of physicians in mass
murder. . . . [For] he or she is still supposed to be a healer—and
one responsible to a tradition of healing, which all cultures revere
and depend upon."[95]

German children were the first victims of euthanasia. By law,
doctors, nurses, teachers, and social workers had to report "defective" children to local health authorities. Cerebral palsy and
Down syndrome, learning and discipline problems, epilepsy and
stuttering—all put children in jeopardy. A panel of doctors promised parents to treat their youngsters in "special pediatric units."
If parents refused the offer, officials could take a child by force.
Sometimes parents unable to cope with severely impaired children
asked the authorities to end their suffering.[96]

These pediatric wards were hellish places. There doctors conducted ghastly experiments on children with Down syndrome—for example, replacing their spinal fluid with air. After a child's death, his or her brain was sent to a laboratory for further study. To illustrate the importance of "racial purity," members of the Hitler Youth and the League of German Maidens took day trips to the pediatric wards. Before going, they were coached to feel no pity for "defectives." During what some called "freak shows," they saw children awaiting death, often by starvation. In one ward, a pediatrician-turned-killer referred to disabled children as "these creatures," ordering a nurse to pull an infant out of a cradle and display it "like a dead rabbit." He said, "With this one, for example, it will take two or three days [to die]." Other "patients" were overdosed on the sedative Luminal, were given poisons, or were suffocated. Afterward, parents received a notice saying their child had died of natural causes and the body had been cremated for "health reasons." Approximately five thousand German children were murdered for reasons of "racial hygiene."[97]

The Nazis extended their killing program to adults. This top-secret program, called Aktion T4 (Operation T4), took its name from the address of its offices in Berlin: 4 Tiergartenstrasse. Following carefully designed procedures, orderlies loaded people with epilepsy, Alzheimer's disease, and other mental and physical conditions aboard buses bound for killing centers. Upon arrival, orderlies led sixty victims at a time into sealed rooms set up as showers. But instead of water streaming from overhead nozzles, carbon monoxide—a colorless, odorless, and tasteless

gas—flowed out of steel cylinders. When our red blood cells absorb carbon monoxide, they lose the ability to carry oxygen, and the result is suffocation. Families of the deceased received official condolences, a death certificate, and an urn filled with ashes, which may or may not have been those of their relative.

Eventually, rumors about the adult euthanasia program began to circulate, perhaps because the orderlies talked too freely or because people wondered why smoke was billowing from chimneys in hot weather. As word spread, outrage grew. One day, Hitler's personal train had to stop at a station while some people with mental and physical disabilities were put aboard another train. When he looked out the window to see what the problem was, the crowd on the platform recognized him. For the first time since he had taken power, angry Germans jeered their Führer.[98]

Meanwhile, a handful of Catholic and Protestant clergymen condemned euthanasia from their pulpits. Clemens August Graf von Galen, the Catholic bishop of Münster, was the most outspoken. There is no such thing as a "worthless life," His Eminence said, in a now-famous sermon from the summer of 1941. He warned: "Woe to mankind, woe to our German nation if God's Holy Commandment 'Thou shalt not kill,' which God proclaimed on Mt. Sinai amidst thunder and lightning . . . is not only broken, but if this transgression is actually tolerated and permitted to go unpunished." The Führer retaliated by having three parish priests beheaded but left Bishop von Galen alone; he did not want to make a martyr of such a well-known figure. Instead, he

ended the T4 program in August 1941, after it had taken two hundred thousand innocent lives. By then, World War II was raging, and the T4 staff easily found other employment—in Poland and Russia. Nevertheless, the secret killing of "unfit" German children continued until the collapse of the Third Reich in 1945.[99]

The Heart of the Tragedy

Warsaw symbolized all that was both sublime and tragic during the war—and the ghetto was at the heart of the tragedy.

—Israel Gutman,
Resistance: The Warsaw Ghetto Uprising (1994)

And the War Came

During the 1930s, ordinary Europeans dreaded another war. Reminders of World War I were all about: in the vast cemeteries and in the bodies of veterans, millions without limbs and some so disfigured they wore aluminum face masks in public. Yet, at the same time, millions of Germans bitterly resented the "wrongs" of the Treaty of Versailles, especially the loss of the Baltic Sea port of Danzig (now Gdańsk) and nearly two hundred towns in the surrounding area to newly independent Poland.

A great speechmaker, Adolf Hitler was also a great liar. In public, he promised Germans work and peace. After all, as a wounded veteran, he'd experienced war's horrors, and he did not want to inflict them on anyone! Rebuilding the nation's war machine, he told cheering crowds, showed his peaceful intentions in two ways.

First, government spending on weapons would spark the economy, lifting the country out of the Great Depression by creating millions of jobs. Second, rearmament promised peace through strength. Hitler vowed to make the military so strong that no nation would dare menace Germany. Thus, for the sake of "peace," the Nazi leader set about creating the strongest and most technically advanced armed force of modern times.

Hitler's peace talk masked his true intentions. In private conversations and speeches before Nazi groups, he told a very different story. As ever, he framed every issue in terms of his ideology of race, struggle, and anti-Semitism. The Führer denounced the ideal of peace as a Jewish-Christian swindle, a violation of the natural order. Moreover, he declared, the Third Reich must have *Lebensraum,* living space for its expanding population. Its destiny, therefore, lay to the east, in the Soviet Union. That country had vast fertile plains where German colonists, all pure "Aryans," could grow crops and graze cattle to feed the Fatherland. There, too, were the raw materials to supply German industries: oil, metals, minerals, timber. With Russia's boundless food and raw materials at his disposal, Hitler would have the means to conquer the world.

The map of Europe dictated the Führer's strategy. It showed that the most direct route into the heart of the Soviet Union lay across Poland. To open that route, in 1938 Hitler seized Poland's neighbors to the south, Austria and Czechoslovakia (today's Czech Republic and Slovakia), by threatening war. Emboldened when Great Britain and France, allies in World War I, did nothing but "deplore" his actions, he turned his attention to Poland. Still

hoping to avert war, Britain and France hesitantly signed defense treaties with Poland.

The one thing Hitler feared was fighting in the east and the west at the same time, which had been so disastrous for Germany in the last war. To avoid splitting his forces, he turned to Joseph Stalin, the Communist tyrant whose country he secretly planned to destroy. Stalin, who had killed and enslaved millions of his own people on suspicion of disloyalty, thought he could outwit the Nazi leader. Though he hated the Nazis, Stalin was a cynical man, ready to do anything to advance Soviet interests. He wanted to expand Soviet power westward. So, in return for Hitler's promise of eastern Poland, on August 23, 1939, he signed a Nazi-Soviet nonaggression pact. In it, Stalin agreed to stay neutral in a war between Germany and the Western powers, thus giving Hitler the go-ahead to strike Poland.

Because Hitler was expecting Stalin's agreement, on the previous day he'd met with his senior commanders. Already Nazi forces were massed along the German-Polish border, awaiting the attack signal. Before the generals left to join their units, the Führer gave them a pep talk. "I have put my [Waffen-SS] formations in place with the command ruthlessly and without compassion to send into death many women and children of Polish origin and language," said Hitler, his voice rising. "Only thus can we gain the space we need. . . . Poland will be depopulated and settled with Germans. . . . As for the rest . . . the fate of Russia will be exactly the same. . . . We will break the Soviet Union. Then there will begin the dawn of the German rule of the earth."[1]

Hitler ended with this farewell: "And now, on to the enemy. In

Warsaw we will celebrate our reunion." As the generals cheered, Hermann Göring could not contain his joy. The official transcript states that the portly thug "jumped on a table . . . and made bloodthirsty promises. He danced like a wild man."[2]

Poland Struck Down

At dawn on September 1, over 1.5 million German troops, supported by 3,000 tanks and 1,600 planes, struck Poland. They were in high spirits. At last, their Führer had unleashed them to punish the Poles and the Jews. On their vehicles many had painted cartoons of Jews with hooked noses and the slogan "We're off to Poland—to thrash the Jews." Elsewhere, officials raised their glasses for a toast: *"Sterben Juden!"*—"May the Jews die!"[3]

They had reason for optimism. Hitler and his generals had learned from the failures of World War I. Back then, along the Western Front, both sides got bogged down in trenches stretching over a thousand miles, from the Swiss border to the English Channel. For four and a half years, the opposing armies shot, burned, blasted, and gassed each other, losing thousands of men to gain, if anything, a few yards of devastated land. Lesson: In the next war, speed and mobility must rule the battlefield. German armies must move *through* the enemy, *around* him, and *over* him. They must wage *blitzkrieg*, or "lightning war."

German and Polish civilians reacted differently to news of the war. By and large, Germans were subdued, dreading a repeat of 1914–1918. William L. Shirer reported from Berlin: "No excite-

ment, no hurrahs, no cheering, no throwing of flowers, no war fever, no hysteria." A German woman whose father had been crippled in the trenches in France recalled her family's reaction to the news over the radio. "They all sat down and cried. And then my father prophesied terrible things would happen."[4]

A twelve-year-old Polish girl with her fourteen-year-old sister, who was killed by the Luftwaffe during a German air raid. (1939)

Many Polish civilians were serene, even confident. News of the British and French declaration of war on Germany raised their spirits, arousing their national pride. Unfortunately, as time would tell, the Allies were too far away, and too unprepared, to have any impact on the fighting. The only action the Allies took was to drop five million leaflets on German cities, denouncing Nazi aggression. Meanwhile, Warsaw Radio played the Allies' national anthems endlessly, and public buildings displayed their flags to cheering crowds.

Polish propagandists went overboard. Without any evidence, newspapers made absurd claims. They said, for example, German aircraft and tanks were made of cardboard and ran on low-grade fuel unfit even for cigarette lighters. "Eyewitnesses" reported seeing bodies of German airmen clad in paper clothes and shoes. Warsaw street peddlers sold a paper toy that looked like a pig but, if unfolded a certain way, turned into a cartoonish picture of Hitler's face. "Attention! Attention!" announcers cried, interrupting radio broadcasts. "Tonight Berlin was attacked by 300 Polish bombers, which resulted in many fires. All our planes returned safely." Polish, French, and British forces would meet in the German capital within days![5]

Events showed these reports for what they were—fantasies to boost morale. The Nazi blitzkrieg ran like clockwork. Without warning, swarms of dive-bombers and fighters destroyed Poland's air force on the ground. Next, fast-moving tank divisions punched holes in the Polish front lines, encircling the defenders and pinning them down as the infantry destroyed them at leisure. Polish forces were already retreating when, on September 17, Stalin's Red Army crossed Poland's eastern border.

Having destroyed Poland's air force, the Germans launched an air campaign of unequaled savagery, striking even civilian targets at will. Fighter planes flew at treetop level, machine-gunning buses, automobiles, ambulances, columns of refugees, individuals—whatever pilots saw moving below. Fleeing the advancing Germans, fifteen-year-old Mary Berg and her parents joined a refugee column. No one imagined the ordeal that lay ahead. "Mile after mile it was the same," Mary wrote in her diary. "Again and again we flung ourselves into the ditches on the side of the road, our faces buried in the earth, while planes roared in our ears. During the night huge patches of red flared up against the black dome of the sky. The fires of burning cities and villages rose all around us." Warsaw was among them.[6]

Hitler loathed the Polish capital, calling it the "City of Bandits" and its residents "more animals than human beings." At the thought of striking Warsaw, he became a man possessed by a demon of destruction. General Franz Halder, German Army chief of staff, was amazed as the Führer described his vision during a meeting. The Nazi leader thrilled at "how the skies would be darkened, how millions of shells would rain down on Warsaw, how people would drown in blood." As Hitler ranted and raved, his "eyes nearly popped out of his head [and] he was suddenly seized by a lust for blood."[7]

The Führer's vision became reality. His planes bombed Warsaw's hospitals and shot up first-aid stations. Incendiary bombs dropped in clusters started fires; the wind carried clouds of hot embers, which landed on rooftops, igniting buildings over a wide area. Hitler relished newsreels of Warsaw's agony.

A German airplane bombing Warsaw. (September 1939)

"That is how we will annihilate them!" he cried, pointing to the screen.[8]

Nazi pilots studied Warsaw street maps, pinpointing Jewish targets, chiefly synagogues. Squadrons of what Jews called "air demons" came day and night. The severest raids took place on the

two holiest days in the Jewish calendar: the first day of Rosh Ha-shanah (that year September 14), the Jewish New Year; and Yom Kippur (September 23), the Day of Atonement—a solemn day of prayer and fasting, when Jews ask God's forgiveness for their sins. A Jewish youth saw the Yom Kippur bombing as a wide-awake nightmare. "Until today, I haven't seen adults gathered together and crying from the depths of their hearts," he wrote. "People's voices were choked as they held their heads in their hands. They did not take into consideration the fact that children were present, or perhaps the sight of the children was an even greater reason for their emotional reactions and tears."[9]

Bombs hurt children as well as adults. Gentile children, though usually not directly targeted, died by the hundreds. However, Germans intentionally bombed a large Jewish orphanage in a Warsaw suburb. "When I arrived," a welfare official reported, "the scene that unfolded before my eyes was shocking. Houses were in ruins; blood and pieces of the murdered children's brains were splattered over the floors and the remains of the walls. The children who survived and most of the staff were overcome by fear and were on the verge of despair."[10]

Janusz Korczak rose to the challenge. This was the educator's fourth war, and ever the patriot, at the age of sixty-one, he again put on his army uniform. Invited to return to Warsaw Radio, he gladly agreed. The familiar, calm voice of the Old Doctor returned to the airwaves. He spoke of patriotism and Poland's honor. The call to duty had energized him. "Yesterday I was an old man," he told listeners. "Today I am ten years younger—maybe even twenty." As for the young, let them buck up, be active, be useful!

"Don't stay inside cowering and crying about what might happen. Go out into the streets and dig fire lanes. Go to the Tomb of the Unknown Soldier who died for Poland and put flowers on his grave."[11]

Korczak took his own advice. At Dom Sierot, he and a few of the older boys and girls stood guard on the roof with buckets of sand, ready to douse incendiary bombs and windblown embers. When a cannon shell exploded outside the dining hall, the director ran to investigate. Just then, another shell exploded nearby, shattering the windowpanes. It happened so quickly that the children had no time to run to the shelter in the basement, where Madame Stefa ran a first-aid station, so they dove under the heavy oak tables. Where was the Old Doctor? Was he dead? Moments later, Korczak appeared, a sly grin on his face. So as not to alarm the children further, he joked about his close call. "I had to make a quick retreat," he said. "My bald head would have been a perfect target for those planes."[12]

Korczak did not think of his bald head during daytime air raids. He went into the streets to find lost and hurt children and take them to first-aid stations and shelters. One time, a woman saw him walking along a bombed-out street, carrying a little boy in his arms.

"What are you doing here?" she asked.

"Looking for a shoe store," he replied.

"But all the shops are destroyed or closed," she said, pointing to the smoking rubble.

"Then I'll find a shoemaker," he replied. "This boy can't walk on all this glass without shoes."

"Who is he?" she asked.

"I don't know. I just found him crying in the street. I have to carry him until I find something for his feet."[13]

When bombs knocked out Warsaw's power plants and waterworks, fires raged out of control. The situation became hopeless. Finally, on September 27, Poland surrendered; by then most government officials had fled the country. Hitler's forces, wrote an American journalist, had crushed Poland "like a soft-boiled egg."[14]

Victory came "cheaply" for Germany: 11,000 men killed and 30,000 wounded. The Poles had 65,000 soldiers killed and 144,000 wounded. As for Warsaw, more than 6,000 soldiers died defending the city; another 40,000 civilians died in air raids and artillery bombardments. One in five houses was damaged or destroyed. When Varsovians emerged from their shelters, they found a frightful new world. "Everything is over," one wrote. "People with tragic faces wander aimlessly about the streets. They stare at the destruction of the city, searching through it for their dear ones. . . . People burst into sudden sobbing. They go crying through the streets; crying through their homes."[15]

Varsovians grew more downcast when the conquerors marched into their city. There was not a paper uniform among them! Chaim Kaplan, the principal of a Hebrew school in Warsaw, wrote in his diary that he was "amazed to see how well fed, sleek, and fat" they were. Yet there was also something menacing about the Germans. A Polish woman, Maria Szubert, never forgot the sight: "I froze as I watched the enemy troops moving in perfect harmony like a shining block of steel: left, right, left, right, left, right,

German troops march through Warsaw. (1939)

their helmets, guns, boots, even uniform buttons all shining. They sang: '*Heili, heilo, heila, heili, heila, heili, heilo, heila.*' Over and over: '*Heili, heilo, heila.*' I felt an overwhelming fear. What are they going to do to us, those automatons?"[16]

Night Descends

The dark night of occupation began with the abolition of the Polish state. As they had agreed, Hitler and Stalin divided their

prey into German and Soviet zones. Stalin took the eastern third of Poland. As his forces moved in, Nazi officers greeted their Soviet "comrades" with smiles, handshakes, and victory toasts. Hitler took the western third of Poland, with its large ethnic German population, absorbing it into the Third Reich. Within a year, the Nazis uprooted 1.5 million Polish Christians and Jews, driving them into the middle third of Poland. This area, which included Warsaw, became a German colony known as the General Government. Hans Frank, Hitler's lackey, ruled this territory from Kraków, Poland's second-largest city. Governor Frank relished his position. He lived with his wife and two sons in a castle, amid elegant furniture, precious antiques, and liveried servants. A vain man with delusions of grandeur, Frank knelt down before his wife and declared, "Brigitte, you will be the Queen of Poland."[17]

Though head of the Nazi administration in the General Government third of Poland, Frank did not set policy; Hitler, working through his inner circle, did. The Führer viewed Christian Poles through the lens of racism, seeing them as "more animals than human beings." His policy, simply put, was to enslave the Polish people. As SS chief Heinrich Himmler put it, Poles would become a "leaderless working class," slaves incapable of thinking or acting for themselves. To that end, Himmler ordered Reinhard Heydrich, his top aide, to make detailed plans, carry them out, and have Hans Frank help in any way possible.[18]

With diabolical efficiency, Heydrich set out to "decapitate" Poland. In effect, he would kill its natural leaders—people with the stature, character, education, and will to challenge Nazi authority.

He was so brutal that even die-hard Nazis referred to him, in anxious whispers, as "a young, evil god of death."[19]

Acting on the SS chief's orders, the Gestapo compiled lists of thousands of educators, doctors, lawyers, landowners, writers, journalists, trade union leaders, civil servants, and police officials. With these lists in hand, mobile death squads hunted down their victims. As a result, Poland's educated classes were decimated. The nation lost 45 percent of its doctors, 40 percent of its university professors, and 56 percent of its lawyers. Also, 2,800 Catholic priests out of a total of 18,000 vanished into unmarked graves. Another 4,000 priests were deported to concentration camps in Germany, where most died of starvation and brutal treatment. In Warsaw alone, one in twenty elementary school teachers, and one in six university faculty members, lost their lives. Over the next five years, the Nazis built more than 2,000 concentration camps in Poland. These housed both political prisoners and Polish slaves used on various construction projects. Extermination camps for Jews, as we will see, were entirely different.[20]

Meanwhile, experts in eugenics set out to cleanse Poland of "lives unworthy of life." Hospital wards for the mentally ill, intellectually disabled, and physically disabled were closed and their patients murdered. When, for example, a Polish physician asked a nurse about the fate of psychiatric patients, she replied: "All the mentally ill were shot with machine guns, but under penalty of death, the hospital personnel were forbidden to talk about this crime." We know about these crimes because German officials sent up-to-date reports to SS headquarters in Berlin, which the Allies seized after Germany's defeat.[21]

Nor were Polish children spared. They suffered in various ways. To increase the death rate of "racial inferiors," the Nazis closed clinics offering care to pregnant women and newborns. According to Himmler, all children allowed to live were destined for slavery. They must have no education beyond the fourth grade. "The sole goal of this schooling," he said, "is to teach them simple arithmetic, nothing above the number 500, writing one's name, and the doctrine that it is divine law to obey the Germans. . . . I do not think that reading is desirable." For good measure, the Nazis took over all bookshops, libraries, publishing houses, and printing shops.[22]

Certain Polish children were placed in a separate category. When Himmler and his aides toured Poland early in the occupation, the number of blond, blue-eyed, and fair-skinned children they saw startled them. Such youngsters, the SS chief said, likely had "racially valuable blood." Though born to Polish parents, they must have had "Aryan" ancestors, and therefore their blood belonged to the Third Reich. Himmler was brutally open about his plans. "I really intend to take German blood from wherever it is to be found in the world, to rob it and steal it wherever I can," he declared. He meant it—literally. German medical teams made the rounds of Polish schools, forcing blond, blue-eyed children to give blood for transfusions for wounded soldiers.[23]

"Racial fitness examiners" selected Polish children between the ages of two and twelve for "return" to their true "Fatherland." Their parents' wishes, let alone their feelings, counted for nothing. Teams of SS doctors visited hospital nurseries, taking any

newborns showing traces of "Aryan" blood. If an SS man saw a girl or boy playing in the street, or a woman wheeling a baby carriage, he could seize the child for the same reason.[24]

"I saw children taken from their mothers," a Polish woman recalled. "Some were even torn from the breast. It was a terrible sight: the agony of the mothers and fathers, the beating by the Germans, and the crying of the children." Fifty years later, Małgorzata Twardecka wept as she recalled the day the Germans took away her son Alojzy and other children from her town. Police with fierce guard dogs kept the parents outside the train station. "You can't imagine," she said, "what it is like to have a child stolen. We didn't give them our children, they stole them. Such a thing has never happened before. My mother told me that in her lifetime she had seen wars . . . but nobody had ever done anything as terrible as this."[25]

"Brown Sisters," SS nurses wearing brown uniforms, took stolen infants and toddlers to Lebensborn homes. Without delay, "Aryan" families adopted them. The children adapted to their new families and learned to speak German. The Nazis destroyed all records of their origins and wrote German names on their forged birth certificates. The certificates described them as orphans, their mothers having died in childbirth and their fathers killed in the war. Gitta Sereny, a writer who identified stolen children after the war, praised their new parents. Though they were Nazis: "I never handled or heard of a single case in which the German foster or adoptive parents had treated the kidnapped child with anything but love."[26]

Officials sent children over age eight to special schools for

"Germanization." There they learned the country's ways, were indoctrinated with racism, and spoke only German; anyone caught speaking Polish paid a price. "They stuck us in the arms and back with needles," a boy recalled. Because the Nazis changed their names and destroyed their records, it is impossible to know how many Polish children were stolen. Historians estimate the number at 200,000, of whom only 25,000 returned to their real parents after the war.[27]

Jews Under Nazi Occupation

For Polish Jews, the German occupation began with abuses reminiscent of Kristallnacht. Regular German troops were highly disciplined. For the most part, they would not act without direct orders or the knowledge that superiors would turn a blind eye to abusive behavior. Many tormented Jews simply because they were Jews, and they could do so without fear of punishment. Yet there was another, more sinister reason for everyday brutality. By stripping away Jews' sense of human dignity, the Nazis meant to condition them to accept abuse, and ultimately destruction, as a matter of course.

The streets became unsafe. In Jewish neighborhoods, Germans often drove their cars onto the sidewalks, hitting pedestrians who could not get out of the way in time. Jews had to behave "correctly"—or else. When encountering a German in uniform, for example, a man had to whip off his hat, bow low, and step into the gutter until the member of the "master race" passed. Even

that might not be enough. Soldiers made Jews kiss the pavement, they forced the elderly to do deep-knee bends, and they ordered men to drop to their knees while they urinated on them. Under threat of death, rabbis had to spit on sacred Torah scrolls. If a rabbi could not produce enough saliva, a Nazi made him open his mouth, spat into it, and then had him spit on the holy text.[28]

Because beards signified piety, Germans amused themselves by "bearding the Jew." They might stop a religious Jew on the street, set his beard on fire, cut it off with scissors, or pluck out clumps of hair with pliers. This was all a big joke to them. Itzchak Belfer, a child at the time, recalled how beard cutting broke his grandfather's spirit:

One of the soldiers grabbed and pulled my grandfather's beard.... The other took out a large pair of scissors, and began to cut off his beard.... The locks of hair began falling, piling up at their feet. They carried on with their task, cutting with precision, taking care to cut only one side of the beard, all the while laughing hysterically.... [When they finished] my grandfather locked himself in his room, refusing to see anyone except my grandmother.... After several days, when my grandfather came out of his room, he was unrecognizable. Grandfather, the hero of my childhood, had once been an upright, long-bearded, well-groomed, and good-looking man who carried his age gracefully, courageous in his actions and thoughts. Instead, out of the room emerged an old man, his face shaven, wrinkled, his eyes extinguished.[29]

Jewish women were subjected to even worse indignities. Soldiers rounded them up for forced labor designed to destroy their self-respect. Diarist Chaim Kaplan recorded how two young women were ordered to remove filth from a barracks latrine and clean it until it sparkled. When they asked what they should use, soldiers shouted, "Your blouses." So, shaking in fear, they took off their blouses and began. When they finished, "the Nazis wrapped their faces in the blouses, filthy with the remains of excrement, and laughed uproariously." In looking for hidden valuables, wrote Mary Berg, soldiers strip-searched women in front of their husbands and children. In one case, "the women were kept naked for

two hours while the Nazis put their revolvers to their breasts and private parts and threatened to shoot them if they did not give up dollars or diamonds."[30] Even worse was to come.

In the fall of 1939, Reinhard Heydrich issued a "strictly secret" order to SS commanders in Poland. Titled "The Jewish Question in Occupied Territory," the order was menacing not only for what it said but also for what it implied. Heydrich drew a line

Grinning German soldiers "bearding" a pious Jewish man. (Date unknown)

between the Nazis' "final goal" and the "preliminary measures" needed to "facilitate subsequent measures." He deliberately used vague terminology, for reasons that he kept to himself. His wording, however, suggests that his bosses, Hitler and Himmler, had already decided to destroy Poland's Jews. (Note: *suggests,* not *proves,* as we have no written evidence that they made the fatal decision at this time.)[31]

"Preliminary measures" meant concentrating, regulating, and segregating Poland's Jews. The process began with dissolving all Jewish communities of fewer than five hundred and moving their residents to cities located along railway lines. Each community then had to select a Jewish Council (Judenrat) made up of prewar community leaders. The councils had to supervise the carrying out of essential day-to-day activities. For instance, they conducted censuses, noting Jews' names, family sizes, occupations, and addresses. They also organized medical and welfare services, assigned people to forced-labor details, and collected taxes to pay for the Nazi-mandated activities. Above all, councils had to carry out every Nazi order promptly, efficiently, and without protest.

Jewish Council members were not Nazi stooges. Most were practical, responsible men (never women) committed to helping their people. They took their cue from the Talmud, a collection of laws and learned commentaries on the laws' meaning. The Talmud says: "Be pliable like a reed, not rigid like a cedar." High winds topple rigid trees, so be flexible, bend, adapt to changing conditions. This made sense. Over the centuries, Jews had devised ways of coping with their oppressors, always more numerous and

violent than themselves. Coping did not involve preventive attack, armed resistance, and revenge. Instead, it involved bribing oppressors, bargaining with them, placating them, then procrastinating when it came to following through. The idea was to play for time, until the oppressor tired or the situation changed for the better. What Jewish Council members failed to comprehend, at first, was the Nazis' dedication to a murderous ideology.[32]

Warsaw's Jewish Council had twenty-four members, more than any other, and over twenty-five hundred employees, mostly office workers and administrative staff. Its president, Adam Czerniaków, was a civil engineer and longtime friend of Janusz Korczak. Unlike the Old Doctor, however, Czerniaków seldom smiled—for good reason. The Nazis watched him closely; a photo shows a Gestapo man standing behind him in his office. His vocabulary had no phrases like "I cannot" and "I will not." Failure meant death, as some council members learned. When Czerniaków made a blunt remark about the SS, Gestapo men beat him up. "My head, arms, and legs were bandaged," he wrote in his diary. "I am barely able to move but I will go to the council tomorrow." After that, Czerniaków hid cyanide capsules in his desk drawer, in case life became unbearable.[33]

Meanwhile, hope for an Allied victory faded. In the spring of 1940, the Nazi blitzkrieg roared through Denmark, Norway, Belgium, and Holland and into France. The Battle of France lasted six weeks, ending on June 14 with the fall of Paris. Millions of Germans took these victories as clear proof of "Aryan" superiority and their Führer's brilliance. People hailed the ex-corporal

Adam Czerniaków, the president of Warsaw's Jewish Council and a longtime friend of Janusz Korczak. Note the Gestapo member standing behind him. (Date unknown)

as a military genius, calling him "Grofaz," short for the "greatest commander of all time," in German. The German victories shocked Poland. In Warsaw, Chaim Kaplan wrote in his diary: "Everywhere, both among the Poles and among the Jews, there is weeping and wailing."[34]

Segregated

Governor Hans Frank made life ever more wretched for Poland's Jews. "My attitude toward the Jews," he told his staff, "[is] based solely on the expectation that they must disappear. They must be done away with. . . . We must annihilate the Jews wherever we find them and wherever it is possible." He was as good as his word.[35]

Hardly a day passed without Frank's signing a savage decree. A few examples: Jews could not enter public parks, travel by train, buy or sell cloth, practice medicine or dentistry, or go to school. Jews had to put all their money into banks, but they could not withdraw more than 250 zlotys a week or have more than 2,000 zlotys at a time (five zlotys equaled one U.S. dollar). This meant that Jews could buy what they needed only if they broke the law, risking severe punishment if caught. Since they had no other choice, they hid any cash or valuables they held when the decree went into effect. If caught, they lost everything.

It was almost impossible to evade the armband decree. It required every Jew over the age of ten to wear a white armband with a blue six-pointed Star of David printed or stitched onto it. (In 1941, Hitler ordered German Jews to wear a patch on their clothing, a yellow Star of David with the word *Jude* stitched in black.) The armband had to be worn on the right sleeve of a garment. Wearing a dirty or wrinkled armband was an offense that provoked a beating and a fine. Some Jews joked about their armbands. Certain Warsaw streets, they said, resembled Hollywood: "Wherever you go, you see a star." Most, however, did not see the

A Warsaw ghetto Jewish police armband. (Early 1940s)

humor. Instead, they were mortified at having to wear the "ribbon of disgrace." For this strip of cloth separated them from the rest of the population, making them easy to identify and, therefore, easy prey for Nazis and Polish anti-Semites.[36]

In Warsaw, as in every Polish city, segregation became the rule. If you were a Pole of German ancestry, or a German from the Reich working in Poland, you lived quite well. The Nazis divided Warsaw into three districts called "quarters." The most desirable quarter was entirely German; Poles and Jews living there had to vacate their apartments, often on a half hour's notice. The apartments had to be left spotless, the beds made, and every stick of furniture in its proper place. Evicted Poles moved into the quarter known as the "Aryan side," shorthand for the non-Jewish area. Jews living there and Poles living in the Jewish quarter had to switch apartments. Located in existing Jewish neighborhoods, the Jewish quarter was overcrowded even before the move.

Under Nazi rule, Polish cities had three police forces: German officers; Polish officers, nicknamed "the Blue police" for the color of their uniforms; and Jewish officers recruited and paid by the Jewish Council. Warsaw had twenty-two hundred Jewish police officers to keep order and direct traffic. Selected from among the "better classes," chiefly lawyers and law students, each man wore a blue cap and a metal badge with the Star of David and carried a rubber club. At first, this pleased the Jews, because prewar Poland had had no Jewish policemen. Many Jews had an "utterly illogical feeling of satisfaction" at seeing them patrol the Jewish quarter. All spoke Yiddish and seemed to relate to Jews better than

Jewish policemen in the Warsaw ghetto. (1941)

gentile officers did. Some residents got carried away, "beginning to think they are in Tel Aviv." However, everyone knew who was in charge. To show their authority, Germans "exercised" Jewish officers, making them do push-ups until they collapsed.[37]

Uprooting

In his secret order, Heydrich used an ominous term: *ghetto*. Originating in the early 1500s, ghettos were walled-off sections of European cities that Jews settled or were forced to live in by authorities. In an era of anti-Jewish riots, such areas offered safety and made it possible for Jews to worship freely and follow their trades. Ghetto residents were not prisoners. They could leave the ghetto to shop, work, or do business during the day, then return before the curfew, when night watchmen locked the gates. During the 1800s, "enlightened" rulers, notably Napoléon Bonaparte of France, abolished ghettos and tore down their walls.[38]

The Nazis brought back the ghetto. Nazi ghettos, however, were not the ghettos of the history books. According to historian Michael Burleigh, the Nazis had a sinister reason for establishing Jewish ghettos. They served as "interim warehousing," pending the decision to empty them by mass murder. Joseph Goebbels said as much. With untypical honesty, the propaganda minister called ghettos "death boxes."[39]

Though Hitler meant to destroy the Jews, he did not want to arouse world opinion against Germany. As ever, he would bide his time, going all out only when the moment was right. Until

then, ghettos would take a slow but steady toll. By creating harsh conditions, Hitler knew many Jews would succumb to "natural" causes: disease, starvation, exhaustion, emotional stress. For that reason, the Nazis created more than four hundred ghettos in the area of Poland under German control. They ranged in size from several hundred to tens of thousands of residents. The largest were located in the five cities with the most Jews: Kraków, Łódź, Lublin, Lviv, Warsaw.[40]

In April 1940, residents of Warsaw's Jewish quarter saw workers building brick walls in odd places. One wall would close off a street in the middle of the block; another would run lengthwise down a street, dividing it in two. Traffic, forced to take detours,

Construction of the Warsaw ghetto wall in 1940.

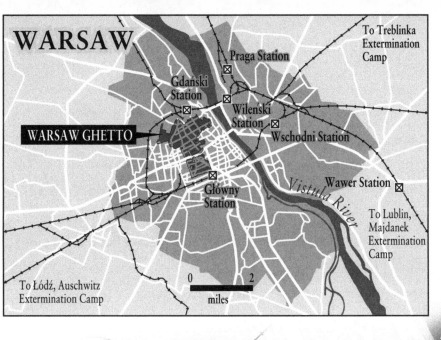

slowed to a crawl. Often, a destination only a few feet away required a half hour's detour. The Nazis called these structures
"epidemic walls" and claimed they were intended to contain an
outbreak of typhus, a disease carried by lice. The Nazis were
lying to quiet people until they revealed the true purpose of the
walls. As for typhus, scientists had already developed an effective
vaccine to prevent infection. The Germans, however, refused to
make the vaccine available to Jews, thus allowing the spread of
the epidemic they said they wished to halt. Throughout Warsaw,
gruesome posters showed the face of a Jew and a large louse and
the words "Jew = Lice = Typhus."

Gradually, workers connected the scattered wall segments. The
completed wall stood nine feet high and was two bricks thick. It
was topped with barbed wire or broken bottles cemented into
place. Zigzagging for eleven miles, it enclosed a hundred-square-
block area totaling 1.3 square miles, almost exactly the size of Central Park in New York City. It had twenty-two entrances, which gave
access to the Polish quarter, the so-called Aryan side. The Jewish
Council had to pay construction costs out of taxes it collected, so
the Jewish community, in effect, paid to imprison itself.

The Warsaw ghetto had two sections. The "large ghetto," at
the northern end, consisted of narrow streets lined with blocks
of shabby apartment houses. Each block was built around a central courtyard. A gateway led from the street into the courtyard,
where doors opened onto flights of stairs. At the southern end, the
"small ghetto" had wide streets and well-kept buildings; prosperous families had lived there before the war. A wooden footbridge
over Chłodna Street, an "Aryan" street, linked the two sections.[41]

The footbridge over Chłodna Street, an "Aryan" street, connecting the two sections of the Warsaw ghetto. (1940)

The Nazis calculated their next move for maximum shock effect. On Yom Kippur—October 12, 1940—loudspeakers, leaflets, and posters gave the order to move. Jews living outside the walled area had to vacate their apartments, many for the second time, and move into the ghetto by October 31. Similarly, about three thousand Jewish converts to Catholicism, and Jews married to Catholics and their children, had to leave their homes. According to Nazi ideology, any trace of "Jewish blood," whatever one's religion, made a person a "biological Jew." Nothing could change that. Two churches in the ghetto served the spiritual needs of converts.[42]

Moving tested the sanity of otherwise calm, levelheaded people. Bernard Goldstein, a veteran trade unionist, recalled:

It is impossible to describe the hellish scenes which took place in Warsaw's streets. . . . Everywhere there was wild panic, unashamed hysterical terror. People ran frantically through the streets, a deathly fear unmistakable in their grim, weary eyes. They searched desperately for any kind of conveyance to transport their belongings. The multitude filled the streets, a nation on the march. Long, long rows of little carts and all sorts of makeshift vehicles heaped with household possessions, wailing children, the old, the sick, the half-dead, moved from all directions toward the ghetto, pulled or led by the stronger and healthier, who plodded along, tearful, despairing, bewildered.[43]

With the weather turning cold, families had to find shelter quickly. The lucky ones moved in with relatives already living in the area that had become the ghetto. However, panic resulted as most searched for living space. The Jewish Council tried to help people relocate but could not cope with the flood of humanity. Frantic Jews went from house to house, Goldstein wrote, asking about "an apartment, a room, a corner of a room, anything. They searched the cellars, the hallways, the rubble of bombed-out buildings, for a place to lay their heads or shelter their children. They lay on the streets or roamed through the gutters, soaked by the rain, shivering from the cold, hungry, worn-out, helpless."[44]

All child services in the Jewish quarter also had to relocate to the ghetto. These included roughly thirty orphanages, boardinghouses, and day-care centers and twenty feeding stations for

children whose parents could not afford to feed them adequately. When the order to move arrived at Dom Sierot, gentile friends worried about the Old Doctor. Already ailing, he seemed less energetic than in all the years they'd known him. Igor Newerly, a rising author and Korczak's former secretary, offered to hide him. Newerly, a Catholic, knew people who could keep him out of the ghetto—for a price.[45]

Newerly had a revealing conversation with his friend. "Everyone's worried about your going into the ghetto with the children," he said. "Just say the word and we'll get you false papers to live on our [Aryan] side [of Warsaw]."

"And the children?" Korczak asked.

"We'll try to hide as many as we can in monasteries and private homes."

"But can you guarantee me that every child will be safe?"

Newerly shook his head. "I'm afraid that's impossible. We can't guarantee anything, even our own safety."

"My friend," said Korczak, "it is best that I keep the children with me." There was no other way, for him. The Old Doctor considered himself their father, and like a good father, he could not abandon his loved ones.

Yet this decent man was also naive. The author of *The Senate of Madmen* could not fathom—*really* fathom—the racist ideology that drove Hitler and the Nazi leadership. "Don't worry, the Germans won't harm us," he told Newerly. "They wouldn't dare. I'm much too well known here and abroad."[46]

The Jewish Council assigned Dom Sierot quarters at what was formerly the High School of Commerce in the small ghetto. So as

not to alarm the children, Korczak and Madame Stefa decided to make moving day a fun day.

Korczak wore his army uniform, but without the required armband. "I accept only the laws of nature and God—not man-made laws," he said grandly. Dressed in their best clothes, the children marched toward the ghetto singing, their few possessions in cloth bags slung over their shoulders. An older boy led the column. Proudly, he carried the green flag of King Matt, with a blossom embroidered on one side and a blue Star of David on the other. Green symbolized hope, the blossom youth, and the star the Jewish people. A cart loaded with potatoes followed the column.[47]

Trouble began at the entry gate. A German sentry looked very cross. Those sacks of potatoes in the cart are *verboten*—forbidden. I must confiscate them! Korczak lost his temper. When he shouted that his children needed those potatoes, the sentry hustled him off to Gestapo headquarters. There he faced a dapper officer sitting at a desk beneath a portrait of Hitler. Why, the Gestapo man politely asked, was this little bald man dressed as a Polish Army major? When Korczak explained that he'd earned the rank by serving in four wars, the officer offered him a chair, thinking him a person of importance.

Another question: "You're not a Jew, are you?"

"I am," the prisoner replied.

"Then where is your armband? Don't you know you are breaking the law?"

"There are human laws which are transitory, and higher laws which are eternal," Korczak said.

But the Gestapo recognized only Hitler's laws. Infuriated,

the officer had Korczak beaten and thrown into a cell in Pawiak, a prison already notorious for its torture rooms and execution yard. His cellmates were Polish criminals, cutthroats swept off the streets. The Old Doctor had known their kind during his student ramblings. Despite their menacing appearance, they seemed so needy, even childlike, that he decided to treat them as children. For hours, he told them stories, and they sat quietly, enchanted. Luckily, after four months, Newerly or another gentile friend put the right sum of money into the right hands, gaining Korczak's release. Still, the experience left him shaken. Following a joyous welcome back at Dom Sierot, he had the street entrance sealed with bricks. From then on, a friend recalled, "when a German policeman came to the house, he was absolutely terrified. This happened only rarely, when the police found a wandering or lost child at night and brought him in." As for the armband, Korczak mastered his fear; he never wore one, regardless of the danger.[48]

During the first two weeks of its existence, the ghetto remained open; people could come and go during the day. Those with jobs on the Aryan side continued to report for work each morning and return by 6:00 p.m., when the curfew went into effect. Everyone wondered: Would the ghetto remain open?

The answer came on November 15. Before daybreak, early risers found the gates closed and guarded; German and Blue police officers stood outside, Jewish police officers inside. Panic! The concert pianist Władysław Szpilman saw "the dark streets swarming with figures wearing white armbands. They were all in an agitated state, running back and forth like animals put into a cage and not yet used to it." (Szpilman's struggle to survive in the

ghetto was made into the 2000 Oscar-winning movie *The Pianist*.) Diarist Chaim Kaplan thought, correctly, "We have entered into a new life. . . . We are segregated and separated from the world and the fullness thereof, driven out of the society of the human race."[49]

A New Life

The Nazis planned to make the ghettos unbearable. We learn the results of their efforts from their victims. Diarists like Chaim Kaplan and Mary Berg were sensitive, verbal people who recorded daily life as they lived it. So did Janusz Korczak, whose diary has become a classic of Holocaust literature. Jewish Council head Adam Czerniaków also kept a diary, documenting his dealings with the Nazi authorities. Keeping a diary was a form of self-expression and also a way of educating future generations. As Kaplan wrote, "In our scroll of agony, not one small detail can be omitted. . . . Our existence as a people will not be destroyed. Individuals will be destroyed, but the Jewish community will live on."[50]

Emanuel Ringelblum saw ghetto life through the eyes of a scholar; without him, there would be wider gaps in our knowledge. A professional historian, Ringelblum organized a secret group of fifty or sixty historians, writers, teachers, doctors, and social workers. Under the code name "Oneg Shabbat" (Hebrew for "joy of the Sabbath"), the group met secretly on Saturday afternoons. Members brought anything having to do with ghetto

life. "Collect as much as possible," Ringelblum advised. "They can sort it out after the war." Pamphlets, illegal newspapers, posters, handbills, Nazi decrees, poems, popular songs, beggars' chants, interviews: all went into the Oneg Shabbat archive. Later, as hopes of survival faded, Ringelblum had the archive buried in stainless steel milk cans, most of which searchers found after the war. By then, he and nearly all his colleagues were dead, killed by the Nazis. This treasure is our chief source for the study of ghetto life. It includes Ringelblum's own writings. Translated into English, his *Notes from the Warsaw Ghetto* is a must-read for anyone interested in that dark time.[51]

The sources portray ghetto life as a daily struggle for survival. Because one-third of Warsaw's prewar population lived in little more than 2 percent of its built-up area, the ghetto was jammed to bursting. It was the densest urban environment on the planet. In 2015, the world's most crowded city, Manila in the Philippines, had 111,002 people per square mile. The Nazis penned 450,000 Jews behind the ghetto wall. Chaim Kaplan was not exaggerating when he wrote, "There is no room in the ghetto—not an empty crack, not an unoccupied hole."[52]

Space was so limited that six or seven people, families and strangers, might share a small room. Often, young children shared a bed with their parents and siblings. All lived amid a "deafening clamor" that seemed to jangle every nerve. Overcrowding and a lack of fuel for heating water and soap for washing made it impossible to keep clean. Dirty clothing, bedding, and bodies gave off "a chilly odor of decay," pianist Władysław Szpilman noted. The streets were just as bad. Kaplan tells us

that, when walking ghetto streets, "you feel that you have been catapulted into a pot that is boiling over. People push and shove and elbow you. . . . The fear of lice obsesses all of us, for the tiny creatures are the carriers of typhus." And there was no way to avoid the nimble creatures if you brushed against another person.[53]

The ghetto wall was so confining that toddlers had no idea what a natural landscape looked like, nor any grasp of the notion of distance. In "A Talk with a Child," Władysław Szlengel, dubbed "the Poet of the Ghetto," asked:

> *But how to explain it to a child,*
> *what does it mean the word: afar*
> *while he does not know what is a mountain,*
> *and he does not know what we call a river . . .*
> *and he has not like mother . . . and has not like me*
> *the images under the eyelids,*
> *then how to explain it to a child,*
> *what does it mean the word: afar?*

Szlengel and his wife would later be shot by the Nazis.[54]

Despite the general misery, one group was worse off than any other. We recall that under Reinhard Heydrich's "strictly secret" plan, Jewish communities of fewer than five hundred had to relocate to cities on railway lines. Families that had lived in their villages for generations were forced to report to their local train station with just a few pieces of hand luggage. After a journey of many hours in dirty boxcars, SS guards left them stranded in the

freight yard of an unfamiliar city. Then, on their own, with no money or jobs, they streamed into the city's ghetto.

Of the Warsaw ghetto's 450,000 inhabitants, 150,000 were utterly destitute refugees. The Jewish Council placed them in shelters called "special houses" but commonly known as "death points." A "point" might have been anything from a corner in a dank basement, to a burnt-out synagogue, to a horse stable. The conditions young Janusz Korczak had found in the slums in the 1890s were almost mild compared to such places. "Ragged and torn, covered with tatters, these human shadows inhabit cellars, basements and pantries," a social worker reported. "Often those dwellings consist of nothing but the four naked walls, without a single article of furniture or a single garment. People are often lying on the bare ground, on straw; beds are conspicuous by their absence. Whatever bedding one finds is the color of mud. Some-times they lie on a heap of feathers, the pillowcases having been sold a long time ago [to buy food]."[55]

Smugglers

Getting enough to eat was the most serious, and most persistent, challenge. The Nazis issued three types of ration cards in occu-pied Poland. They specified the amounts and types of food that holders could get each day. Reich Germans and ethnic Germans received the largest ration: 2,613 calories, the normal daily re-quirement for an adult. Poles were entitled to 699 calories daily. Ghetto Jews got 184 calories! In Warsaw, all "legal" shipments

came in through a transfer station in the rail yard in the northeast corner of the ghetto. When shipments arrived—they were often delayed a week or two—the Jewish Council paid for the food and distributed it to those with ration cards. Because refugees did not qualify for ration cards, they ate once a day at charity-run soup kitchens, where they were given a bowl of watery potato soup and a slice of black bread.[56]

Nazi nutritionists designed a diet lacking in essential vitamins and minerals—no butter, eggs, meats, fruits, or vegetables. Children could not have milk. Usually, the "official" daily meal consisted of moldy potatoes and three ounces of black bread. This "bread" was half sawdust and potato peels, making it all but indigestible. A diarist wrote: "A dybbuk [evil possessing spirit] has entered my belly. My belly talks, shouts . . . and drives me mad."[57]

Hitler's henchmen aimed at the deliberate and systematic starvation of ghetto Jews. Governor Hans Frank admitted as much; he told aides that Poland's Jews "must disappear." Ludwig Fischer, governor of the Warsaw district in the General Government third of Poland, echoed his boss. Fischer said of the Jews: "We will destroy that breed. They will disappear through hunger and want . . . and of the Jewish question only a cemetery will remain."[58]

Ghetto Jews had no hope of surviving on the official ration. Wretched, facing lingering death by starvation, they turned to food smuggling from the Aryan side of Warsaw. There were two types of smugglers. Children working alone or in small groups brought in meager amounts of food. Adult gangs of professionals smuggled large quantities of food and other goods.

Often, a child as young as six became his or her family's sole breadwinner. Everyone faced the problem of getting out of, and back into, the ghetto. The wall was a difficult obstacle to overcome but not an impossible one. In places, children cut the barbed wire and flattened the broken bottles. In remote corners, they removed several bricks to create narrow openings, replacing the loose bricks behind them. Wherever the wall crossed a roadway, builders had left narrow gaps at the base so rainwater would flow from the ghetto into sewers on the Aryan side. Small children could wriggle through these gaps. Children might also try to slip past the guards at the gates.[59]

Upon reaching the Aryan side, the children begged for food on the streets. If they had a few zlotys, Polish boys might steer them to a supplier. "There was," memoirist Ruth Altbeker Cyprys wrote, "a great decency in dealings among these little merchants; one did not cheat the other." What is remarkable is that, despite rampant anti-Semitism, there were those who could see beyond bigotry to their common humanity. Ghetto diarist Abraham Lewin was amazed at how many Poles "showed, and continue to show, pity and kindness to Jews who were destitute, especially towards beggar-children."[60]

Diarist Chaim Kaplan painted a word portrait of the young smugglers sneaking into the ghetto through a gate:

Whoever sees them recognizes them immediately. Their bodies are clothed in rags and tatters—and even their feet are wrapped in torn rags—and their faces attest to abysmal poverty. Besides their poverty they have another characteristic.

Jewish children climb the wall of the Warsaw ghetto. If caught by German guards, they would be beaten or shot on the spot. (1941)

All of them bear humps on their backs after the custom of camels. Anyone who didn't know their occupation would think them deformed. But the connoisseurs of smuggling know their secret. This is an artificial, manufactured hump whose inside is filled with potatoes and onions.[61]

These pint-size "criminals" had no childhood; they had to grow up too fast for that. Henryka Lazowert, a Polish poet of Jewish descent who was eventually murdered in Treblinka, captured their spirit in her poem "The Little Smuggler," which was widely read, recited, and praised in the ghetto:

Through walls, through holes, through sentry points,
Through wires, through rubble, through fences:

Hungry, daring, stubborn
I flee, dart like a cat.

At noon, at night, in dawning hours,
In blizzards, in the heat,
A hundred times I risk my life,
I risk my childish neck.

Under my arm a burlap sack,
On my back a tattered rag;
Running on my swift young legs
With fear ever in my heart.

Yet everything must be suffered;
And all must be endured. . . .

And if the hand of sudden fate
Seizes me at some point in this game . . .
Mama, don't wait for me.
I won't return to you,
Your far-off voice won't reach.
The dust of the street will bury
The lost youngster's fate.

And only one grim thought,
A grimace on your lips:
Who, my dear Mama, who
Will bring you bread tomorrow?[62]

Governor Hans Frank called child smugglers "rats" and ordered them killed on sight. Those caught begging on the Aryan

side were almost certainly doomed. One day, for example, a beggar boy of four or five sat on a main street, his hand stretched out. "An elegant German came by, opened a sewer-grating, took the child, and threw him into the sewer," a Pole reported. At night, SS men whom the Jews called "corpses" hid in dark corners near the wall. The moment a child appeared, bullets flew. Josef Blösche, a German police officer nicknamed "Frankenstein," held the record for killing youngsters. Emanuel Ringelblum described him as "a bloody dog who kills two or three smugglers a day. He just can't eat his breakfast until he has spilled the blood of a Jew." Frankenstein, at least, killed quickly. Others did not. Diarist Ludwik Hirszfeld noted: "A child smuggler caught by a German begged— 'Don't kill me'—'Don't worry, I will only make sure you won't smuggle again.' . . . and shot the child in both legs. Later they had to be amputated."[63]

Yet not all Germans were brutes. A few sentries—sadly, too few—acted decently. Unfortunately, we do not know their names or what became of them. When children walked through a gate, their clothes bulging with food and "looking like balloons," these men smiled knowingly and turned their backs. Most likely, they were not SS men but German police officers assigned to duty in Poland.[64]

Professionals made smuggling a business. Before the war, most had belonged to the Jewish underworld: thieves, swindlers, receivers of stolen goods. They went by names like "Berl the Souse," "Solly the Skirt," and "Izzy the Face." With the closing of the ghetto, they formed alliances with gentiles on Warsaw's Aryan side. Emanuel Ringelblum called "Polish-Jewish cooperation in

the field of smuggling . . . one of the finest pages in the history of mutual relations between the two peoples during the present war. . . . Ghettos would most certainly have swiftly perished without the help of Polish smugglers."[65]

Working together, Jews and Poles shared secret warehouses on the Aryan side. Poles with travel permits went into the countryside, bought food from farmers, and brought it to Warsaw. One fellow had a sense of humor; he sat in a train compartment with a dead pig that he had dressed as a peasant woman. When railway police saw the "woman," they broke up laughing. But they let him go.[66]

Smugglers also set wooden troughs in the windows of houses bordering the Aryan side of the wall and poured grain down, which accomplices on the Jewish side caught in sacks. Similarly, men with metal cans collected milk poured through sheet-metal pipes. Gangs used makeshift cranes and hooks attached to ropes to hoist heavy crates over the wall. To smuggle live cattle, they built mobile ramps against both sides of the wall; one gang brought twenty-six cows across in a single night. Better yet, Ringelblum noted, heavy trucks brought smuggled goods through the entry gate.[67]

How was this possible? How could Germans shoot small children taking scraps of food to their families, while waving big-time smugglers through the gates in broad daylight? The answer is that the Nazi occupiers, despite their claims of racial superiority and higher morality, were hypocrites who corrupted everything they touched. Bribery became a way of life in the ghetto. Smugglers and Germans wisecracked: "If you want to hear the music, you have to put a coin in the slot." It was true. What Jews

called *dos gesheft,* Yiddish for "the business," was so profitable that smugglers gladly offered, and Germans greedily took, a share of the profits.[68]

Smugglers were not philanthropists. They were men out to enrich themselves, and consumers had to pay the high prices they charged. Many, particularly the elderly, sold any valuables they'd managed to hide from the Germans. Many others sought an *Ausweis,* a permit to work at a German-approved job. German firms took advantage of the cheap labor abundant in the ghettos. Under contract to the military, they produced a wide variety of items: caps, helmets, belts, boots, brushes, mess kits, canteens, and camouflage suits. Though bosses offered long hours at low wages, workers earned enough to scrape by on smuggled food.

The Warsaw ghetto also had Jewish-owned industries, all illegal. These depended on smugglers supplying raw materials, workshops turning them into finished goods, and smugglers selling them on the Aryan side. Jews, too, salvaged and repaired items already in the ghetto. Tinkers made scrap metal into pots, pans, bowls, and spoons. Fat smuggled from Polish slaughterhouses became soap and candles. Cobblers made shoe-soles out of scrap wood and uppers from rags. Six-year-olds mass-produced toys. Understandably, the ghetto attracted visitors. Big buses took German tour groups through it to see how "degraded" the Jews were. On their days off, Germans came for bargains; soldiers took dates to see the sites and sniff the "ghetto smell" of "those people." Even Governor Frank's wife made frequent trips to buy "the most beautiful camisoles," loose jackets worn as dressing gowns.[69]

Smuggling was big business, and its big shots became an

aristocracy. It seems fantastic, but it is true. These people lived in apartment houses on choice streets in the small ghetto. Their wives and lovers were ladies of fashion. "In the evening," Emanuel Ringelblum noted, "you could see well-dressed women, wearing lipstick and rouge, strolling down the street with their dogs, as though there were no war." They favored long jackets, full skirts, hats, and high-heeled shoes. Luxury shops catered to their demand for scented soaps and perfumes; fancy groceries and bakeries sold vintage wines, real coffee, chocolate bonbons, canned caviar, and savory pastries. On warm days, diarist Mary Berg saw the newly rich on "a beach—a piece of ground on which deck chairs have been placed. For two zlotys one can bask in the sun here for an entire day. Bathing suits are obligatory, apparently to create the atmosphere of a real beach." Jews with spare cash did not walk to their destinations but went by pedicab, a two-seat tricycle pedaled by a man.[70]

More than ninety restaurants, cafés, and nightclubs catered to wealthy smugglers. These businesses had elegant names: Café Sztuka (Art Café), Melodia, Casanova, Splendid, and Britannia. Celebrated Jewish musicians, singers, and actors performed nightly for tips and a free meal. Café Tira advertised daily concerts, lamb on the luncheon menu, and a rear garden. Mary Berg, whose family was well off, described Café Hirschfeld's daily fare: "the most expensive liqueurs, cognac, pickled fish, canned food, duck, chicken and goose." Its patrons wore fine clothes, the women sporting gaudy makeup and dresses with plunging necklines.[71]

Over tables laden with food and drink, big-time smugglers

Actors stage a performance in the Warsaw ghetto. (1941)

bought favors from SS and Gestapo officers in civilian clothes. Payoffs took the form of cash, gold, and jewelry. Jewish police officials might also sit at tables nearby, meeting contacts and taking bribes. These men had a *schmaltz-grub* (literally, a "hole filled with chicken fat"—schmaltz is a Jewish delicacy, a yellow mixture of rendered chicken fat, often with added onions, spread on bread in place of butter), Yiddish slang for a profitable racket.

Ghetto restaurants and nightclubs did a booming trade. Despite the 6:00 p.m. curfew, their Nazi contacts allowed them to stay open all night. The last customers, bloated and bleary-eyed, staggered out before daybreak. One recalled how "my companion was warning me not to step on a corpse. I jumped. Underfoot lay a human form covered with newspapers." They were returning to the reality of the Warsaw ghetto.[72]

Starvation

Big-time smugglers handled an estimated 80 percent of the food eaten in the ghetto. Refugees from small towns relied on charity for their single daily meal. But a bowl of watery potato soup and a crust of black bread were not nearly enough to sustain life. Similarly, Jews who'd spent all their cash and sold their possessions could not afford smugglers' prices.

Hunger drove the needy to begging. Entire families begged in the streets. The saddest sights, however, were small children clad in rags, walking skeletons with gray, pinched faces and bulging

Starving Jewish children begging in the streets of the Warsaw ghetto. (Date unknown)

eyes. Though better-off passersby might avert their gaze, they could not make themselves deaf. Children pleaded, in crackly voices, *"A schtickele broit, a schtickele broit!"*—"A little piece of bread, a little piece of bread!" Little ones stood at building entrances, singing:

> *Have pity, have mercy, good people!*
> *Drop me a piece of bread,*
> *A tiny, tiny piece of bread.*[73]

Children might snap under the stress of hunger. Emanuel Ringelblum saw an eight-year-old boy become hysterical. He screamed: "I want to steal, I want to rob, I want to eat, I want to be a German!" Asked what she hoped to become, a little girl answered: "I'd like to be a dog because the Germans like dogs and I wouldn't have to be afraid that they'd kill me."[74]

The most pitiful were the pleas of starving children at night. Ignoring the curfew, these doomed ones stood in courtyards crying their hearts out. Dawid Wdowiński, a physician, heard them. "One who has not heard the crying of hungry children at night outside the windows of apartment houses has not heard the piercing anguish of an animal in peril," he wrote. "These were not human cries, nor human weeping. It was the haunted baying of creatures facing death, clinging to life with the only physical effort still left to them—the whistling howl that ripped out of their empty bellies and contracted entrails to fill the troubled night with frightful tremor."[75]

We also read about small children, themselves starving, showing qualities normally expected of mature, caring adults. Their actions were the stuff of poetry, a major form of expression in the ghetto. Every situation inspired its poems, which today are valuable historical documents. Poetry, as scholar Frieda W. Aaron observes, "helped to keep the soul alive." Poets wrote not only to express themselves but also to reaffirm human decency and transmit their experiences to future generations. Yet the ghetto poets are not easy to read, for they tug at our hearts and still have the power to bring tears.[76]

Grown up emotionally, if not in years, children showed sensitivity and wisdom their tormentors could not have understood. Racist indoctrination had deprived these men of empathy, the normal person's ability to imagine another's feelings. For poet Itzhak Katzenelson, who was to lose his wife and sons, and finally his own life, these little ones were angels with hollow cheeks and sad eyes. He writes in "The Song of the Murdered Jewish People":

> *I watched the two-year-old grandmother,*
> *The tiny Jewish girl, a hundred years old in her*
> *   seriousness and grief.*
> *What her grandmother could not dream she had*
> *   seen in reality. . . .*
>
> *Don't cry I saw a five-year-old girl. . . .*
> *She fed her younger, crying brother . . .*
> *She dipped hard breadcrumbs in marmalade*
> *And got them cleverly into his mouth . . . I was lucky*
> *To see it, to see the five-year-old mother feeding him,*

And to hear her words. My mother, exceptional
though she was, was not that imaginative. . . .

They, the Jewish children, were the first to perish, all
of them,
Almost all without father or mother, eaten by cold,
hunger, and vermin,
Saintly messiahs, sanctified by pain. . . .
Why were they the first to pay so high a price to evil
in the days of slaughter?[77]

Most people in the West have seldom, if ever, seen a dead body, let alone several corpses at a time. But in the square mile of the Warsaw ghetto, starvation and disease took thousands each

A dead Jewish man in the streets of the Warsaw ghetto. (1942)

month. In January 1941, for example, nine hundred people died every day in the "points" and on the streets. People of all ages got used to the sight of death. Bodies lay in full view, naked and covered with newspaper, for the rags worn by the deceased still had some value. The Jewish Council hired men to collect them in carts for burial in the Jewish cemetery at the northern end of the large ghetto.[78]

Korczak's Children

An orphanage in the small ghetto once sent a wreath to the funeral of children from another orphanage. The inscription read "From children who are starving to children who have died of starvation." We cannot say if the Old Doctor knew about this, but if he did, surely he would have seen a similarity to the situation of his own children.[79]

Korczak could not find it in himself to turn away the neediest. As a result, Dom Sierot grew from 100 children when the war began to 192 in 1941. By 1941, they were living in more cramped quarters, having been forced to move to an even smaller place at the southern end of the small ghetto.

Nevertheless, the educator stuck to his routines, trying to keep things as normal as possible. To rouse creativity and sharpen their minds, he encouraged children to read the few books that were available and to keep diaries; like their young authors, none of those diaries survived. Though the Nazis banned schools in the ghetto, residents secretly ran them in apartments; teachers

were usually paid in food. At Dom Sierot, classes were taught in history, geography, mathematics, and science. Given his many contacts, Korczak also invited noted scientists and historians, including Emanuel Ringelblum, to lecture on whatever subject they pleased. They gladly accepted, even knowing what might happen if the Gestapo found out.[80]

Drama teachers helped put on plays; Korczak sold tickets to raise money for various activities. Poetry promoted unity and courage. The most popular poem was "Ale Mentshn Zaynen Brider" (All Men Are Brothers), a 1915 work by the famed I. L. Peretz. Sung or recited in chorus, this hymn to brotherhood rejected racism in all its forms:

White, Brown, Black, Yellow—
mix the colors all together!
All people are brothers,
From the same father, from the same mother!

And one god has created them all,
and one homeland: the world!
all people are brothers,
that is absolutely certain![81]

Humor, too, soothed the soul. Even in the midst of hardship and horror, people tried to raise their spirits with laughter. For example, a father teaches his son to say grace before meals:

"Today in Germany the proper form of grace is 'Thank God and Hitler,'" says the father.

"But suppose the Führer dies?" asks the boy.
"Then you just thank God."

My favorite ghetto joke: A teacher asks a pupil, "What would you like to be if you were Hitler's son?" He answers, "An orphan!"[82]

The Old Doctor's main job was to feed his children. To do so, he turned beggar, venturing into the large ghetto, which he called "the district of the damned." He found the streets a swirling panorama of misery. Roving musicians, opera singers, and revered synagogue cantors performed for a copper coin or a crust of bread. A blind accordion player sang, as did a walking skeleton who wheeled his paralyzed wife in a child's stroller. Scrawny, hollow-cheeked women stood in doorways, offering clean armbands for sale.[83]

Then there was Rubinstein, the ghetto's *meshuggener*—its lunatic. Nobody knew his first name or where he came from. Among the poorest of the poor, Rubinstein occasionally wore a dress. "I don't have a wife," he'd explain, "so I guess I have to be my own wife today; not bad, eh?" Passersby chuckled when he bawled in Yiddish, *"Ale glaych"*—"All are equal!" All in the ghetto were equal in the face of death is what he meant. To scare people into giving him handouts, he'd shout at the top of his voice, "Down with Hitler! Down with the German murderers!" The kindly Old Doctor, thinking Rubinstein "madly wise," pressed a coin into his hand.[84]

Korczak was most disturbed by children's indifference to the horrors around them. They had grown so used to death that the

sight of bodies seemed normal. Children held make-believe funerals and pretended to dig graves; some tickled corpses to "awaken" them. A gruesome incident made so deep an impression on the Old Doctor that he recorded it twice in his diary. "A young boy, still alive or perhaps dead already, is lying across the sidewalk," he wrote. "Right there three boys are playing horses and drivers; their reins have gotten entangled. They try every which way to disentangle them, they grow impatient, stumble over the boy lying on the ground. Finally one of them says: 'Let's move on, he gets in the way.'"[85]

Korczak set an exhausting pace for himself. "It's difficult," he'd say. "But one can't be squeamish in these matters." With a sack over his shoulder, he knocked on the doors of likely donors. Sometimes they gave him a hard time, forcing him "to shout, reprove, beg, and lose his temper." Yet his fame and goodness commanded respect, so few sent him away empty-handed. If a well-off person gave too little, he'd growl, "Not enough! Put a few more potatoes into the sack! I need a little cash!" When visiting a nightclub, he wore his army uniform. He'd make the rounds of the smugglers' tables, shouting: "Is there someone here with a bag of potatoes to get my children through the winter?" Thanks to him, meals at Dom Sierot, though poor in quality and amount, were lavish by ghetto standards; they included potatoes, black bread, and horsemeat sausage mixed with horse blood. From time to time, Korczak was able to wangle a barrel of tiny salted fish called "stinkies," which were used to make soup.[86]

Each night, the doctor-beggar returned to the children's home "shattered." By 1941, after nearly two years in the ghetto, time was

catching up with him. Now sixty-three, he showed signs of aging. "There isn't a bit of me left in sound health. Adhesions, aches, ruptures, scars. I am falling to pieces," he wrote in his diary. His eyes hurt, and he had high blood pressure. He also smelled awful, something new for him. "It is a long time since I have had a bath. Yesterday I caught on myself and killed without turning a hair— with one dexterous squeeze of a nail—a louse." Nevertheless, he respected lice, honest creatures that earned their blood-meals and took no more than they needed. For, as he observed, "a louse is not like a man; it will not suck up every last drop of blood."[87]

His nights were filled with morbid thoughts. Revved up from begging and by a hundred worries, Korczak tossed and turned in bed. To help himself fall asleep, he drank a glass of raw alcohol mixed with hot water. And still the nightmares came: "What ghastly dreams! . . . Bodies of dead children. One dead child in a bucket. Another skinned, lying on the boards of the mortuary, clearly still breathing." He awoke exhausted, barely able to dress.[88]

But the Old Doctor had not given up hope. He still felt that, with luck, he and Madame Stefa would live to guide their children in happier times.

Late one night in the spring of 1941, Korczak saw something that revived his spirits. He stood with a friend, Michael Zylberberg, a teacher of Jewish history, at a window in Dom Sierot, overlooking the darkened streets. As they watched, German tanks rolled through the ghetto, bound for the Vistula bridges. Many a steel monster bore a chalked slogan on its sides: *"Stalin, wir kommen"*—"We're coming, Stalin!" Instantly, they knew the Führer was massing his armies for a surprise attack on the Soviet

Union. "Dr. Korczak," Zylberberg recalled in his diary, "thought this was a happy omen for the Jews. He was so certain that in a matter of days Russia would crush the Germans. It was a ray of hope for every Jew behind the ghetto walls."[89]

The Old Doctor could not have been more wrong. For those tanks were the worst possible omens, not only for Polish Jews but also for every Jew trapped in Nazi-occupied Europe.

A Dream So Terrible

I am hiding in a pit, lingering on without fresh air . . . but that doesn't matter, because I will finish my account. . . . And they will ask if this is the truth. And I will answer in advance: No, this is not the truth, it is only a small part, a tiny fraction of the truth. The essential truth, the real truth, cannot be described even by the most powerful pen.

—Stefan Ernest, a worker who did not survive (1942)

Lethal Intentions

In his arrogance, Adolf Hitler ignored a basic principle the German military learned from World War I: Never fight on two fronts at the same time. The Führer decided to attack the Soviet Union, though Germany was still at war with Great Britain and clearly not winning. The decision was an unforced error, a colossal blunder that would bring Nazi Germany to ruin.

Late in 1940, Hitler ordered his high command to draw up plans for Operation Barbarossa (Redbeard), named for a German emperor of the Middle Ages famed for his red beard and fierceness in battle. Hitler looked forward to fighting a war without rules or moral limits, the kind of war that he believed nature demands. Speaking with all the hatred and fanaticism he could

muster, he declared, "The law of existence prescribes uninter-rupted killing, so that the better [race] may live." The invasion would be a full-scale race war against a "dull," "dumb," "barely humanlike" enemy degraded by "Jewish Bolshevism."[1]

Pity would have no place in the struggle. "This is a war of ex-termination," Hitler told his generals. He was effectively ordering them to discard an essential aspect of what it means to be human. For pity is an emotion human beings feel for one another, because they see something of themselves in the other person. Hitler, how-ever, regarded pity and conscience as "Jewish inventions," hin-drances in the struggle for existence.[2]

The only Russians allowed to live would be slaves; the rest of the population, tens of millions of human beings, must die of starva-tion, disease, or outright murder. Russian culture—literature, art, music, libraries, museums, universities—would disappear. Nazi forces would level the Communist nation's cities, including its capital, Moscow. Hitler left no doubt about his intentions. "I will raze this damned city to the ground," he swore, "and I will make an artificial lake to provide energy for an electric power station. The name of Moscow will vanish forever."[3]

Hitler gathered the largest invasion force in the history of warfare. At precisely 3:15 a.m. on June 22, 1941, Operation Bar-barossa began. Over 3.5 million troops went into action, sup-ported by 600,000 motorized vehicles, 3,600 tanks, 2,500 planes, and 7,000 artillery pieces of various sizes. In classic blitzkrieg fashion, there was no declaration of war, only massive air strikes and fast-moving tank divisions. Taken completely by surprise, the Red Army reeled under the blows.

Soviet losses skyrocketed. No modern nation had ever suffered so terribly at the outset of a war. During the first week, Hitler's armies stabbed two hundred miles into "Mother Russia." Within days, they destroyed nearly 4,000 aircraft, most parked in neat rows on the ground, and they killed, captured, or wounded some 700,000 Red Army troops. As in Poland, Nazi airmen had no respect for innocent human life, shooting at anyone they saw on the ground. Fighter pilot Hans Hartigs boasted: "We liked to go for women pushing prams, often with children at their sides. It was a kind of sport really." When a Soviet interrogator asked another captured pilot, "Didn't it bother you to bomb defenseless women?" he shrugged and said, "It was fun."[4]

Columns of prisoners, marching five abreast, stretched to the horizon, as far as the eye could see. Under international law, captors must properly feed, shelter, and give prisoners of war medical care. The Nazis deliberately violated the law. Guards used captives "as target practice and set their dogs on them, placing bets on which dog would inflict the worst injuries." They starved Soviet prisoners, just as their comrades were starving ghetto Jews in Poland. Well-fed men thought it hilarious to throw a dead dog into a compound and watch the hunger-maddened Russians tear it to shreds and eat the pieces raw. Of the 5.7 million Soviet POWs held by the Nazis, 3.5 million died of starvation, disease, exposure, or murder. By comparison, as many American and British POWs died in German hands during the entire war as Russian prisoners died in one day. As ever, Hitler blamed the Jews. "It's not my fault," he insisted. "I didn't want this war or the POW camps. Why did the Jews provoke this war?"[5]

Hitler attacked the Soviet Union not only to gain *Lebensraum* (living space) for Germany and raw materials for world conquest but also to strike at the Jews. He meant to use the Soviet war as a device for realizing a goal he'd set at the start of his political career. In writings dating from 1919, he had declared his intention to annihilate the Jews. If nothing else, Hitler was consistent, for his ideology of racism and anti-Semitism led, inevitably, to this murderous outcome.

Historians recognize that the Nazi leader willed the Holocaust, the systematic murder of Europe's Jews. The creation of ghettos in occupied Poland was but the initial stage in this process. To be sure, as Germany rearmed and Hitler grew bolder, he did not mince words in meetings with foreign diplomats. In November 1938, just days after Kristallnacht, he told a South African official that the Jews "would disappear from Europe one day." In January 1939, eight months before the invasion of Poland, he informed the Czech foreign minister: "We shall exterminate the Jews."[6]

On January 30, 1939, Hitler issued a public threat to Europe's Jews. If they started another war, he warned, the result would be "the extermination of the Jewish race in Europe!" Why did he hold the Jews responsible for the war he'd begun by attacking Poland? The answer, it seems, is that, for Hitler, any obstacle that stood in his way had to be part of the Jewish "conspiracy" to rule the world. Whatever the reason, the Führer repeated his dire warning more than a dozen times in public statements, even in radio broadcasts. Given Hitler's ideology, it should come as no

surprise that he dubbed World War II the "war against the Jews."
It was also, as we will see, the war against the Jewish children.[7]

Surviving testimony of the people closest to Hitler leaves no
doubt that the Holocaust was his doing. Joseph Goebbels said
so in his diary: "The Führer is the moving spirit behind the racial solution, both in word and deed." After the war, Nicolaus
von Below, a Luftwaffe officer who served as a personal military
aide to Hitler, said, "There is no question whatever in my mind
that . . . it was Hitler who specifically ordered the extermination
of the Jews." Christa Schroeder, one of Hitler's personal secretaries, who saw him nearly every day for a decade, took his responsibility for granted. "Of course, Hitler knew!" she said in 1977.
"Not only knew, it was *all* his ideas, his orders." The Führer was
in charge—always. As he liked to say, "Every bullet that is now
fired from the barrel of a German pistol is my bullet."[8]

Yet historians have found no paper document proving Hitler's
guilt. Most likely, such a document never existed, because the
Führer gave the order orally to distance himself from blame. We
do know that early in the summer of 1941, he met with Heinrich Himmler "under four eyes"—that is, they spoke alone, and
no written record was made. After the meeting, the SS chief left
Hitler's office. Clearly agitated, he plopped into a chair beside
Christa Schroeder's desk. "My God, my God," he moaned, "what
am I expected to do?" Schroeder added: "Later, much later, when
we found out what had been done, I was sure that was the day
Hitler told him the Jews had to be killed." Evidently, what troubled Himmler was not the morality of the mass-murder order;

a fervent racist, he, too, wanted the Jews wiped out. It seems that Himmler's agitation stemmed from the scale and complexity of his assignment.[9]

Himmler must have relayed the Führer's order to Reinhard Heydrich, who in turn passed it to his underlings. At a secret meeting, Heydrich told SS commanders, "Eastern Jewry is the reservoir of Bolshevism, and is thus to be exterminated, in the view of the Führer." Hitler's "view" was hardly an opinion; SS men took it as a command, though unwritten. Afterward, different SS officers said they'd gotten the order directly from Heydrich, or from other SS higher-ups, at different times, in oral or written form.[10]

Einsatzgruppen

As the blitzkrieg smashed into the Soviet Union, Heydrich sent special operation groups called Einsatzgruppen into action. Heydrich tasked them with following the advancing German armies, securing the rear areas, and shooting any Soviet officials or Jews who fell into their hands. Those killings, Heydrich assured commanders, would be "due exclusively to the personal orders of the Führer, Adolf Hitler."[11]

Four Einsatzgruppen took the field: Groups A, B, C, and D, each with 500 to 700 members divided into companies called commandos. The group leaders were not crude thugs but men of culture and education. Three had the title "Doctor" before their names, with degrees in law and economics, proof again that

formal education is no guarantee of wisdom or decency. Like Hitler, Himmler, and Heydrich, Einsatzgruppen leaders were true believers, diehards driven by racist ideology. Their sub-commanders were also professional men: lawyers, teachers, artists, even a Protestant minister. Nor were the rank and file common criminals, but members of the SS Security Service, the Gestapo, and the German police, as well as foreigners sympathetic to the Nazis. All were volunteers and could have resigned without fear of punishment. So far, researchers have not found a single instance of a member harmed for refusing to obey a murder order.[12]

Before reaching Soviet territory, Hitler's armies overran the three Soviet-controlled nations bordering the Baltic Sea—Estonia, Latvia, Lithuania—and Ukraine. Their long histories of anti-Semitism made it easy for the Nazis to stir up pogroms. As German troops stood by, egging them on, locals butchered Jews in town squares with axes and crowbars; in some places, parents brought their children to watch the mayhem. Volunteers also became auxiliaries, working alongside the Waffen-SS and Einsatzgruppen. In the years ahead, they helped to empty ghettos, carry out mass shootings, and run extermination camps.

The Einsatzgruppen committed the bulk of their atrocities in the Soviet Union, home to 3.2 million Jews. All Jews who had not fled with the retreating Red Army were marked for death. Appearing suddenly, motorized commandos surrounded a village before daybreak, rousing the sleeping residents with shouts and gunshots. After assembling the Jews, they marched them to the edge of a remote ravine or into a forest clearing where Jewish slaves

had dug pits during the night. In the early actions, they made victims kneel at the pit's edge, killing them individually with a pistol shot to the back of the neck; the force of the bullet pitched the person forward, into the pit. Later, they killed en masse, mowing Jews down with machine guns. Before opening fire, executioners ordered everyone to remove their clothing. Experience taught that nakedness made victims more manageable, dulling the instinct for self-preservation. The worst massacre by shooting took place on September 29–30, 1941, at Babi Yar, a ravine outside the Ukrainian city of Kiev. Executioners needed thirty-six hours to murder 33,771 men, women, and children. Shooters kept up such a hectic pace that backup teams had to relieve them every two hours or so.[13]

Children were prime targets, because nothing can destroy a people so thoroughly as the killing of its youngest. In Hitler's ideology, children embodied renewal because they carried their race's traits in, as he liked to say, their "blood" and their "souls." He explained: "If one little Jewish boy survives without any Jewish education, with no synagogue and no Hebrew school, it [Judaism] is in his soul." Himmler agreed, adding that Jewish children not only had "bad blood" but would seek vengeance for their parents' deaths if allowed to live. Therefore, according to his perverse logic, "even the child in the cradle must be trampled down like a poisonous toad."[14]

By 1941, racism had poisoned the German military at every level. Even top generals, bound by a centuries-old code of honor, preached about "cleansing" the east of *Untermenschen,* or "subhumans." Similarly, rank-and-file soldiers took it for granted that,

as "Aryan supermen," they had the right to do whatever they pleased. So many men committed atrocities in so many places that it became impossible to keep these "actions" secret. Soldiers on leave told their parents, wives, and friends about what they'd seen and done in Russia. Though Heydrich banned cameras at execution sites, spectators took "souvenir" snapshots anyhow. Captured soldiers had execution photos in their wallets; some families pasted them into scrapbooks.

Ordinary Wehrmacht fighting men, as well as Einsatzgruppen members, wrote millions of letters home. Many described gruesome crimes, making us wonder how families felt upon reading them. For instance, Walter Mattner, a police officer in civilian life, was proud of his skill with a rifle. Mattner wrote his wife that he was perfectly calm while shooting infants, which comrades tossed into the air like tin cans at target practice. "The babies flew in great arcs and we shot them to pieces in the air before they fell into the ditch." Karl Kretschmer, an Einsatzgruppen member, wrote his wife: *"My dear Soska. Here in Russia, wherever the German soldier is, no Jew remains."*[15]

Mass shootings also affected some of the shooters. These individuals found killing helpless people at close range, day after day, too awful to bear. The weeping, wailing, and screaming of the doomed chilled them to the core. Skulls exploding when struck by bullets spattered them with blood, brains, and bone splinters. Inevitably, there were those—we will never know how many—who cracked up. These men might become speechless, soil their pants, and tremble uncontrollably. To steady their nerves and blot out memories, they got drunk; more than a few became alcoholics.

Scores, possibly hundreds, of distraught men resigned and volunteered for combat duty, seeking suicide by Russian bullets.[16]

Christabel Bielenberg met such a tortured soul one night. She was traveling by train from Berlin when an air-raid alert forced it to stop and put out its lights. She dozed off, awakening when an antiaircraft searchlight pierced the darkness for an instant. In that split second, she caught a glimpse of the man sitting opposite her. His collar had the lightning-bolt insignia of the SS. Softly, he asked the *"Gnädige Frau,"* the Dear Lady, if she had a long journey ahead. Bielenberg tried to make small talk, but he insisted on telling her about his time in the Einsatzgruppen:

Do you know what it means—to kill Jews, men, women, and children as they stand in a semicircle around the machine guns? I belonged to an extermination squad—so I know. What do you say when I tell you that a little boy, no older than my youngest brother, before such a killing stood at attention and asked me "Do I stand straight enough, Uncle?" Yes, he asked that of me; and once . . . an old man stepped out of the ranks, he had long hair and a beard, a priest of some sort I suppose. Anyway, he came slowly towards us across the grass, slowly step by step, and within a few feet of the guns he stopped and looked at us one after another, a straight, deep, dark, and terrible look. "My children," he said, "God is watching what you do." He turned from us then, and someone shot him in the back before he got more than a few steps. But I—I could not forget that look; even now it burns into me.

Then the SS man told Bielenberg that he was going to the front, "*anywhere,* did I hear, where he should be allowed to die," and asked, "You are silent, *Gnädige Frau?* You are horrified at my story?" Bielenberg replied, "No—no . . . I am not horrified, I think I pity you, for you have more on your conscience than can be absolved by your death." Emotionally drained, she fell into a deep sleep. When she awoke, the train was moving, and the SS man was gone.[17]

Clearly, if you were Heinrich Himmler or Reinhard Heydrich, you wanted to find a "better" way of mass killing, more efficient and more "humane"—that is, one less stressful for the killers.

Toward the "Final Solution"

On December 7, 1941, Japanese planes bombed the U.S. naval base at Pearl Harbor in the Hawaiian Islands. The following day, Congress declared war on the Empire of Japan. On December 11, in support of his Asian ally, Hitler declared war on the United States. Fighting the world's leading industrial power would turn out to be a greater blunder than attacking the Soviet Union. But the thought of taking on the "racially corrupt" American giant excited the Führer. Seventy years before terrorists crashed airliners into the towers of New York's World Trade Center on September 11, 2001, Hitler imagined for his aides New York's skyscrapers as immense pillars of fire, burning until they collapsed. As for Europe's Jews, he decided to finish them off.[18]

On January 20, 1942, a select group of fifteen men met in a mansion in the Berlin suburb of Wannsee. Apart from Reinhard

Heydrich, who chaired the Wannsee Conference, they were top civil servants. Eight held doctorates, and all were masters of detail, nuts-and-bolts men who knew how to get things done in the cheapest, swiftest, most efficient way.

Hermann Göring, the Führer's second-in-command, had entrusted Heydrich with "the Final Solution of the Jewish Question in Europe." The purpose of the conference, he explained, was to coordinate the efforts of their departments—police, transportation, finance, foreign affairs, legal—to achieve that goal. Heydrich planned to comb occupied Europe from west to east. Jews—all 11 million of them—would be identified, segregated, arrested, and deported to "transit ghettos." From there, able-bodied men would be sent to work as slaves under conditions sure to kill them. The others, the vast majority, would go to camps that were nothing like Hitler's concentration camps for political prisoners, horrible as they were. Unique in human history, the new camps were true factories designed for murder on an industrial scale. After Heydrich's presentation, according to the minutes of the meeting, the officials "spoke about methods of killing, about liquidation, about extermination."[19]

During the discussions, Josef Bühler, Hans Frank's deputy, had "only one favor to ask." Governor Frank was urging that the "Final Solution" begin in Poland. He had already given it a head start by promoting starvation and disease in the ghettos. Now he hoped to finish off the Jews "as fast as possible." Heydrich agreed. The final stage of the Holocaust would begin in Poland.[20]

Auschwitz, opened in 1940 as a forced-labor camp, became an extermination center, too—the largest that ever existed. Jewish

slave laborers also began work on three purpose-built death factories: Bełżec, Sobibór, and Treblinka. In May 1942, Czech commandos sent from Britain fatally wounded Heydrich in Prague, the capital of Czechoslovakia. To honor the memory of Hitler's "young, evil god of death," the three death factories were code-named "Operation Reinhard" camps.[21]

Setting the Stage

Europe's Jews knew nothing of the Wannsee Conference. In the Warsaw ghetto, the majority had managed to survive despite

Women and children walk toward the gas chambers in Auschwitz. (1944)

every hardship. People knew the war would not last forever, and they hoped to outlast the Nazis, as their ancestors had always outlasted oppressors.

Events seemed to justify their hopes. Teenager Mary Berg noted in her diary that, after America's entry into the war, German sentries at the gates had "long faces." By then, the advance into Russia had stalled, as the Red Army regrouped and pushed back. To make matters worse, Mother Nature turned against the invader. Russia's three legendary commanders—General Winter, General Frost, and General Snow—arrived in the nick of time.[22]

Expecting a quick victory, Hitler had not ordered cold-weather gear for his armies. As a result, the three "generals" caught them in summer uniforms. Endless snow fields glittering in bright sunlight caused snow blindness. In temperatures below $-40°$ F, surgeons worked around the clock, amputating frostbitten ears, hands, and feet. On a single day in December, surgeons cut off the frozen limbs of fourteen thousand German soldiers. Meanwhile, Soviet troops, snug in their quilted jackets, fur hats, and felt boots, inflicted massive losses on the invaders. To end their suffering, German medics may have killed hideously maimed, brain-damaged, and mentally traumatized troops. Though historians have no solid proof of this, we know that nurses told friends that they gave lethal injections to "our own" men. It seems logical that the Nazis, who'd killed disabled German civilians, would do the same to soldiers who'd become "useless eaters."[23]

That winter in Warsaw, a diarist noted, "Jewish spirits soared." Every day saw the arrival of hospital trains crammed

with wounded German soldiers; Poles called them *rubanka*—"chopped meat." Nor did Jews seem to mind all that much when ordered to turn over, on pain of death, their fur coats, gloves, and earmuffs. Before handing them in, many dipped them in boiling water to loosen the hairs so that the garments would later fall apart. Better yet, by the spring of 1942, the underground press reported that scores of newly built airfields dotted the English countryside. American and British bombers began to raid German cities. In the Warsaw ghetto, Emanuel Ringelblum noted, news of Allied bombings "evoked great joy."[24]

Meanwhile, planning for mass murder went into high gear. To ensure secrecy, the Nazis moved cautiously. In doing so, they corrupted language, as racism had corrupted their minds. They devised a special vocabulary to soothe their consciences and deceive their victims. Adolf Eichmann, the SS lieutenant colonel who took the minutes at Wannsee and later directed the roundup and shipment of Jews to death camps, explained the procedure. When asked how it felt to send millions to their deaths, Eichmann replied, "Our language made it easy. My fellow officers and I coined our own name for our language. We called it 'office talk.' In office talk, you deny responsibility for your actions. So if anybody says, 'Why did you do it?' you say 'I had to.' 'Why did you have to?' 'Superiors' orders. Company policy. It's the law.' "[25]

In everyday life, we may prefer to say that a friend "passed away" rather than died, or that a sickly pet was "put to sleep" instead of killed. We use a bland term—a euphemism—rather than a harsh or direct one. Nazis routinely used euphemisms—"office talk"—to veil their crimes. A few examples:

Final Solution of the Jewish Question =
  extermination of European Jews

resettlement action = deportation

evacuation = deportation

transported material = deported Jews packed into
  boxcars

cleansing operation = deportation, murder

deported to the east = sent to death factories

liquidated = murdered

processed = murdered

given special treatment = murdered

disinfected = murdered

special installations = death factories

finished off = murdered

pacification = massacre of Jews in a specific area

was made free of Jews = every Jew in an area was
  killed

unproductive elements = "useless" Jews slated for
  death

treated appropriately = murdered

Jewish resettlement region = death factory

bathhouses and showers = gas chambers

special actions = massive operations to round up
  and kill Jews

During the spring of 1942, as the Operation Reinhard camps
began mass killing, the SS and Gestapo launched "special actions"

in the ghettos in Poland. Acting swiftly, they "evacuated" the Jews of Lviv to Bełżec, and those of Lublin to Sobibór. Before long, rumors that thousands of Jews—forty-four thousand from Lublin alone—had simply vanished reached the Warsaw ghetto. (The Lubliners died in the nearby Majdanek extermination camp.) "What is the significance of the pogrom in Lublin?" Mary Berg wondered. Family friends guessed its Jews must be at forced-labor sites in eastern Poland or Russia. Few imagined that the Nazis, sadistic as they were, would murder thousands of skilled workers when their war effort demanded ever more slave labor and increased production. Besides, Lublin and other ghettos were small compared to the Warsaw ghetto. Optimists thought it too large, too important, and too well known for the Nazis to try to destroy. "To exterminate such a number of people seems impossible, inconceivable," Mary Berg told her diary, echoing popular opinion.[26]

A professor of history, a deeply learned man, insisted that doomsayers suffered from a "distorted sense of reality." He argued from "proved and incontestable facts, by citing innumerable examples drawn from various periods of history . . . [that] a danger . . . did not actually exist." The unnamed historian, a rational man, *should* have been right. However, the trouble with sane people like him was that they could not think like fanatical racists. Where Nazi-style racism ruled, the "sanity" of the victims could be seen as a form of madness, preventing them from grasping the danger they faced.[27]

The Great Action

What the Nazis called Grossaktion Warschau (Great Action Warsaw) unfolded gradually, over a period of three months. Before mass deportations could begin, SS planners decided they needed to further terrorize, confuse, and disorient their victims. The purpose was to paralyze resistance and divide the Jews, forcing each group to look after its own interests at the expense of others.

The initial blows fell on the night of April 17, 1942. After the 6:00 p.m. curfew forced people indoors, four-man Gestapo teams set out in cars, each with a hit list and a Jewish policeman to show them the way. Upon arrival, they knocked on an apartment door. Politely, they asked the man on their list to, please, come downstairs for a moment. With their car's headlights shining into his eyes, they stood him against a wall, shot him, and left his body where it fell. Then they drove off to get their next victim. Fifty-two men lost their lives during this Night of Blood (Nacht des Blutes). At daybreak, early risers found the bodies lying in pools of blood. What had the victims done to deserve this? The only thing they had in common was their religion. Otherwise, they came from different walks of life: artisans, shopkeepers, printers, civic leaders.[28]

The Night of Blood was just the beginning. Day after day, Gestapo men terrorized the ghetto with gangster-style killings. In broad daylight, a car screeched to a stop beside a pedestrian on a crowded sidewalk. Two men emerged and dragged him inside as the car sped off. A few blocks away, the car again screeched to a stop, a door opened, and a corpse tumbled into the gutter. Once,

three children were sitting on the first three steps at the front of a building, each behind the other. A passing German shot them in the head with a single bullet and calmly walked off. Another time, intruders burst into an apartment. Finding a paralyzed man in a wheelchair, they threw both out a window as horrified neighbors watched.[29]

Night, as ever, was the worst time. Marek Edelman, a leader of the 1943 Warsaw ghetto revolt, recalled: "The very basis of ghetto life started to move from under people's feet. Every night filled with the shrill, crisp sound of shots was an illustration that the ghetto had no foundations whatever, that it lived by the will of the Germans, that it was brittle and weak like a house of playing cards. . . . But nobody yet realized that its entire population was destined to die." The SS knew how to keep a secret.[30]

In June, the SS spread confusion by abruptly switching from terror to "goodwill." Unexpectedly, officials gave the Jewish Council permission to organize a "Jewish Children's Festival." Under the slogan "Give the children a little joy in their lives," the council built a playground opposite its headquarters, and a street artist painted a mural, "a symphony of color," on an outside wall. On opening day, the Jewish police band played, and a children's chorus sang "Hatikvah," the Zionist anthem whose title is Hebrew for "hope." Smiling SS and Gestapo men attended as guests. "They actually came to the ceremony and stood there without as much as batting an eyelid or saying a word as they watched the performances," a witness recalled.[31]

Nevertheless, deportation rumors spread. On July 20, Jewish Council president Adam Czerniaków asked Gestapo official

Gerhard von Mende if the rumors were true. Von Mende feigned ignorance. Deportation? He knew nothing about any deportation plan. Perhaps others did. Czerniaków should ask them. So, for hours he went from office to office, asking about the rumored deportation. He got the runaround: Talk of deportation was "prattle and nonsense." Officials gave their "word of honor" as Germans that no deportations were planned. Deportations began the next day.[32]

July 21. At ten o'clock that morning, SS major Hermann Höfle sped off in his staff car, followed by bodyguards in two more cars and two trucks full of soldiers. A tall, fair-skinned "Aryan" dressed in a spotless uniform, Höfle held the title "Chief of Staff for Operation Reinhard." He personally had directed the "cleansing" of the Lublin ghetto. Upon arriving at Jewish Council headquarters, he found Czerniaków, as ordered, in his office. Every window was wide open, because Warsaw lay in the grip of the hottest summer in living memory. From the street, three floors below, came the sound of music; Höfle's bodyguards were playing waltz records on a portable phonograph to pass the time.[33]

Höfle came straight to the point. "Today the deportation from Warsaw begins. You know there are too many Jews," he said. Using "office talk," the major continued: "All Jews, irrespective of sex or age, with certain exceptions, will be deported to the East . . . [for] resettlement." What is more, the Jewish Council must deliver six thousand people each day until further notice. Council members *will* obey—or else. Already, the Gestapo had taken several council members into custody. They would be shot if the action fell short of the Nazis' daily quotas. Czerniaków's wife, Felicia, had not been arrested, but, Höfle said, "she will be

the first one to be shot as a hostage." Something else: The Jewish Council must deliver several large wooden boxes with hinged covers. Only later was it learned that these were for collecting the valuables of the people killed at Treblinka.[34]

By mid-afternoon on July 21, posters titled "Order of Deportation Notice" appeared on walls throughout the ghetto. In minute detail, they listed categories of people exempt from deportation: Jewish Council members and staff and their families, Jewish policemen and their families, people with work permits for German firms and their families. Everyone else had to go. But not to worry, as they would work on various projects to the east. The deportation would begin promptly at 11:00 a.m. the next day. Anyone subject to deportation who failed to report, or reported late, or encouraged others not to report, "will be shot." The reason for the large number of exemptions was to divide the community by giving the illusion that permit holders were valuable to the Germans, and therefore safe. As a historian explained, this kept people on edge by encouraging the idea of self-preservation—"torture by hope." We might call it "torture by wishful thinking."[35]

July 22. The roundup of "unproductive elements" began. Jewish police and Ukrainian auxiliaries raided the "points," the shelters for destitute refugees, and swept many beggars, homeless people, and living skeletons off the streets. "Shocking scenes took place in the streets," wrote social worker Adolf Berman. "The children sensed the danger of death threatening them and resisted the police, struggled with them, and tried to escape. The streets echoed with the heartrending screams and crying of children." Treblinka's gates swung open that evening.[36]

July 23. Though Czerniaków never learned about Treblinka, he'd heard rumors of the mass shootings in Russia and knew about the disappearances from the Lublin ghetto. With good reason, he worried about the fate of Warsaw's deportees. He especially feared for the orphans, who, by Höfle's definition, were "unproductive." Czerniaków asked that the ghetto's orphanages be left alone. The major refused. As the Nazi spoke, Czerniaków glanced out the window and saw children being dragged away from the playground across the street. In that moment, he must have realized that he was powerless. Höfle had his orders. Nothing a Jew said, no appeal to reason or pity, could change them or soften his heart.[37]

When the major left, Czerniaków closed his office door. After scribbling two notes, he swallowed one of the cyanide capsules he kept in his desk drawer for such a time. Aides found his body and read the notes. In the first note, to his wife, Czerniaków gave his reason for leaving her so abruptly: "They are demanding of me that I kill the children of my people with my own hands. Nothing is left for me but to die." The second note, addressed to his colleagues, was a cry of pain: "I am helpless; my heart is breaking with sorrow and pity; I can bear it no longer."[38]

When Höfle learned of Czerniaków's death, he sent aides to offer mourners the SS's condolences! With greater sincerity, Janusz Korczak, a longtime friend of the Jewish Council head, gave the eulogy at the funeral. Facing the casket, the Old Doctor said: "The Lord entrusted you with the honorable task of watching over the dignity of the Jewish people. Now you are honored to bring it back to the Lord."[39]

Other Jewish Council officials had yet to face the Lord. While they lived, they grappled with a grim moral choice. Judaism holds human life sacred, as a gift from God. Its sacred writings teach *pikuach nefesh,* the obligation to save a life at all costs, even violating the sanctity of the Sabbath. The Talmud says, "Whosoever saves a life, it is as if he saved an entire world." Could Jews, then, rightly hand over fellow Jews to the Nazis to spare other Jews? In Warsaw and other ghettos, councils chose what they considered the lesser of two evils. They decided to cooperate in hopes of saving at least a remnant of their community.[40]

Each morning, a Jewish Council secretary gave a Jewish policeman a list of buildings due for "shaking out." Squads of officers, backed by Ukrainian auxiliaries, then burst into a courtyard, shouting, "All Jews must come down. Thirty kilograms of baggage allowed. Those remaining inside will be shot." Moments later, a survivor wrote, "people run from all staircases. Some descend as they are, sometimes straight from bed, others carrying everything they can possibly take along, knapsacks, packages, pots and pans. People cast frightened glances at one another. The worst has happened." Those with valid work permits stood off to the side; they could return to their apartments later. Ukrainian volunteers, serving in the German Army, searched the apartments and shot anyone found hiding in a closet, behind a dresser, or under a bed. Ukrainians and Jewish policemen marched the others away or flung them into horse-drawn wagons.[41]

Though admired in the ghetto's early days, Jewish policemen had long since earned residents' scorn for their callousness and

corruption. Their role in the roundups turned scorn into bitter hatred. To save themselves and their families, they tried to ingratiate themselves with the Nazis and even identified with them, speaking of "those Jews" as if they were a race apart. Though a few helped individuals escape—usually big-time smugglers, and for a price—the vast majority of Jewish policemen did as they were told.

It got worse. In the second week of the Great Action, Major Höfle increased the tempo and scale of the roundups. The SS took charge, aided by the usual Ukrainian auxiliaries and Jewish policemen. Rather than raid a single house, deportation teams surrounded entire blocks, clearing one building after another. *"Alle Juden raus, schnell, schnell, alle Juden herunter!"* an SS man roared through a bullhorn. "All Jews out, quick, quick, all Jews down here!" Hearts pounding, faces gray with worry, all, including those with work permits, assembled in the courtyards. Using clubs and rifle butts, their captors arranged them in columns, five abreast, and got them moving.

New posters promised anyone who volunteered for deportation three loaves of bread, each weighing 2.2 pounds, and a small tin of jam. Thousands of famished people took the bait. A woman wrote: "Some of them are walking slowly, with drooping heads; others move nervously ahead, with unsteady, frightened eyes, seemingly in a hurry as if they were afraid of being forced to go back. . . . Scarcely anyone in the ghetto is surprised at this quiet, resigned marching. . . . How enticing were these three brown loaves!"[42]

The Umschlagplatz, or "collection point," from which Jews were deported from the Warsaw ghetto to Treblinka. (1943)

Deportation

In the summer of 1942, all routes led to the Umschlagplatz, a "collection point" or "reloading point" beside a freight yard at the northern end of the large ghetto. A big square behind an abandoned hospital, the Umschlagplatz was enclosed by walls topped with barbed wire and broken glass. Captain Mieczysław Szmerling, a Jewish police officer dubbed "the hangman with the whip," was a hulking brute. Having won the confidence of the SS, he was put in charge of what a survivor called "a carnival of horrors."[43]

Szmerling's men forced arriving Jews to kneel or squat, the easier to manage them. SS snipers posted on the hospital roof shot anyone who stood up. Early arrivals found places in the shadows

cast by the walls. With the temperature above 90°F in the shade, even many of these collapsed from heatstroke and thirst. Nobody drank, as the SS had closed all the water taps. Nor did modesty have a place; people had to relieve themselves within sight of everyone. Marek Edelman described the scene: "Everybody's eyes have a wild, crazy, fearful look. People look pale, helpless, desperate. . . . A nightmare settles into one's chest, grips one's throat, shoves one's eyes out of their sockets, opens one's mouth to a soundless cry. . . . One wants to yell, but there is nobody to yell to; to implore, to argue—there is nobody to argue with; one is alone, completely alone in this multitude of people." Hermann Höfle, a sneer on his lips, inspected the Umschlagplatz whenever he had a chance. Pleased with himself, the major, an eyewitness wrote, "would climb up to the top of the [hospital] and observe the people slated for deportation calmly and non-chalantly. He stayed utterly impassive to tragic scenes worthy of great writers, film directors, and painters."[44]

Two trains left each day, one in mid-morning, the other in the early evening. Ukrainians pushed late arrivals and those remaining in the square after sunset into the hospital. During the night, people cowered in fear and filth. Sentries posted below amused themselves by shooting at anyone who appeared at a window. Yet, amid the horrors, some might still express love. On a gray wall, someone carved with a penknife a heart pierced by Cupid's arrow. The inscription: "Blima and Chilek, August, 1942."[45]

All deportees endured "the selection." SS men stood at the opening of a narrow funnel lined with barbed wire. As each person approached, a German decided his or her fate. Anyone deemed

"unfit for transport"—the elderly, sick, and handicapped—was taken to a Jewish cemetery nearby, shot, and dumped into a mass grave. Individuals who still seemed able to work went to a holding area; they would continue working in German factories until a later roundup. Everyone else had to pass through the funnel.

Double rows of Jewish policemen stood, shoulder to shoulder, at the end of the funnel, their clubs ready. Beyond, a train waited, steam rising from its smokestack, the doors of its sixty box-cars open. Since the boxcars had no steps, loading crews placed wooden ramps in front of each door. Germans and Ukrainians counted off from eighty to a hundred people per car, then chalked the number on the door. Anyone who hesitated to go up the ramp

At the Umschlagplatz, SS men load Jews onto trains bound for Treblinka. (1942–1943)

was shot on the spot. One man went willingly, perhaps gladly. Legend has Rubinstein, "the madman and joker" of the ghetto, laughing as he ran into a boxcar. When each car was filled, SS men rolled the doors shut and locked them from the outside. Inside each car, small air holes covered with barbed wire were the only source of light. At an officer's signal, the engineer blew the steam whistle three times. The train jolted. It began to move. It gathered speed. Its destination: Treblinka.[46]

Treblinka

A few deportees managed to escape along the way to Treblinka, usually by prying loose the barbed-wire window coverings and wriggling through the narrow opening. Not many survived the fall onto the tracks, or the hail of bullets from the Ukrainians posted on the roofs of the boxcars. A handful of others escaped from the death factory itself. Of necessity, what follows is a composite description based on the recollections of individuals in both groups.

Anyone familiar with the history of the Atlantic slave trade from Africa to the New World would have recognized the conditions in the boxcars. As it had been for Africans locked below-decks in a slave ship, thirst was the great tormentor. Most of the deportees had not had a drink of water since their arrest in the ghetto—and would never have one again. "The children," an escapee said, "were so thirsty they licked their mothers' sweat."[47]

Another escapee told Emanuel Ringelblum's team about the crowding, heat, and filth:

It's impossible to imagine the horrors of that closed, air-less boxcar. It was one big cesspool. Everybody was pushing toward the window, where there was a little air, but it was impossible to get close to the window. Everyone was lying on the ground. I also lay down. I could feel a crack in the floor. I lay with my nose right up against the crack to grab some air. What a stench all over the car! You couldn't stand it. . . . Filth everywhere, human excrement piled up in every corner of the car. People kept shouting, "A pot! A pot! Give us a pot so we can pour it out the window." But nobody had a pot. . . .[48]

The stench from Treblinka-bound trains fouled the air for miles around. It was so bad that farmers living near the tracks had to shut their windows until a train passed. On calm, humid days, the stench lingered for hours. Whenever a German troop train bound for Russia got caught behind a trainload of maltreated Jews, the "pestilential smell" made Waffen-SS men gag and vomit.[49]

Trains often took a day to go little more than sixty miles. After crossing the River Bug and passing through Małkinia Junction, they might have to wait at a siding while the Nazis "processed" (office talk) the people in the trains ahead. When a train reached the Treblinka station, German railroad workers uncoupled twenty of its cars at a time. A small donkey engine pushed these cars,

holding roughly two thousand people, along a single-track spur that ran through a pine forest.

The forest served as a security zone around the camp. Camouflaged machine-gun nests and roaming foot patrols shot outsiders on sight. Secrecy was so tight that it cost several Germans their lives. One day, a transport train arrived from the Reich. The SS did not take German Jews to their deaths in sealed boxcars. To deceive them until the last moment, it sent them in regular passenger trains, complete with sleeper, dining, and baggage cars. Unfortunately, a woman "of pure Aryan stock" and her two little boys had boarded a Treblinka-bound train by mistake. Though they had proper identification, an SS officer decided they'd seen too much. Too bad. An eyewitness said that "her children cried just as the Jewish children did."[50]

Treblinka's commandant, Franz Stangl, called his domain "Dante's Inferno," a reference to hell as portrayed in *The Divine Comedy*, a fourteenth-century poem by Dante Alighieri. Yet this deadly place was surprisingly small and had few staff members. The camp occupied a mile-square clearing in the woods, enclosed by a barbed-wire fence intertwined with tree branches to block any view from the outside. Watchtowers outfitted with machine guns stood at each of the four corners. Barbed-wire fences divided the camp into three sections: staff quarters, Jewish slave workers' barracks, and the extermination area. Around thirty SS men supervised up to 120 Ukrainians, a tiny number relative to the number of their victims at any given time. Like the members of the Einsatzgruppen, the staff at Treblinka were volunteers. Nobody

forced them to become murderers. Postwar interviews reveal that the staff acted out of obedience to orders, racist ideology, and sadism (the thrill of hurting others).[51]

The Nazis modeled their death factories on the factory assembly line. An assembly line is a series of workstations arranged in order, each designed for a specific task. An automobile assembly line, for instance, has stations for placing, securing, and inspecting each part. A vehicle moves on a conveyor belt from station to station, until it rolls off the belt as a finished product. At the Operation Reinhard camps, the end products were corpses.

The moment the engineer braked and the boxcars stopped, a waiting work detail sprang into action. SS men and Ukrainians flung open the doors, shouting the familiar *"Juden raus, schnell, schnell!"* With bursts of gunfire, whips, and attack dogs, they drove the deportees onto the platform.

Speed was essential for two reasons. First, though a few people might suspect their fate, they did not know it for certain. According to historian Yitzhak Arad, an Operation Reinhard expert, "there was almost total unawareness of the aim of the deportations among the large majority of Jews in the ghettos of occupied Poland." Most Jews thought they really were going east to work; some even asked when they would reach their assigned farms and factories. Thus, speed created confusion, preventing them from grasping Treblinka's real purpose until the last moment. Second, moving quickly made new arrivals short of breath, preparing their lungs for the gas that would soon fill them. Usually, the entire process, from exiting the boxcars

to death and disposal, took from half to three-quarters of an hour.[52]

Once deportees left the platform, guards herded everyone into a barbed-wire enclosure. A tall SS man addressed them in a booming voice. "You are in a transit camp from which the transport will continue to labor camps," he announced. "For physical cleanliness, all arrivals must have a bath before traveling on." For the time being, they had to leave their luggage and go on to the "baths."[53]

Ahead lay a gate opening onto an area also enclosed by a

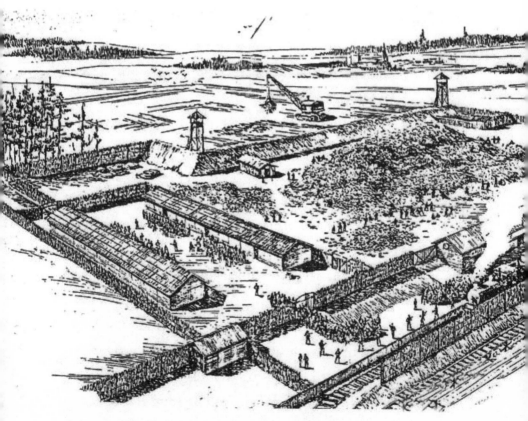

A drawing of Treblinka by Samuel Willenberg, a survivor of the death camp. (c. 1945)

barbed-wire fence. Guards called it "departure square"—an in-joke, because they knew the Jews were about to depart this world. Two long barracks stood on either side of the square. An SS man, less polite than the one before, barked: "Women and children to the left! Men to the right!"[54]

As the men entered the barracks, a guard shouted, *"Ganz nakt!"*—"Strip naked!" The men placed each article of their clothing in a separate pile, tied their shoelaces together, and handed over any valuables they had. A guard walked down the line of naked men standing at attention, not daring to move a muscle. Occasionally, the guard paused to tap someone on the chest with a stick, permission to live a little longer as a slave. The chosen ones put their clothes back on, and camp guards led them away. To show their authority, guards shot or beat to death anyone who failed to keep pace or spoke. After a day's work, the slave laborers received their first drink of water since leaving Warsaw and a slice of black bread.[55]

In the meantime, the women and children entered the barracks on the left. Immediately, guards ordered them to undress and turn in their valuables. That done, they had to run to the "beauty salon," a shed attached to the rear of the barracks. Jewish "hairdressers" sat them on wooden stools for the "Treblinka cut." All women had their hair sheared off and put into sacks on the floor. Hair was valuable stuff. Hitler's navy used it to fill mattresses, line slippers, and weave into socks for submarine crews, because it does not absorb moisture. Treblinka contributed three tons of hair to the Nazi war effort.[56]

A door led from the "beauty salon" to a narrow, barbed-wire-

enclosed path. SS guards with whips and clubs lined each side, beating the women and children to make them run faster. Staff members called this path "the tube" or, mockingly, *Himmel-strasse,* "the road to heaven." A sign at the entrance read THIS WAY TO THE SHOWERS, and guards shouted, "Faster, faster, the water's getting cold, and others will have to use the showers, too." SS planners had timed the killing process so that the men ran along a side path and were gassed while the women and children waited their turn.[57]

At the end of "the road to heaven," victims came to a low gray stone building. Five wide concrete steps, lined with potted geraniums, led to a door made of heavy wooden planks. Suspended from the roof was a carving of a Star of David. Above the door hung a ceremonial curtain looted from a synagogue, also meant as a guards' in-joke. Embroidered in gold thread was a Hebrew inscription: "This is the gateway to God, through which the righteous may enter."[58]

The door opened. Entering, the Jews found themselves in a dimly lit corridor with rooms on either side: gas chambers. Each room was twenty-six feet by thirteen feet, with small white ceramic tiles on the walls and large orange earthenware tiles on the floors. Nickel-plated showerheads protruded from the low ceiling, amid a network of crisscrossing pipes. Guards pushed the naked people inside the chambers with rifle butts, leaving no space to move; sometimes they tossed small children on top of the mass. Then the doors were shut and the lights turned off.

At this point, the Jews realized they were doomed. Panic! Men shouted. Women wept. Children clung to their mothers. Regain-

ing their composure, some prayed in their last moments. "God, my one and only God!" a woman chanted. "God, You One and Only God, take revenge on our enemies for their crimes! We are going to die to sanctify Your name. Let our sacrifice not be in vain! Avenge our blood and the blood of our children, and let us say, Amen!"[59]

"*Wasser!*" a guard bellowed. "Water!" Another guard flipped a switch, and the engine from a captured Russian tank, kept in a shed next to the gas chamber building, began whirring and thumping.

Supposedly, Nazi death camps killed with Zyklon B, a pesticide whose crystals form cyanide gas when exposed to air. This is only partially true. While Auschwitz used Zyklon B, Operation Reinhard camps suffocated victims with carbon monoxide. Experts from Aktion T4, Hitler's discontinued adult euthanasia program, had been transferred to Poland. To kill masses of people in a short time, they devised a way to pipe carbon monoxide, a waste product from burning gasoline, into the gas chambers.

SS men watched the gassing through tiny windows set in the doors. In a tightly packed chamber, carbon monoxide took from twelve to twenty-five minutes to kill, depending on the temperature and humidity. Once everyone was dead, slaves opened a rear door to ventilate each chamber and remove the bodies. A gruesome sight greeted them. A former slave wrote, "The victims held on to one another; they all stood upright and were like one single block of flesh." Because of their death agonies, blood and excrement covered their bodies and the chamber's floor, making it slippery.[60]

While people were dying in the chambers, teams of slaves hurriedly cleaned the empty boxcars before the donkey engine pushed them back to the Treblinka station. A telephone call to the stationmaster summoned the next group of boxcars. Other teams went through the baggage the victims left behind and removed clothing from the undressing barracks.

The Economic and Administrative Main Office of the SS required the camps to ship every useful item to Germany. Its official list of items fills page after page of small type. It includes spectacles, fountain pens, mechanical pencils, penknives, scissors, eyeglasses, flashlights, pots, pans, umbrellas, baby carriages, cigarette lighters, pipes, razors, mirrors, briefcases, and artificial limbs. Among men's clothing items were shirts, shoes, socks, pants, jackets, handkerchiefs, wallets, belts, and underwear. Women's clothing included skirts, dresses, blouses, shoes, stockings, cotton underwear, silk panties and bras, and handbags. Treblinka alone sent fifteen hundred boxcars of belongings to Germany. The camp staff was ordered to "check that all Jewish stars have been removed from all clothing before transfer." The Nazis gave this plunder to needy Germans, especially those who'd lost their belongings in Allied bombing raids. Babies' clothing went to Lebensborn homes. The rest was sold at knockdown prices, and the money deposited in SS bank accounts.[61]

The death camps also yielded valuables such as foreign currency, diamonds, pearls, fine watches, and gold coins. After the gassing, Jewish "dentists" opened each adult victim's mouth to extract teeth with gold fillings and gold false teeth, which were then melted down into gold bars. Camp commanders prided

Wedding bands taken from Jews on their arrival at a death camp. (1945)

themselves on the amount of gold sent to Germany. Once a week, Treblinka sent two suitcases filled with it.[62]

Disposal was the final stage on the assembly line of death. Using hand-drawn carts, teams of slaves wheeled bodies from the gas chambers to immense burial pits. The pits, dug by a steam shovel, were 160 feet long, 82 feet wide, and 33 feet deep. Big though they were, the pits filled up quickly.

After inspecting Treblinka in 1943, SS chief Heinrich Himmler ordered the bodies dug up and burned, along with those of all Jews killed later. Slaves stacked the rotting corpses in layers on iron rails set over deep pits, like immense barbecue grills, and doused them with gasoline. "The result," survivor Jankel Wiernik wrote, "was one huge inferno, which from the distance looked

like a volcano breaking through the earth's crust to belch forth fire and lava. The pyres sizzled and crackled. The smoke and heat made it impossible to remain close by." Afterward, mechanical steel rollers crushed any remaining bones into tiny slivers, which the "Ashes Gang" poured into ditches or spread over a forest road.[63]

After his capture by American troops, Franz Stangl discussed the killers' mentality. He and his staff at Treblinka had no sense of guilt or shame. They saw themselves not as responsible actors but as cogs in a vast, impersonal machine. They had done their duty and "followed orders," the outcomes of which were others' concern. As for their victims, they were not human beings in the racists' eyes. "Cargo," said Stangl. "They were cargo." Though Stangl and his wife had two young daughters, he saw no similarity between them and those put to death in Treblinka. "You see," he explained, "I rarely saw them as individuals. It was always a huge mass. I sometimes . . . saw them in the tube. But—how can I explain it—they were naked, packed together, running, being driven with whips like . . ." He fell silent, unwilling or unable to say "cattle."[64]

Stangl's Führer also knew about the camps and had no regrets about them. Comparing Jews to a ghastly infection, Hitler admitted, "I gave the order to burn out the abscesses of our inner well-poisoning and the foreign poisoning down to the raw flesh."[65]

Even so, the Führer never spoke of mass murder at social gatherings, and guests thought it would be "rude" to bring up the subject. Henriette von Schirach, who had known Hitler since childhood, broke the unwritten rule. While visiting Amsterdam,

she'd seen terrified Jewish women boarding a train under SS guard. "My Führer," Henriette said during a dinner party at the Berghof, his mountain vacation home. "Those poor people—they look terrible. I'm sure they're being very badly treated. Do you know about it? Do you allow it?" The room fell silent; you could hear a pin drop. Hitler sprang to his feet, his face white as a sheet. "You are sentimental, Frau von Schirach!" he said, his voice rising. "You have to learn to hate! What have Jewish women in Holland to do with you?" Moments later, a servant asked her to leave the Berghof—right away! That was the last time she saw Hitler in person.[66]

The Righteous

The Nazi occupation tested the Poles' attitudes toward Jews. This remains a sensitive topic, even though three-quarters of a century has passed since the end of World War II. All the same, certain facts are recognized parts of the historical record. Fact: Anti-Semitism was rife in prewar Poland. Fact: Poles often shunned assimilated Jews, treating them as outcasts. Even humanitarians like Janusz Korczak were subjected to verbal abuse. We all know the saying "Sticks and stones may break my bones, but names can never hurt me." It is nonsense. Words can be as painful as blows. Those who insult others aim to wound, shame, and diminish them, shattering their self-respect.

Studies suggest that, on the whole, Poles did not aid Jews in their darkest hour. Indeed, there were instances where entire

villages took part in organized "Jew-hunts," scouring the countryside for victims to kill or hand over to the Nazis for a reward. Former Israeli prime minister Menachem Begin grew up in prewar Poland. He claimed: "What concerns the Jews, the Poles were collaborating with the Germans. . . . Only at most one hundred people have been helping the Jews. Between ten and twenty thousand Polish priests did not even save one Jewish life. All these death camps were [therefore] established on Polish soil." Author Elie Wiesel echoed the Israeli politician: "It was not by accident that the worst concentration camps were set up in Poland, worse than anywhere else." Both men claimed, as some still do, that the Polish people were innately anti-Semitic, that they drank anti-Semitism "with their mothers' milk." Thus, it made sense for the Nazis to select Poland for their death camps, believing that Jew-hatred there was so intense that Poles would condone mass murder.[67]

Yet there is another side to the story. No German document I know of says that Poles wished for anything like Treblinka on their soil. To be sure, Johannes Blaskowitz, a senior Nazi general, reported the opposite. Early in 1940, more than a year before Hitler ordered the Holocaust, Blaskowitz wrote: "The acts of violence against the Jews which occur in full view of the public inspire among the religious Poles not only deep disgust but also great pity for the Jewish population, to which up to now Poles were more or less hostile."[68]

True, there were instances of Polish villagers hunting Jews. But though Polish police helped guard the ghettos, no Poles joined the Waffen-SS or served as guards in any extermination camp. Units of French, Dutch, Belgian, and Norwegian volunteers *did* wear

Waffen-SS uniforms and fight in Russia. The Nazis built death camps on Polish soil not because Poles wanted them but because Poland had the highest concentration of Jews in Europe. Poland, too, had a fine railway system, and large tracts of forested countryside with small populations, ideal for masking atrocities.[69]

In his taped recollections, made in 1974, Yitzhak Zuckerman, a leader of the 1943 Warsaw ghetto revolt, warned against making blanket statements about an entire people. "You can't generalize about the Poles. There were all kinds of Poles," he said, adding, "Anyone who fosters total hatred of the Polish people is committing a sin!" Yad Vashem, Israel's memorial to victims of the Holocaust, reinforces Zuckerman's warning about blanket statements. Since 1963, its "Righteous Among the Nations" program has been honoring non-Jews who risked their lives to save Jews during the Holocaust. As of 2016, Yad Vashem had honored more than 22,000 "Righteous Gentiles." Of those, 6,620, by far the largest group, were Poles. As Zuckerman explained: "One swine could betray a hundred Jews to the Germans. But to save one Jew you needed the participation of a hundred Poles." Scholars estimate that more than 1,200,000 Poles helped Jews in ways big and small.[70]

Rescuers came from all walks of life and, as we might expect, had different motives. Many acted instinctively, apparently without thinking, in the same way passersby rush to aid a person who has fallen on a sidewalk. Help could be whispering a warning about lurking danger, giving a bite of food, showing the way, or offering shelter for a few hours.

There are many examples of rescuers acting on the spur of the

moment. While fleeing, teenager Janina Bauman and her mother found safety several times by randomly knocking on doors and having a stranger take them in until the coast was clear. At the age of seven, smuggler Marysia Szpiro was on Warsaw's Aryan side when a Pole shouted that she was a Jew. A Blue policeman grabbed Marysia, but when others yelled that she was Polish, he let her go. When Germans chased young smugglers, a Polish woman upset her apple cart in front of the pursuers, allowing the children to escape. While fleeing from a Ukrainian patrol, my wife's cousin Jack hid in a church basement. The priest found him, fed him, blessed him, and told him the way to a nearby forest.[71]

Then again, a gutsy person might confront a Nazi head-on and live to tell about it. Halina Martin's family were prosperous landowners. One day, German police arrested her on suspicion of hiding a Jewish boy. She had. At headquarters, a Gestapo man demanded that she reveal the boy's whereabouts. Martin looked him in the eye, hard. "Listen, you," she snapped in broken German. "I'm a mother. For me, a child's a child whether it be German, Turkish, Jewish, Chinese, or Polish. If I find one lying in a ditch, I'll always feed it. You threaten death? Fine! I'd rather not live in a world where a woman, a mother, can't help a child. You can shoot me, hang me. Do you have children? Where? Are they in Berlin? Under the falling bombs? Who's going to help them when they're lying wounded in a ditch somewhere?" Enough said! Martin must have touched a nerve, for he let her go.[72]

In Warsaw, Poles helped Jews escape from the ghetto and hide on the Aryan side. Historian Gunnar S. Paulsson believes this effort involved so many people that they formed a "secret city"

consisting of individual rescuers, hidden fugitives, and the criminals who preyed on them. Nearly all those who were rescued were assimilated Jews who'd had gentile contacts before the Nazis sealed the ghetto: friends, colleagues, business associates, former employees. Orthodox Jews, however, had few if any gentile contacts. Besides, their mannerisms, poor command of Polish, and Yiddish accents made it impossible to conceal their identity.[73]

Escapees used the same routes as the smugglers: over, under, and through the ghetto wall. Rescuers then took them into their own homes. Though Jews might pay for their keep, they realized their presence burdened their hosts. Yitzhak Zuckerman explained that while "there were . . . Poles whose motive was money and took large sums for sheltering Jews, there were also people who knew their job was to rescue, that that was their human obligation. Some of them were simple folk who were content to receive pennies and saved Jews simply out of human kindness; and even when Jews ran out of money, they went on supporting them." Zuckerman added, "These people [were] glorious." No fewer than 28,000 Jews hid on the Aryan side of Warsaw, aided by an estimated 70,000 to 90,000 Poles. Of the 28,000 Jews, approximately 11,500 survived the war.[74]

As for the hidden Jews who did not survive, it seems that the majority were betrayed by "greasers," members of criminal gangs that specialized in finding them. Numbering between 3,000 and 4,000, the greasers blackmailed Jews, taking whatever valuables they had. After milking them dry, they betrayed them to the Gestapo for a reward. What is worse, a number of Jew-catchers were Jewish themselves. Nicknamed the "Jewish Gestapo," these

human bloodhounds "sniffed out" hidden Jews for their pay-masters. In her memoir, Ruth Altbeker Cyprys records a children's rhyme circulating at the time:

> *Mummy, Daddy, listen do*
> *With the Gestapo came two by two*
> *What a shame, what a disgrace*
> *The first was a Pole, the second a Jew!*
> *Mummy, Daddy, listen do*
> *Here come the Gestapo, do you know who?*
> *What a shame, the worst disgrace*
> *The first is a Jew, and the second is too!*[75]

Poles risked their lives to save Jews. In occupied Western Europe, the Germans might send a gentile who helped Jews to jail, often freeing him or her after a short time. Not in Poland. There, Governor Hans Frank decreed that helping Jews in *any* way, even with a drink of water, meant death for one's entire family. Moreover, Frank said, "[those who] attempted deeds will receive the same punishment as those who carry out the deed." The case of the Ulma family illustrates this perfectly. Józef Ulma was a farmer who lived with his wife, Wiktoria, and their six children. Horrified at seeing Jews shot by local people, the Catholic couple decided to hide fugitives on their farm. Betrayed by a neighbor, the Ulma family, including Wiktoria, who was seven months pregnant, were killed by the Germans.

Elsewhere, Germans wiped out entire villages in reprisal for a family's sheltering Jews. When, for example, the Germans raided

the village of Aleksandrów, near Lublin, they shot 446 people and burned the place to the ground. Historians estimate that as many as fifty thousand Poles were executed for the "crime" of acting humanely.[76]

Like the Ulmas, these were usually devout Catholics, whose church held two views of Jews. Traditionally, it blamed the Jewish people for the death of Jesus Christ; as punishment, it was said, God exiled the Jews from the Holy Land. But the Catholic Church also taught that God created humans in His image and that one must "love thy neighbor as thyself." Jesus says, "Inasmuch as ye have done it unto one of the least of these my brethren, ye have done it unto me" (Matthew 25:40). Obviously, what the Nazis were doing to the Jews violated God's law. Poet Maria Hochberg-Marianska left no doubt about the duty of faithful Catholics:

> O Christ, crucified on the bloody Polish roads . . .
> Where is Thy place in these times of crime and
>   dread;
> Is it not behind the walls of the ghetto and the wire
>   of the camps?[77]

Incredibly, several rescuers were both staunch Catholics *and* anti-Semites. The most important of these, Zofia Kossak, is a testament to human decency in the face of evil. Born in 1889, Kossak was an author who spent most of her career writing for Catholic newspapers. Also a hard-line anti-Semite, before the war she called Judaism the "dismal and grotesque faith" of a people "completely foreign" to Poles. Kossak never changed her opinion;

in 1942, she declared Jews "political, economic and ideological enemies of Poland." Yet one day she witnessed an incident on a bridge over the Vistula River. A German sentry saw a Pole giving a coin to a ragged Jewish boy. Calmly, he told the Pole that the little beggar must die. "You can go free, if you drown him, or I will kill you, too. Drown him or die. I will count . . . 1, 2 . . ." The Pole broke down, grabbed the child, and threw him into the Vistula. The soldier patted him on the shoulder, said, "Stout fellow," and walked away. Two days later, Kossak heard that the Pole had hanged himself.[78]

Nazi savagery outraged Kossak as a person, a Pole, and a Catholic. She joined the Polish underground, or resistance movement. The underground was a vast "secret state" with branches in every corner of Polish life. It spied for the Allies, collected taxes, and had a system of courts. Underground schools taught all subjects and even awarded doctoral degrees. As editor of *Poland Lives,* an illegal newspaper, Kossak wrote a leaflet titled "Protest!" Appearing in August 1942, at the height of the Great Action in Warsaw, "Protest!" was an impassioned declaration grounded in religious belief:

In the Warsaw ghetto, behind a wall that is cutting them off from the world, several hundred thousand condemned people await death. . . . In the face of murder it is wrong to remain passive. Whoever is silent witnessing murder becomes a partner to the murder. Whoever does not condemn, consents. . . . We protest from the bottom of our hearts filled with pity, indignation, and horror. This protest is

demanded of us by God, who does not allow us to kill. It is the demand of our Christian conscience. Every being calling itself human has the right to love his fellow man. The blood of the defenseless victims is calling for revenge. Who does not support the protest with us, is not a Catholic.

We protest also as Poles. We do not believe that Poland could benefit from the horrible Nazi deeds. Just the opposite. . . . The forced participation of the Polish nation in the bloody spectacle taking place on Polish soil may breed indifference to unfairness, sadism, and, above all, the belief that murder is not punishable.

Whoever does not understand this, and whoever dares to connect the future of the proud, free Poland, with the vile enjoyment of your fellow man's calamity—is, therefore, not a Catholic and not a Pole.[79]

Kossak took a leading role in forming the Council for Aid to Jews, an organization sponsored by the Polish underground. Code-named "Żegota," it was the only organization in occupied Europe entirely devoted to helping persecuted Jews. Jointly run by Catholics and Jews, Żegota was divided into sections, each dealing with a specific need: escape and evasion, housing, finance, medical care, propaganda, and child welfare. For security, each section was further divided into "cells," whose five to ten members did not know each other's real names and used aliases. Kossak's alias was "Weronika" (Veronica).

Żegota set up a network of safe houses, places where a cell could hide fugitives and attend to their needs. According to an

old Russian saying, a person is made up of three elements: a body, a soul, and a passport. To build a new identity, a person needed "papers." In occupied Poland, these included an identification card with a photograph, a birth certificate, a work permit, and a travel permit. In meeting this need, Żegota would have won the admiration of the criminal world anywhere. Only the photo on a document was genuine. Everything else—the name, address, date of birth, marital status, occupation—was fabricated. Żegota had several secret workshops in and around Warsaw. There forgers, photographers, seal and stamp makers, papermakers, and printers churned out thousands of lifesaving documents each month.[80]

Żegota's funding came from American Jewish groups and the Polish government-in-exile in London, where hundreds of officials fled after the Nazi invasion. The underground relied upon young women to smuggle bundles of cash—Polish zlotys, British pounds, American dollars, German marks—into the country and get them into the right hands. These women were Polish, usually with fair skin, blue eyes, and blond hair. "Never before have I seen oversized busts as in Poland at this time," a male agent remarked. Some of the women pretended to be pregnant, with belly bumps formed by sacks of money. Jan Karski, a hero of the resistance, thought women better suited to secret work than men. "They were quicker to perceive danger . . . more cautious and discreet, had more common sense and were less inclined to risky bluffing." Most, too, were handy with a revolver.[81]

Despite all precautions, Żegota operatives lived on the edge; there was no telling when the Gestapo might pounce. Late in 1943, "Weronika" was arrested on suspicion of having under-

ground contacts. She wound up in Auschwitz, the labor camp, not the adjacent death factory. Luckily, the Gestapo missed her connection to Żegota. She was sent back to a Warsaw prison for further questioning, and well-placed bribes bought her release. She went into hiding but continued working for Żegota. Zofia Kossak is the only anti-Semite honored by Yad Vashem as one of the "Righteous Among the Nations."[82]

Many, if not most, child-survivors of the Warsaw ghetto owed their lives to another woman. From the look of her, Irena Sendler, at four feet ten inches, was not an imposing figure. Yet looks are only skin-deep; a person's true nature is inward, invisible to the naked eye. Born in 1910, the only child of a doctor and his wife, Sendler combined unshakable moral principle with daredevil courage. Her parents were her role models. "My parents taught

me," she wrote, "that if a man is drowning, it is irrelevant what is his religion or nationality. One must help him."[83]

Sendler had always identified with the underdog. As a student at the University of Warsaw, Korczak's alma mater, she joined Jewish students in protesting segregated seating in lecture halls. "Why are you standing?" a snooty classmate asked a Jew. "Because I am Jewish," he answered. "Why

Irena Sendler, a Polish social worker famous for saving Jewish children from the Warsaw ghetto. (1942)

are *you* standing?" he asked Sendler. "Because I am Polish," she snapped.[84]

After graduation, Sendler joined the Warsaw City Council's Health and Care Department as a social worker. Promoted to senior administrator, she supervised programs to aid orphans, the elderly, and the poor. With the Nazi occupation and creation of the ghetto, she focused her efforts on helping needy Jews.

For more than a year before Żegota got under way, Sendler visited the ghetto as often as three times a day, armed with a pass from Warsaw's Epidemic Control Department to check for typhus. What she saw shocked her sense of decency. "There were children on the street . . . starving . . . begging for a piece of bread. I'd go out on my rounds in the morning and see a starving child lying there. I'd come back a few hours later, and he would already be dead . . . covered with a newspaper."[85]

During her visits, Sendler brought medicine, food, and clothing, which she gave to the needy without charge. Sewn into her bra were small pockets in which she hid vials of typhus vaccine. To show her solidarity with Jewish people, she put on a Star of David armband the moment she passed the checkpoint at a gate. During these visits, she sometimes met with the Old Doctor, who steered her to poor families he knew of but for whose children Dom Sierot had no room. Later, she joined Żegota, heading its children's section under the code name "Jolanta."[86]

When the Great Action began in July 1942, Sendler turned to rescuing children. Because swiftness meant lives, she recruited twenty-five Polish social workers to help get as many children as possible out of the ghetto; each social worker had a typhus-

inspection pass. Yet the hardest part was not finding helpers but persuading parents to part with their children. Parents had two reasons for hesitating. First, Sendler recalled, they worried about safety. "Can you guarantee they will live?" they'd ask her. "No," she'd reply, "but if they stay here, I guarantee they will die. You shouldn't trust me. But what else can you do?" Often, to allow them to think it over, she left, promising to return the next day. When she did return, she found many an empty apartment; the Germans had dragged everyone to the Umschlagplatz.[87]

Second, the possibility of rescue triggered a moral and spiritual crisis among Jews. The road to safety led from the ghetto to a brief stay with a Polish family and, finally, to sheltering with nuns in a convent. Even if the nuns promised not to convert their children, would they keep their word? How could an intensely Catholic environment *not* affect children's loyalty to Judaism? Would rescued children become Catholics, forever lost to their faith and people?

Parents held different views on these questions. Some rejected any notion of placing Jewish children with Christians, let alone nuns. "We won't let our children be handed over to convents for spiritual destruction," they'd declare. "Let them share the fate that God has ordained for us." There are accounts of parents who kept their children with them, fully knowing that deportation lay ahead.[88]

Other parents took the opposite view. Even if some children became Catholics, they argued, it would still be worthwhile to send away all they could. Emanuel Ringelblum quoted a parent: "The soul of each and every Jew is precious, and we must try to

take pains to preserve it. . . . Sending a handful of Jewish children into monasteries will enable us to rescue those who will be the creators of a new generation of Jews. We have no right to take away the next generation's right to live. . . . If we do not carry out this child-rescue operation with the aid of the clergy, in a short time none will remain." These parents entrusted their children to Irena Sendler.[89]

Sendler and her group used two buildings that straddled the border between the ghetto and the Aryan side as escape routes for older children. The Warsaw Municipal Law Courts building and All Saints Church were busy places but lightly guarded. A child, escorted by a social worker, would enter the courthouse by one door, remove his or her armband, and exit through the other door. At All Saints, Father Marceli Godlewski, formerly an anti-Semite who'd attacked Jews from the pulpit, had had a change of heart. As an act of mercy, he provided child-fugitives with new, Catholic birth certificates. The child then walked out through his church's door on the Aryan side, holding the hand of a social worker.[90]

A different route was used for infants and toddlers. Before setting out, Sendler gave them a sedative to keep them still, then had them carried past a checkpoint hidden in a suitcase, handbasket, gunnysack, or toolbox. "Some children were placed in coffins, their mouths taped so they wouldn't cry," she recalled. One toddler got out under a man's long coat, with his feet on the man's shoes and hands gripping the man's belt. A woman walked out with a little girl hidden between her legs, under her voluminous skirt. So the parents of rescued children could find them after the

war, Sendler wrote their names on sheets of thin paper, which she buried in a jar under an apple tree in a friend's backyard. The friend lived across the street from a German Army barracks.[91]

Sendler's humanity caused her much pain. In October 1943, a tip led the Gestapo to arrest her. Taken to Pawiak, the prison the Old Doctor knew all too well, she refused to name her helpers. During an especially brutal session, interrogators fractured both her legs and feet. Sentenced to death, she expected a bullet to come crashing into her skull at any moment.

When the time came for her execution, a Gestapo officer threw her into a car and drove to a secluded spot outside the city. Then he punched her in the face, pushed her out of the car, and drove away, leaving her alone. Unknown to Sendler, Żegota had given him a hefty bribe to let her go. In searing pain, her legs and feet swollen, somehow she made it back to Warsaw. There she found her name listed on public bulletin boards as among those executed that day. Using her code name "Jolanta," she continued to work for Żegota. In her nineties, Sendler wrote about what she had done. "Every child saved with my help and the help of all the wonderful messengers, who today are no longer living, is the justification of my existence on this earth, and not a title to glory." Yet the modest heroine could not forgive herself. "I could have done more," she said. "This regret will follow me to my death."[92]

We cannot imagine what more she could have done. The woman known to Jews as the "Polish Angel" was responsible for rescuing twenty-five hundred children from the Warsaw ghetto—more than any other individual, anywhere in Nazi-held Europe, saved during the Holocaust. Oskar Schindler, the more famous

German industrialist, saved twelve hundred Polish Jews, nearly all of them adults. Hollywood made *Schindler's List*, an Academy Award–winning film about his exploits. Sendler's work was no less heroic. Though she has been called the "female Schindler," it might be more accurate to call him the "male Sendler."

As for the rescued children, Sendler and her helpers took them to "emergency care units," private homes where caregivers taught them the basics of Catholicism. Familiarity with the Catholic religion was essential, because ignorance of it among gentile Poles was almost unheard of. Unless they could "pass" for Catholics, Jews were doomed, along with all who sheltered them. Żegota volunteer Magda Rusinek recalled how she taught her charges "little prayers that every child knows in Polish. I would wake them up during the night to say the prayer. And then I had to teach them how to behave in a church, a Christian Church." Eventually, a Żegota guide brought the child to a convent that had a small orphanage or boarding school. Historians have located 189 convents, about a third of them in the Warsaw area, that hid Jewish children.[93]

Not every child found sanctuary by such organized means. Survival could be a matter of being at the right place at the right time. For example, a ferryman brought nuns a baby he'd fished out of the Vistula, and a Blue policeman brought a baby he'd found in a basket in an empty apartment. Desperate relatives also delivered children, like the old man who tossed a baby to a nun, saying, "Bring him up! He's yours now!" Poles found lice-infested toddlers wandering the streets and took them to a nearby convent. A nun saw a little girl climbing out of a sewer and brought

Several nuns and a priest with Jewish children who were hidden at a convent in Łomna, Poland, during the German occupation. (1946)

her to her Warsaw convent. Just minutes after seeing her parents shot, a little girl threw her arms around a Mother Superior's neck and cried: "Germans have just killed my Mommy and Daddy; Sister, please be my mother!" Historians have found no record of nuns turning away any child.[94]

Normally, nuns voted on important convent matters, so the decision to harbor fugitives was a collective one. Yet, before voting, the Mother Superior might gently guide them by reading the Lord's charge (John 15:17): "These things I command you, that ye love one another." Given Nazi savagery, the nuns knew the risks they ran. One recalled the impact of this passage: "Silence. No one stirred. Not a single breath. We were ready. We would not give up the Jewish children. We would rather die, all of us. The

silence was overwhelming—we did not look at each other. . . . We did not even pray together as we normally do. We went to Chapel. We felt light and joyful, though we realized the gravity of the situation. We were ready."[95]

Many children came with forged birth and baptismal certificates provided by Żegota. Yet, the nuns knew, they would have to blend with their surroundings. This meant teaching them a lot more than they'd learned thus far: Catholic dogma, prayers, hymns, rituals. This was also necessary to keep them from standing out from the other children, who did not know they were Jewish. Feeling safe at last, some identified with the nuns to the point where they wanted to convert. As a rule, nuns made it clear that they had no intention of converting them; they just hoped to save their lives. Conversion, if they still wished, had to wait until after the war, when, as young adults, they could make a mature decision.[96]

In this regard, the experience of Miriam Klein is likely typical. Miriam asked a nun she admired to prepare her for conversion, but Sister Bernarda deftly changed the subject. Somehow a *siddur*, a Jewish prayer book, found its way into the convent. Sister Bernarda asked Miriam what it was; the sister had never seen such a book and could not read Hebrew. When Miriam told her, the nun took it for safekeeping. Whenever she had time, she invited Miriam to her room, closed the door, and had her read aloud from the siddur. "Pray to the Jewish God, and we will pray to Lord Jesus," the nun said warmly. "If we all pray, then perhaps we will survive the war."[97]

Survival was the nuns' goal and their chief challenge. The Gestapo knew that convents sheltered Jewish children, but not which ones. Hence, Gestapo agents showed up without warning, at all hours, hoping to catch the children in an unguarded moment. And the nuns, who knew the Gestapo knew, drilled the children constantly to keep them alert. At the first hint of a raid, perhaps a word from a sympathetic Polish policeman, they were to flee to designated hiding places. For example, Sister Bernarda gave Miriam Klein a key to the chapel so she could hide in the altar, among the holy relics. Other nuns quickly bandaged the heads and faces of children with Jewish features, feigning injury. This was not odd; unable to afford a dentist, the poor often "treated" toothaches by bandaging their cheeks and jaw. If spoken to by a German, children with Yiddish accents acted as though they were mute. "Why are you risking the lives of so many people because of me?" Anna Clarke, a hidden Jewish child, asked a nun. "For the love of the God we have in common," the Sister answered.[98]

The Polish clergy paid dearly for the love of God and their fellow humans. The Nazis killed 289 nuns for sheltering Jewish children. In Warsaw, the Gestapo raided a boarding school run by the Salesian Brothers. Finding several Jewish boys, they hung them and their protectors from the balcony of a wrecked building opposite the Warsaw Municipal Law Courts building. "Their tragic bodies were left hanging for several days," wrote Ruth Altbeker Cyprys, who saw them as she passed by. "People tried desperately not to look, yet they were compelled to see them, to think about them."[99]

Of the nearly one million Jewish children alive in Poland in 1939, barely five thousand survived the Nazi terror. Historians estimate that nuns rescued twelve hundred of these. Their efforts, however, could not save the Old Doctor and his children, or the Warsaw ghetto, or the city of Warsaw itself.[100]

Written in Smoke and Ashes

See, see, the slaughtered calves, so smitten and so laid;
Is there a price for their death? How shall that price be paid?

—H. N. Bialik,
"The City of Slaughter" (1904)

Korczak's Last Walk

By the summer of 1942, the Old Doctor was nearly a broken man. Overwork, stress, and malnutrition were sapping the sixty-four-year-old's last reserves of energy. He was in constant pain. His joints ached, and his eyes were puffy from a chronic infection. Swollen feet and legs signaled poor blood circulation due to a weakened heart muscle. Always tired—no, exhausted—he had dizzy spells, and it hurt to urinate. It was hard to concentrate. He was often forgetful. His condition shocked Igor Newerly, his friend and former secretary. Having not seen Korczak for some months, he found him "ill, wasted, and stooped."[1]

Dom Sierot's children were sliding downhill, too. Though Korczak and his staff tried to keep up their spirits, reminding them that despite loss and hardship, where there is life, there is hope, it

was a losing battle. "The children moon about," he wrote in his diary in July. "Only the outer appearances are normal. Underneath lurks weariness, discouragement, anger, mutiny, mistrust, resentment, longing." He stopped weighing them every Saturday, his usual practice; it was too depressing, as they grew thinner and thinner, despite his best efforts. The air in the home smelled putrid, like diarrhea. Bedbugs were a plague; their bites left red, itchy blotches. Spoiled food made everyone sick. "The result of the consumption of bread of unknown composition and make was mass poisoning." A dish made of "stale eggs," sprinkled with pepper to hide the taste, caused general vomiting and "moaning with pain."[2]

Korczak could have made things easier for himself. The ghetto had thirty orphanages, boardinghouses, and day-care centers, serving four thousand children. Those who ran them faced the same problems as he, but evidence suggests that contacts on the Aryan side offered at least several of them a chance to escape.

Escape made sense if one thought solely in practical terms. As in the case of the rescue of children, certain skilled people—managers, educators, physicians, nurses, social workers, rabbis—would be essential to rebuilding the Jewish community after the war. Few in the Warsaw ghetto had ever heard the name Treblinka, and none, as yet, knew what went on there. What seemed certain was the ultimate fate of the poorest children. Their chances of survival dwindled by the day. It seemed only a matter of time before starvation and disease carried them off. Yet, despite it all, the directors and staffs of childcare facilities chose to stay at their posts, no matter the outcome.[3]

Like them, Korczak opted to remain in the ghetto, and we are lucky to have evidence that allows us to follow his train of thought. Perhaps a month before the mass deportations began, Igor Newerly snuck into the ghetto with fake passes for a master plumber and a drainage engineer. A Polish "friend" had rented a room for Korczak in a house on the Aryan side; forgers had prepared a full set of documents under a false name. All he need do was leave Dom Sierot and walk out of the ghetto with Newerly.[4]

Though he trusted Newerly with his life, he called his offer "despicable." Korczak's temper flared. "You wouldn't abandon your own child to disease, misfortune, or danger, would you?" he growled. "And how could one live with the thought of what [one] . . . had done?" As they shook hands for what would be the last time, he promised to send Newerly his diary if the Germans seemed likely to do their worst.[5]

"Will there be an outbreak of mass hysteria?" Korczak asked himself. Not in Dom Sierot, he thought, if the children "believed that as long as the doctor was calm, there was no danger." It all depended on him. Since they looked to him for guidance, he had to keep calm, whatever happened. However, he also had to prepare them for the end, and do so as gently as possible.[6]

How?

The Old Doctor thought of euthanasia, poisoning his children to spare them from agony. "The right to kill as an act of mercy belongs to him who loves," he wrote. Though he loved them with his whole being, that he could not do. "I saw it as a murder of the sick and feeble, as an assassination of the innocents."[7]

While Korczak never said it outright, his actions suggest that

he wanted his children to understand that death is not final, not the end of existence. Instead, he imagined death as a kind of doorway, a passage from one form of existence to another. "You may not believe in the existence of the soul," he wrote, "but you must acknowledge that your body will live on as green grass, as a cloud. For you are, after all, water and dust." Like all else, this was nature's way.[8]

On July 15, 1942, a week before Treblinka's gas chambers began operating, Korczak sent invitations to people he admired. Among them were Irena Sendler and poets Itzhak Katzenelson and Władysław Szlengel. The Old Doctor invited them to see, free of charge, a play that "transcends mere acting—being the work of children."[9]

His children were to act in *The Post Office* by Rabindranath Tagore (1861–1941), a renowned Indian poet and educator. The play is about Amal, a dying boy confined to his bed in a dark room. Amal longs to wander amid trees and flowers, to hear birds singing and brooks burbling. He believes the village headman when he pretends to read a letter from the King, who promises to visit him soon. Astonishingly, the royal physician arrives. Irate at Amal's isolation, he orders the windows of the room thrown open. Amal, his pain gone, falls into a deep sleep. Amal's friend, Sudha the flower girl, asks when he will awaken. "Directly the King comes and calls him," the physician says as the curtain falls.[10]

On July 18, the audience watched *The Post Office* with rapt attention. The children saw themselves in little Amal, for they,

too, were in a dark room—the ghetto—longing for freedom and beauty. Sobs filled the room. The Old Doctor sat in a corner in the rear, listening, his eyes "bottomless wells of sadness," a woman who saw him recalled.[11]

Afterward, a guest asked why he'd chosen such a sad play. "Korczak replied that he wanted his children to learn how to welcome the Angel of Death calmly," just as little Amal welcomed the angel that took him in his sleep. The play was the Old Doctor's "way of imparting to the little helpless ones the calm wisdom in the moment of tragedy which in his faith did not mean the end."[12]

But the end of earthly existence was near. On July 30, Major Hermann Höfle, the Operation Reinhard deportation expert, ordered the ghetto's orphanages to be emptied on August 5. The day before, the Old Doctor rose early and, looking out his window, saw a German sentry in the street. He wrote this in his diary:

I am watering the flowers [in a window box]. My bald head in the window. What a splendid target.

He has a rifle. Why is he standing and looking on so calmly?

He has no orders to shoot.

And perhaps he was a village teacher in civilian life, or notary, a street sweeper in Leipzig, a waiter in Cologne?

What would he do if I nodded to him? Waved my hand in a friendly gesture?

Perhaps he doesn't even know that things are—as they are?

He may have arrived only yesterday, from far away . . .[13]

Korczak left the sentence unfinished. Perhaps something interrupted him, and he meant to return to it later. We can never know for sure, but it seems likely that he had no idea that these would be his last written words.

August 5. Similar scenes took place at all the children's homes at various times throughout the day. At Dom Sierot, during breakfast, two shrill blasts of a whistle pierced the air, followed by shouts of *"Alle Juden raus! Schnell! Schnell! Zehn Minuten!"*—"All Jews out! Fast! Fast! Ten minutes!"

Madame Stefa, with her usual efficiency, had already rehearsed the children for such an eventuality. Quietly, without fuss or tears, 192 children formed a column, all in their best clothes, holding a favorite storybook, a diary, a toy, a doll. Ten staff members, including the director and his assistant, took their assigned places.

"Vorwärts marsch!"—"Forward march!"

The Old Doctor led the column. He wore his old army uniform, boots with his trousers tucked into them, and a blue cap. A few paces ahead, a boy held up the green flag of King Matt, with the blue Star of David set against a white field on one side.[14]

"A Page from the Deportation Diary" captures what the poet Władysław Szlengel saw at the start of Korczak's last walk:

I saw Janusz Korczak today. He was walking
at the head of his children in line.
They were dressed in clean clothes, as if for an
    outing
on Shabbat [the Sabbath], when the weather's fine.

They wore their holiday jumpers—today
if they're dirtied no one will scold—
as if through the woods the orphanage walked,
five by five, through the haunted crowd. . . .

Bareheaded, with fearless eyes,
Janusz Korczak walked on before.
One child held on by his pocket,
And two in his arms he bore. . . .[15]

One should never take an eyewitness account at face value; that is why historians and lawyers collect and compare testimony from as many sources as possible. They assume that people, especially in stressful situations, are prone to view the same event differently. Moreover, with the passage of time, people forget certain details and imagine others. In this way, a historical event can take on the qualities of a myth. If enough people believe the myth, it becomes the "truth."

Korczak certainly carried two small children; several observers agreed on this point. But he could not have done so for long. After a while, even small children get heavy, and the day was brutally hot. With children of various ages, some sick, others needing to relieve

themselves, and all malnourished, the going must have been slow. And Korczak himself was sick and in pain. Some eyewitnesses said the three-mile walk to the Umschlagplatz lasted two hours; others said four. That they noted the timing and other details differently does not mean any of them were wrong, let alone lying. It means they saw the procession at different times and places along the route. Depending on where they were, they estimated the pace differently. Only the participants walked the entire route. The guards chose not to write about the event, likely because it had become routine, and the Dom Sierot people did not live to write about it.

In places, onlookers lined the pavement; the Germans ordered them to watch the procession to show the Jews' helplessness. Elsewhere, the streets were empty. Terrified people peered from behind closed curtains. What could have gone through their minds?

Some thought in narrow, personal terms. Removing the orphans meant the Nazis would fill their quota, sparing adults who had work permits for another day at least. Others were heartbroken. Hillel Seidman, a historian employed by the Jewish Council, watched the procession set out from Dom Sierot. He grieved at the dreadful human waste. "The column of children begins to move, marching to their unknown destination," Seidman wrote in his diary. "Who knows how much potential, skill, talent, and Jewish treasures are contained within these precious young souls, now condemned to death. . . . At their head marches Janusz Korczak—the symbol of selfless love and charity overwhelmed by the cruel and evil enemy who knows no mercy. Humanity has been beaten by the beast of prey." Like others, Seidman guessed those driven to the Umschlagplatz were doomed. For if the deportees

were really going east to do hard physical work, the Nazis would not be sending young children.[16]

The pianist Władysław Szpilman claimed to have seen "the smiling children . . . singing in chorus" while a boy accompanied them on his violin. But Irena Sendler saw nothing of the sort. As the column turned a corner, her eyes met the Old Doctor's for an instant. He did not acknowledge her—no greeting, no nod of the head, no sign of recognition. His face "was a frozen mask of hard-won self-control." Only once, Sendler said, did she lose her nerve during the war: "I really wonder how the hearts of the eyewitnesses, myself included, did not break in two. . . . I used my last ounce of strength to walk into [my] house. Then I had a nervous breakdown. . . . Of all my dramatic war-time experiences . . . including my . . . torture in the Pawiak prison . . . not one left so great an impression on me as the sight of Korczak and his children marching to their death."[17]

Żegota operative Marek Rudnicki saw the column approach the Umschlagplatz. Years later, he recalled, "There were no gestures, no singing, no proud spring in the step. . . . There was an overwhelming, weary silence. Korczak dragged his feet with an effort, appeared smaller than usual, as if shrunk, mumbling something to himself. . . . One of the children hung on to Korczak, gripping his coat, perhaps his hand. They walked as if in a trance. . . . I followed them to the gate of the 'Unschlag' as we called it. I cannot describe the scene in front of our eyes. I lack adequate words; perhaps such words do not exist."[18]

Groups of children from orphanages across the ghetto straggled into the Umschlagplatz throughout the day. The only account

Jewish children boarding a truck to the Chełmno death camp. (Date unknown)

we have of them is by Nachum Remba, who revered the Old Doctor.

Remba, later to die in a gas chamber himself, was the secretary of the Jewish Council. When the Great Action began, Remba ran a "first-aid" station just outside the Umschlagplatz. Since the Germans still held to the lie that Jews were "going east" to work, they allowed "Dr. Remba" and a few nurses to treat the sick until they were well enough to travel. Remba, however, used his position to rescue Jews. Wearing a doctor's white coat, he searched for people with prestige or special skills—rabbis, scholars, members of Jewish resistance groups. These he sent to his two-room "first-aid" station. At the end of the day, he'd take them out of the Umschlagplatz by horse-drawn ambulance, claiming they needed further treatment before going east. Remba returned them to the ghetto—the only place he had access to—hoping to keep them alive for a while longer.[19]

As the children filed into the Umschlagplatz, "Dr. Remba" took the Old Doctor aside. Anxious to help, he asked Korczak to go with him to the Jewish Council. Perhaps it could persuade the Germans to postpone at least the departure of Dom Sierot?

Korczak refused to leave the children for even an instant. In his absence, they might panic, precisely what he'd tried to avoid by staging *The Post Office*.[20]

All of a sudden, Captain Szmerling, the brute in charge of the Umschlagplatz, gave the order: "Load the orphanages!" Remba described the scene:

> *The loading of the carriages now began. . . . A teeming, closely packed crowd was being pushed toward the direction of the carriages with whips. . . . Heading the procession was Korczak. No, I shall never forget this scene as long as I live. Indeed, this was no march to the carriages, but rather a mute protest organized against the murderous regime. . . . It was a procession the likes of which no human eye has ever witnessed. The children were arranged in fours; Korczak marched at the head with raised eyes, holding the hands of two children. . . . They were going to their death with eyes full of contempt for the murderers. Seeing Korczak, the ghetto policemen jumped to attention and saluted him. The Germans asked: "Who is this man." At this point I could no longer contain myself. With both hands I tried to hide the stream of tears running from my eyes.*[21]

Legend has it that an SS officer handed Korczak a paper at the last moment. "You may stay, Doctor," he said, clicking his heels. "And the children?" asked Korczak. "Ah, *unmöglich* [impossible], the children must go." Korczak replied, "You are wrong, Sir, the children matter most," as the boxcar door slammed shut.

To repeat, this is a legend. It would be amazing if it were true, but we have no evidence—none whatsoever—that it is. Nevertheless, the story spread throughout the Allied world. The Polish government-in-exile in London soon published an official report, *The Mass Extermination of Jews in German Occupied Poland,* based on information gathered by secret agents. It said that Korczak refused to abandon his children, "although he was given the alternative of remaining behind."[22]

What is certain is that Janusz Korczak, Madame Stefa, and everyone else from Dom Sierot and the other orphanages died in Treblinka. A day or two later, a redheaded boy Igor Newerly had never seen before handed him his friend's diary and fled without saying a word. Newerly cemented it into a wall, where it remained until he retrieved and published it after the war.

The Great Action Ends

Meanwhile, the agony of the Warsaw ghetto continued. After a brief pause while workers built ten new, larger gas chambers at Treblinka, the roundups resumed. On September 5, 1942, the SS ordered all Jews to report to an area of several square blocks, enclosed by barbed wire, next to the Umschlagplatz. Germans called it "the cauldron," a large kettle for cooking on an open fire. Even the two thousand Jewish policemen and their families had to enter it the next morning. There would be another "selection," in which only the healthiest would receive fresh work permits marked "Not Subject to Resettlement." All others would be deported.[23]

The order doomed children under the age of fourteen. Any parent with a young child automatically went to the boxcars. It was a no-win situation: Whatever a parent did would result in someone's death. Many parents chose, like Korczak, to stay with their children no matter what happened. Some children, sensing danger, tried to separate themselves to save their parents. In one instance, horrified onlookers saw a ten-year-old boy run away from his mother. "Mamma, Mamma, keep right on going. Don't look back at me," he cried. She ran after him, so SS men sent them both to the boxcars. Other parents abandoned their children before entering the selection lines, leaving them for the SS and Ukrainians to shoot or bayonet. Abandonment was not for lack of love. Nothing parents did could save their young children—that they knew. Also, their will to live was still strong, even if it meant such a dreadful sacrifice.[24]

Adina Blady Szwajger was a pediatrician at the Bersohn and Bauman Children's Hospital, where the Old Doctor had worked early in his medical career. Since the creation of the ghetto, she had treated seriously ill children sent there from Dom Sierot. Now she had to act quickly. Korczak had rejected "mercy killing" out of love; Szwajger did the opposite for the same reason. She knew the SS would murder every child in her ward. To give them a calm death, she decided to overdose them with morphine, a strong painkiller made from opium. She later wrote:

I took the morphine upstairs. Dr. Margolis was there and I told her what I wanted to do. So we took a spoon and went into the infants' room. And just as, during those two

years of real work in the hospital, I bent down over the little beds, so now I poured this last medicine into those tiny mouths. . . . Downstairs, there was screaming because the [Ukrainians] and the Germans were already there, taking the sick from the wards to the cattle trucks. After that we went to the older children and told them that this morphine was going to make their pain disappear. They believed us and drank the required amount from the glass. And then I told them to undress, get into bed and sleep. So they lay down and after a few minutes . . . they were asleep.

This act of mercy left a deep yet invisible scar. From that day forward, Szwajger was not the same person, constantly beset by pangs of guilt: "I was always different from everybody else. And nobody ever understood this."[25]

This round of deportations ended within a week, on September 12. During that time, roughly 10,000 Jews were driven to the Umschlagplatz each day. The Great Action, better called the "Great Liquidation," officially ended on September 21. The number of lives it claimed boggles the mind. Between July 21 and September 21, the SS sent (by its own count) 310,322 Jews to Treblinka and murdered 5,961 within the ghetto. Roughly 55,000 Jews remained, of whom 30,000 were in the ghetto legally; they had "life tickets"—work permits—or were family members of a ticket holder. Two hundred Jewish policemen and their families also remained. These officers, all picked men, were the most loyal to the Germans, and the cruelest toward their fellow Jews.[26]

The original Warsaw ghetto, once crowded and bustling, was

gone. What remained were streets littered with discarded luggage, glass from broken windows—and feathers. Feathers swirled even in the gentlest breeze, settling into drifts. When searching for valuables, the Germans slashed feather blankets and pillows, emptying them out the windows. One could walk for hours along "snowy" streets, seeing only stray dogs and cats. The SS ordered the small

Ruins of the Warsaw ghetto. (1945)

ghetto, the final location of Dom Sierot, cleared and its walls torn down. In the large ghetto, troops cleared more streets every few days. It became three separate areas, each surrounded by fences and barbed wire, sealed off from its neighbors.

Within these "islands," Jews worked and lived with their families in German factories, or they lived in adjoining blocks of apartment houses. "Every factory is a prison, locked and bolted," diarist Abraham Lewin wrote. "We go in a group to and from work, before seven in the morning and at six in the evening." Workers in different factories could not speak to each other or go out alone, on pain of death. They were slaves, the property of

the SS. Their employers paid the SS a daily fee per head; in return each slave got a little food, a place to sleep, and the privilege of living—for the time being.[27]

Roughly twenty-five thousand Jews were in the ghetto illegally. Having refused to report for the September selections, they had no "life tickets," and thus no right to live. Nevertheless, they hid in the houses in the wasteland between the factory areas. The SS called them "wild people," denizens of the "wild houses" in the "wild ghetto." SS patrols shot them on sight. To survive, they roamed at night, darting among the shadows, scavenging from abandoned apartments. Smuggling continued, though greatly reduced, so they traded household goods for food. Polish thieves, too, stole into the wild ghetto to take anything with resale value to the Aryan side.

States of Mind

Whether factory slaves or wild people, the living bore emotional scars. All knew the ravages of starvation, disease, and fear. Even after seven decades, survivors' accounts remain deeply moving human documents. Loss of loved ones is the dominant theme. Itzhak Katzenelson's "The Day of My Great Disaster" is typical of these accounts and, I believe, the most expressive. Here the poet describes his despair upon returning to the tiny room that his family shared, only to find his loved ones gone:

> I [enter] the four bare walls of my dark home
> and I wring my hands—

Hannah is not here and my two boys gone too!

Gone—there's no trace of them

Hannah! I call your name out loud. . . .

Hannah my Hannah my only one you!

Where are my boys, my Benzion? My Benjamin?

Their bright eyes, their beautiful heads

Oh my fine ones where have you been dragged? . . .

Hannele tell me where you've been taken

I cannot stand not to know where you are. . . .

I cannot rest day or night

Something in me has finished. Stop!

And something chases me and chases me downhill

Am I going insane? . . .

Hannah . . . you

my dear know nothing of that![28]

Like Katzenelson, many had "survivor guilt," a sense of having done wrong by surviving an ordeal while others, equally or more deserving, perished. "I'm sorry I'm alive," said a survivor. "Why was I saved?" asked a young woman. "Why did I get out of the ghetto? I committed treachery. I shouldn't have gotten out while other, more noble people remained."[29]

Survivors might also look beyond their private sorrows. In doing so, they asked two questions, one philosophical, the other practical. First: Where is God amid all this horror? Second: Can we fight the Nazi evil, and if so, how? There were (and are) no easy answers.

The first question is as old as monotheism, the belief in one

God, the master of all. If the Creator of the Universe is all-powerful, all-knowing, all-just, and all-good, why does He allow evil? Believers answer that He has given humans free will, the ability to choose their paths. So if we choose wrongly, it is our fault, not the Almighty's. If our choice causes suffering, it is punishment for our sins, brought upon ourselves, or a mystery because we cannot understand the ways of the Almighty.

The reality of the ghetto challenged this view. For many, the Jews' sins, however grave, in no way matched those of the Nazis. And even if they did, young children had never wronged anyone. Agonized, Itzhak Katzenelson asked:

> Oh, God in heaven!—
> Shuddering I shall cry:
> what for and why
> did my people die?
> What for and why
> in vain did it die? . . .
> What for, my Lord,
> dear God, why?[30]

Others answered these questions for themselves. God, they decided, had let the Jewish people down. Jews had kept faith with Him, praying to Him and obeying His laws. Though the Nazis had demolished synagogues, forbidden prayer, and banned religious education, Jews held fast to their faith. Nevertheless, God let the oppressor sacrifice them on the altar of racism. To express their bitterness, a prisoner scrawled graffiti on a wall: "If there is

a God, He will have to beg my forgiveness." Władysław Szlengel echoed this cry. In "It's High Time," the poet portrays a topsy-turvy Judgment Day. Here God does not judge His children; they judge Him:

And You, up there, almighty convict
There in the awesome silence of the galaxies,
You'll hear every single word of ours,
When sentenced by us, Your chosen people.
There is no absolution, no absolution!!! . . .

We won't forgive You now
That You have delivered us
into the hands of killers,
because during the millennia
We had been Your loyal children. . . .

For tortures in the ghettos, specter of the gallows,
We, the degraded, we, the exhausted . . .
We'll pay You back!! We'll pay You back!! . . .
Then they'll burn You
And You will be ash.[31]

The calamity made even Orthodox Jews question, and some lose, their faith. "We lived by the Torah; is this the reward?" one asked. Defying tradition, some men shaved their beards, put away their prayer books, and left the clandestine synagogues. A number seem to have lost their minds completely. We read, for instance, of a Hasidic man spitting at heaven and eating pork, banned by

Jewish law as unclean. A fellow Hasid shook his raised fists, shouting, "Jews, collect large stones and throw them up to heaven! Why has God picked on us for this torment? Give me stones to throw in defiance of heaven!" The poor man's wife apologized: "He has had neither food nor water for three days. He is terrified. He is not responsible for what he is saying."[32]

Terror might also have the opposite effect, renewing and deepening faith. Examples abound. Graffiti chalked on ghetto walls urged, "Jews, Never Despair!" People sang, "I believe, I believe, I believe." After boxcar doors slammed shut, some Hasidic men burst into song because "[we] are going to meet the Messiah." Others recited a Bible passage: "Though He slay me, yet will I trust in Him" (Job 13:15). In a boxcar, two elderly women knelt beside the praying Jews. They were Catholics, housekeepers who had been with their employers for ages and could not think of abandoning them. As the boxcar rattled and swayed, their prayer, "You have suffered wounds for us, O Jesus Christ," mingled with the traditional Jewish cry, "Hear O Israel, the Lord our God, the Lord is one."[33]

To Fight or Not to Fight?

After the Great Action, survivors asked themselves why they had not resisted. Emanuel Ringelblum captured their mood:

Why didn't we resist when they began to resettle 300,000 Jews from Warsaw? Why did we allow ourselves to be led

like sheep to the slaughter? Why did everything come so easily to the enemy? Why didn't the hangmen suffer a single casualty?. . . . We should have run out into the streets, have set fire to everything in sight, have torn down the walls, and escaped to the Other Side. The Germans would have taken their revenge. It would have cost tens of thousands of lives, but not 300,000. Now we are ashamed of ourselves, disgraced in our own eyes, and in the eyes of the world, where our docility earned us nothing.[34]

Before discussing why Jews did not fight back at first, we must examine their attitudes toward violence. This is a complicated issue, which ghetto leaders began debating on July 23, just as the Great Action got under way.

During the debate, the Orthodox voiced age-old ideas. Believing that only God can decide the struggle between good and evil, they ruled out violence as useless and unworthy of the pious. Real courage, in their view, was not shown in battle, with weapons in hand and blood spattered. It was spiritual courage expressed in study, prayer, and faith in the Holy One. Yes, the Nazis were brutal racists. Yet Jews must trust God. "I believe in the Almighty and a miracle," as one put it. "He will not allow his people to be destroyed. We must be patient and a miracle will occur. Fighting the enemy makes no sense." Plainly, the Orthodox would not fight under any circumstances.[35]

Leaders of the Bund (League), an organization of Jewish labor unions, took the middle ground. Bundists should fight, they said, but only when the Polish underground began a general war of

liberation. Until then, it would be unwise to attack individual Germans in the ghetto, because the oppressor, holding the entire community responsible, would slaughter scores in retaliation for each offense. And if they took you alive, they'd murder your entire family.[36]

Zionists were the most militant. For years, they had run training camps to prepare young men and women to immigrate to Palestine. A major part of their training involved learning to farm the land. Another part, as important, taught the use of firearms to defend settlements against Arab raiders. In dealing with the Nazis, Zionists urged armed resistance, regardless of what others might or might not do.

The meeting ended with a decision not to decide. Representatives would wait, as one delicately put it, "until the situation was clarified." Translation: Get the facts before you make up your mind. Though they, like Hillel Seidman and Nachum Remba, might think that the men, women, and children taken from the Umschlagplatz went to their deaths, they had no proof. Until they knew

A poster promoting Zionist cultural schools in Poland. (1930s)

for sure, they could not commit themselves to violent resistance. Nevertheless, they needed to be prepared. So on July 28, several Zionist youth groups formed the Jewish Fighting Organization—or ZOB, from its Polish initials. In the following weeks, the Bund and other groups joined forces with the ZOB. If it came to fighting, they reasoned, Jews must create a united front.[37]

Almost immediately, the ZOB began unveiling Treblinka's secrets. Fortunately, a few Jewish policemen played a double game. While helping the Germans at the Umschlagplatz, they also fed information to the ZOB. Each day, they copied the serial numbers of the waiting locomotives and boxcars. The next day, they compared these with the serial numbers on the trains that had just arrived in Warsaw. To their amazement, the numbers were identical. The Germans said the deportees were "going east," to distant work sites in Ukraine and Russia. However, in peacetime, the round-trip journey took from three to four days. Obviously, the trains' destination lay close to the Polish capital.

Zalman Friedrich, a Bund activist, was assigned to find out where the trains went. A blond giant with fair skin and blue eyes, Friedrich looked to be the perfect "Aryan." Early in August, only days after the Old Doctor's last walk, he escaped from the ghetto. Traveling on foot, he followed the tracks from the Umschlagplatz, often dodging German railway police patrols.

Upon reaching Sokołów, a town on the main line northeast of Warsaw, Friedrich questioned the locals in flawless Polish. Had they seen trains with boxcars packed with Jews? Where had those gone? He was told that a few miles up the line, at Małkinia Junction, the trains were rerouted to a village called Treblinka.

From there, farmers in the area said, a single-track spur led into the forest. Whatever the forest hid was well guarded, and an awful stench hung in the air. While in Sokołów, Friedrich also met a man he knew. This in itself was miraculous, as less than 0.01 percent of Jews sent to Operation Reinhard camps survived. The fellow was in bad shape, famished, bleeding, and in shock. He said he'd escaped from a work gang in Treblinka and had seen everything, from the Jews' arrival to the disposal of their bodies.[38]

Back in the ghetto, Friedrich gave the grisly account to *Storm*, an illegal newspaper. "Do not be deceived," *Storm* warned readers in a special one-page edition. "Throw off your illusions! You are being taken to death and extermination. Do not let them destroy you! Do not give yourselves voluntarily into the hands of your executioners." In late September, two escapees reached Warsaw from Treblinka; they'd hidden in a boxcar loaded with victims' clothes bound for Germany. They confirmed Friedrich's account, and soon an anonymous verse swept the ghetto:

> *Treblinka village,*
> *The last resort for every Jew;*
> *Whoever comes here, remains here:*
> *Remains forever.*[39]

Despite these reports, there were those who clung to their illusions. It is hard to imagine one's own death, and they could not believe the Germans meant to wipe them out. ZOB activist Zivia Lubetkin recalled that Hitler's prewar threats to annihilate the

Jews seemed so outlandish that most dismissed them as merely the "barking of a mad dog." They thought mass murder "could never happen in the heart of Europe, in Warsaw," so therefore "nobody believed him. Nobody wanted to believe him." Besides, it was one thing to get rid of the ghetto's "unproductive," but murdering thousands of skilled workers defied reason. Those workers helped keep the Nazi war machine running, just when the war was turning against Germany. Jews in ghetto factories produced all sorts of military gear, including 60 percent of the winter clothing worn by the troops in Russia.[40]

However, for most, the reports about Treblinka broke a mental barrier. In a way, the awful truth cleared the mind. Any illusions about Nazi intentions vanished. The Nazis meant to kill them all, not because of anything they'd done, but because of who they were—the evil "race enemy." That realization freed people to choose. They had an either-or choice. Either the Jews could continue as before, "letting them take us to death like sheep to the slaughter," as the pianist Władysław Szpilman put it. Or the Jews could fight back. "Don't die with a Torah in your hand," said ZOB leaflets, "die with weapons in your hand."[41]

But it would be wrong to say resisters expected to check, let alone defeat, Hitler's war machine. Realists, they would fight not for survival but for things they deemed more precious than life itself. As Zivia Lubetkin put it: "We said to ourselves: 'We must see the truth for what it is. The Germans want to annihilate us. It is our duty to . . . struggle for our honor and the honor of the Jewish people. . . . We would not go helplessly off to slaugh-

ter. We would no longer die without a struggle.'" The aim was not to save themselves, for it was all but certain that few if any would come out alive. What they wished to save was their human dignity.[42]

First Blood

The ZOB began by forming fighting groups ranging from twenty to twenty-five men and women, nearly all in their late teens and early twenties. The groups' overall commander was Mordechai Anielewicz. Born in 1919, "Angel," as friends called him, was a child of the tenements Janusz Korczak had explored in his student days. Polish gangs roamed the streets, robbing Jews and beating

them up. But Angel was no angel, as thugs learned to their dismay. A natural leader, he had his own gang of toughs. He would lure a thug into an alley, where his "boys" would beat him with brass knuckles. Upon graduating from high school, Angel became a Zionist organizer. After the

Mordechai Anielewicz, the leader of ZOB, the Jewish Fighting Organization. (c. 1943)

German invasion, he set up underground youth groups and newspapers. His role in the ZOB was to devise a fighting strategy and coordinate the activities of its fighting groups.[43]

Fighting required weapons. To obtain them, ZOB agents operated on two fronts. To buy weapons, they needed money, which they raised within the wild ghetto. Since big-time smugglers still had plenty of money, ZOB "taxed" them. In one case, it kidnapped a smuggler's son and held him until his father paid up. At the same time, ZOB agents snuck out of the ghetto using smugglers' routes. On the Aryan side, they contacted the Home Army (Armia Krajowa), the military arm of the Polish underground. The Home Army had nearly four thousand resistance groups throughout the country; it was the largest underground force in occupied Europe.

Home Army leaders loathed the Nazis, but they had doubts about arming the Jews. On the one hand, some of them were anti-Semitic and had no intention of aiding Jews; indeed, guerrilla units sometimes killed Jews who had escaped to the forests. On the other hand, Home Army leaders who were sympathetic to Jews were unsure they would fight; so far, they had not shown that they would. Besides, the Home Army needed weapons and had to build up its stocks before attacking the Germans. Yet, as a gesture of goodwill, its Warsaw command gave ZOB, as a gift, between twenty and thirty pistols and a few hundred bullets— hardly enough for a revolt.

ZOB used the pistols against Jewish traitors. An assassin would waylay an informer and shoot him. Because every bullet

counted, a gunman known only as Hershel shoved a twelve-year-old informer out a window instead. As for the remaining Jewish policemen, resisters declared war on them. An assassin shot Józef Szeryński, the hated police commander, crippling him. Jacob Lejkin, his deputy, was killed. Israel Shahak recalled that he "together with a few [other] children and teenagers present danced for joy round the dead body and then ran home as quickly as I could to carry the glad tidings to my mother." No wonder ZOB gained its reputation as "the people's avengers."[44]

On January 9, 1943, Heinrich Himmler inspected the Warsaw ghetto. Never known for physical courage, the SS chief had a "delicate" stomach, and the sight of blood gave him agonizing cramps. Now the man who'd ordered infants killed took no chances with his own safety. Two armored cars preceded his limousine, and two others covered the rear, each bristling with machine guns. Upon meeting his commanders, Himmler ordered the ghetto workforce cut severely, in preparation for the final liquidation in the spring.[45]

On January 18, SS units made workers assemble outside their factories for another round of selections. Those who showed a work permit stamped "Not Subject to Resettlement" had it torn up and their faces slapped. Soldiers then began herding columns of terrified people toward the Umschlagplatz.

Things did not go as smoothly as expected. As the columns got under way, Mordechai Anielewicz sent three fighting groups to mingle with the crowd. By then, the ZOB had 143 pistols, each

with seven rounds of ammunition. At Angel's signal, the resisters started shooting. Though taken by surprise, the SS guards returned fire with their rifles. Amid the confusion, hundreds fled into the wild houses. The shooting stunned the Germans, making them leery about entering the area except with overwhelming force. Within four days, they withdrew, ending the operation. Still, they'd sent 6,500 Jews to Treblinka, while killing perhaps 250 resisters, a stunning blow to the ZOB. The SS counted 20 dead and 50 wounded.[46]

Despite their losses, Angel's fighters had scored a victory. Never before had Warsaw Jews shot SS men. Denied any worth or dignity as human beings, Jews, in Nazi minds, were merely "meat," placid beasts easily led to slaughter. Now the Nazis knew better. Władysław Szlengel captured the Jews' elation in a ferocious poem titled "Counterattack":

> Bullets whirl in their joyous song,
> REVOLT OF THE MEAT,
> REVOLT OF THE MEAT,
> REVOLT OF THE MEAT! . . .
> Hear, O German God,
> How the Jews, in the "wild" houses pray,
> Clenching in the fist a stick, a stone.
> We beg You, O God, for a bloody battle,
> We implore You for a violent death,
> Let us not see, before we expire,
> The stretch of the train tracks.[47]

The setback infuriated Himmler. From his Berlin headquarters, he sent the order to SS commanders in Warsaw: "I hereby order that the Warsaw ghetto be destroyed," and that its population of "subhumans . . . should completely disappear."[48]

The ZOB did not have to read Himmler's order to know what was coming. Angel's fighters had humiliated the SS, and sure as day follows night, the SS could not rest as long as the ghetto existed. Home Army leaders agreed: the January clash proved that Jews would fight. Accordingly, they stepped up arms deliveries, though still on a small scale. The ZOB had to find additional sources.

Polish smugglers dealt in guns as well as food. These included Polish Army weapons hidden prior to the nation's surrender in 1939. Surprisingly, smugglers also obtained weapons from German soldiers on leave from the Russian front. Hundreds of fighting men, disgusted with the endless slaughter, sold their guns to pay for a good time in Warsaw or to send money to their folks back home; they told superiors they'd "lost" the weapons. ZOB purchasing agents hid the guns in safe houses before smuggling them into the ghetto. Catholic nuns helped. The Barefoot Carmelites, who lived in a convent on Wolska Street, near the ghetto, hid guns in the basement.[49]

Agents also sent bomb-making materials. With the advice of Home Army technicians, ZOB workshops in the wild ghetto fashioned them into grenades and mines. Though explosives were never plentiful, scavengers brought empty bottles to the workshops, where they were made into Molotov cocktails. Named

for Soviet foreign minister V. M. Molotov, those gasoline-filled bottles were ignited and thrown, exploding upon impact and engulfing their targets in flames; they were especially effective when aimed at the air intakes of German tanks. Similarly, burnt-out light bulbs were injected with sulfuric acid; the bulbs were easily broken on contact with skin, and the acid inside caused blindness and ugly burns.

Since there still would not be enough weapons to go around, most Jews could not join the combat units even if they'd wished to. They would have to stay safe and out of the fighters' way in hundreds of bunkers, hiding places for noncombatants. Bunker building required special skills. Though there were a few Jewish engineers, Jewish craftsmen had never played a large role in Warsaw's construction trades. Now they served as helpers; the experts—electricians, carpenters, plumbers, masons—were Poles. "There were many gentiles loyal to us," a fighter noted. "Most of them weren't paid for their work. Some people could be counted on just as much as the most loyal Jew . . . and most of the builders were loyal Poles."[50]

Under cover of darkness, workers built bunkers beneath cellars, the floors of apartments, courtyards, and mounds of rubble. As one might expect, some of the bunkers were better equipped than others. Structures varied in size, with space for from thirty to two hundred people. Many had tiers of bunks, electric lights, flush toilets, and water faucets. Several had freshly dug artesian wells. So that the "wild people" would continue to have water, a man from the Warsaw waterworks connected a bunker's pipes to

the pipes of a German factory. The "thieves' bunker" was extraordinary. Built by a criminal gang under 18 Miła Street, it could hold three hundred people and a large store of smuggled food. The system of bunkers, a fighter noted, "resembled a subterranean Jewish city."[51]

Builders concealed bunker entrances behind false walls, trapdoors, and even ovens that one had to wriggle through. To allow residents to move about indoors, hidden passageways linked apartments, rooms, staircases, roofs, and cellars. Luckily, ghetto houses were mostly uniform, built up against each other and three to five stories high. Topping each was a tiled roof that covered an attic running the length of the building. Ladders connected the rooftops. Once across, a person could duck into an entryway cut into the roof tiles, then use the attic as a concealed "highway," moving from house to house through holes made in the common walls. Ghetto fighters would need every advantage.[52]

Revolt!

Himmler set April 19, 1943, as the date for the liquidation of the Warsaw ghetto. The SS chief planned to present his Führer with a Jew-free Warsaw on April 20, his fifty-fourth birthday.

Hitler needed some good news. Reports from the eastern front told of a shattering disaster at Stalingrad, a major industrial center on the west bank of the Volga River. When the German Sixth Army entered the city, Soviet forces sprang a trap, surrounding

the troops and preventing outside help from reaching them. After a three-month siege during which 300,000 Germans were killed and 90,000 taken prisoner, the invaders surrendered on February 2. In Warsaw, Jew and gentile mocked the Germans, dubbing Stalingrad (Stalin City) Stalingrab (Stalin Grave). The Home Army plastered Warsaw with posters of skeletons carrying swastika flags and the caption *"Deutschland Kaput!"*—"Germany Is Broken!"[53]

April 19. At 5:00 a.m., ZOB lookouts saw German troops moving toward the ghetto in battle formation. The coming clash, said a ghetto resident, would be "between a fly and an elephant." The Nazi "elephant" had 2,100 men, scores of machine guns, several short-range cannons, and two tanks. The Jewish "fly" mustered 750 fighters. This would not be the mass uprising later portrayed in novels and schoolbooks. The vast majority of Jews did not take part; they stayed in their bunkers, as intended. ZOB had more weapons than ever, though still not nearly enough. Each fighter carried a pistol, from ten to fifteen rounds of ammunition, four or five hand grenades, and several Molotov cocktails. In all, the force had ten rifles of different makes and quality, and one or two submachine guns, probably of German make.[54]

Mordechai Anielewicz knew the ZOB stood no chance against the Germans in open battle. To counter their advantage in numbers and weapons, he decided to fight at close quarters. "We shall wear out the enemy," he said. Jewish fighters would "hug" the Germans, battling them on stairways, in alleys, and in narrow passageways.[55]

Three Jewish women who fought in the Warsaw ghetto uprising and were captured by SS soldiers. (1942)

Angel's strategy worked. At first, the Germans advanced boldly, led by their tanks. Then it happened: A fighter, darting from a doorway, threw a Molotov cocktail at an SS man. The bottle landed at his feet and broke, engulfing him in flames. A human torch, he screamed, panicking the rest of his squad. Elsewhere, Jews shot from windows, attics, and piles of rubble, turning streets into killing grounds.

The fighters stunned the Nazi "supermen." A soldier yelled as he took cover, *"Juden haben Waffen! Juden haben Waffen!"*—"Jews have weapons! Jews have weapons!" A comrade, scarcely able to believe his eyes, cried, *"Hans, eine Frau schiesst!"*—"Hans, a woman is shooting!" To make matters worse, the tanks proved useless. Molotov cocktails set one ablaze, roasting its crew alive. The Germans retreated, regrouped, returned, and got more of the same before leaving the ghetto at two o'clock in the afternoon.[56]

Elation! After dark, "wild people" emerged from their bunkers, laughing, cheering, hugging and kissing the fighters. A woman recalled: "[We] saw German blood pouring over the streets of Warsaw, after we saw so much Jewish blood running in the streets of Warsaw before that. There was rejoicing."[57]

April 20. Adolf Hitler did not get his Warsaw birthday present. Though his troops returned better organized and more cautious, they met the same determined resistance. To drive home their failure, a large mine was detonated under an advancing unit. The result, a ZOB fighter wrote, was "a tremendous explosion . . . crushed bodies of soldiers, limbs flying . . . complete chaos. I saw and I didn't believe: German soldiers screaming in panicky flight, leaving their wounded behind." Again the enemy withdrew, having been fought to a standstill. Again the rebels had a victory. It would be their last.[58]

Heinrich Himmler was furious. When Ludwig Hahn, Warsaw's police commander, phoned in his report, the normally soft-spoken Himmler "used the most vulgar language again and again." What had happened in the ghetto, he shrieked, was a "shame" and "a stain on the SS's good name." Himmler ordered Waffen-SS general Jürgen Stroop to take over the operation at once. Stroop personified the Nazi ideal. Six feet tall, lean and fair-skinned, the forty-eight-year-old was a ruthless killer who'd learned his trade in the trenches of the First World War. Regular army officers despised Stroop, calling him an "arrogant SS pig," a brute without common decency or soldierly honor.[59]

The general vowed to stamp out "this rabble and subhumanity," his term for ghetto Jews. Stroop's daily reports, published after the war as *The Stroop Report: The Jewish Quarter of Warsaw Is No More!*, are gifts to historians. In over one hundred typed pages, he describes his actions in detail. A photographic section contains fifty-three iconic images, examples of which appear in most histories of the Holocaust.[60]

MIRS
LIBRARY

Es gibt keinen
jüdischen Wohnbezirk
in Warschau mehr!

INTERNATIONAL MILITARY TRIBUNAL
NÜRNBERG, GERMANY
USA Exhibit
Filed

The cover page from a copy of *The Stroop Report.*
The German title reads, "The Jewish Quarter of
Warsaw Is No More!" (1943)

Stroop changed German tactics. Instead of fighting the "subhumans" at close quarters, as the ZOB preferred, he kept his distance. "All our plans were now useless," said Zivia Lubetkin. "We had dreamed of a battle face to face with the enemy. . . . But the Nazis avoided open battle, sending fire instead to destroy us. We had never expected this."[61]

Stroop's combat engineers ignited gasoline barrels at building entrances. Men with flamethrowers shot streams of burning oil through windows. Roaring, rolling, churning waves of fire swept the ghetto. Bunkers became ovens in which residents roasted or suffocated. Driven from one fighting position after another, Marek Edelman, a unit commander, described the inferno in the streets:

> The flames cling to our clothes, which now start smoldering. The [asphalt] pavement melts under our feet into a black, gooey substance. Broken glass, littering every inch of

the streets, is transformed into a sticky liquid in which our feet are caught. Our soles begin to burn from the heat of the stone pavement. One after another we stagger through the conflagration. From house to house, from courtyard to courtyard, with no air to breathe, with a hundred hammers clanging in our heads, with burning rafters continuously falling over us, we finally reach the end of the area on fire. . . . The flames chased the people out of their shelters. Thousands staggered about in the courtyards, where they were easy prey for the Germans. . . . Hundreds committed suicide [by] jumping from the fourth and fifth storeys of

SS general Jürgen Stroop (fourth from right) watches buildings burn during the suppression of the Warsaw ghetto uprising. (1943)

apartment houses. Mothers would thus save their children from terrible death in flames.[62]

How did Varsovians react to the struggle? They could not ignore it, as it became the background of everyday life. The rumble of exploding shells, the chatter of machine guns, echoed across their city. At night, they stood on rooftops, watching plumes of smoke rise amid the glare of raging fires. It seems that many, perhaps the majority, were indifferent, looking out for themselves, just trying to survive. However, some were downright gleeful, declaring that the Jews deserved their fate. For Christians, it was Holy Week, and crowds in the streets were going on foot to visit family and friends. "The Yids are frying," said a passerby. "They're spoiling our holiday. It's because of them that we have to walk." A woman exclaimed, "The one and immortal favor by the Germans toward the Poles is the fact that they had cleansed [our country] of Jews." A man even urged Poles "to donate money in order to put up a golden statue of Hitler for freeing us of Jews."[63]

Poles—how many we cannot say, as there were no public opinion polls in Warsaw—also pitied the victims of Nazi racism. An underground newspaper spoke for them, saying, "This is a battle of the lost versus the beasts of prey." Various incidents showed the decency of ordinary folk. If, for example, you stood outside the ghetto, you could see Jews jumping from burning buildings. "As the ghetto was burning, I would mix with the crowd assembled to watch the ghetto walls," recalled Yitzhak Zuckerman. "With my own eyes, I saw Poles crying, just standing and crying." Helena Elbaum Dorembus, a Jew hiding with a Catholic family, saw a

woman leap from a burning building with a child in her arms. As she did, a Polish woman cried out, "Jesus, Jesus, have mercy. After all, they are human beings."[64]

Polish history is filled with heroes who defied oppressors, and there was plenty of heroism in the ghetto. Ruth Altbeker Cyprys recalled hearing "an elderly man speaking gravely and making the sign of the cross. 'Serves them right, those vile German cowards.'" And when Poles saw German ambulances speeding from the ghetto, sirens wailing, they paid resisters the highest compliment they could imagine. They christened the ghetto Ghettograd, after Stalingrad, the scene of the recent German disaster. On the other side of the wall, in Ghettograd, SS men, whom Poles called *Shwabs,* from the German word for cockroaches, were tasting their own medicine.[65]

Jürgen Stroop thought the fighting was as intense as any he'd seen in the First World War. Defiantly, people leaped from burning buildings, "shaking their fists" while "cursing against Germany, the Führer, and the German soldiers." A captive held a few feet away from the general whipped out a pistol but was shot by the general's bodyguards. Stroop stood over the dying man, watching his life ooze away. The general reported that with eyes blazing with hatred, and "with all his remaining strength, he spat at me." Women fighters amazed him even more. "Not infrequently these females fired pistols from both hands. Repeatedly, they concealed pistols or hand grenades in their underpants to use at the last minute against the men of the Waffen-SS, Police, and Wehrmacht."[66]

Home Army leaders refused to join the revolt, fearing that premature action would cripple their ability to mount an attack

later. Nevertheless, resister David J. Landau wrote, "our Polish friends stood by us." Acting on their own initiative, small groups of Home Army fighters supported the embattled Jews. General Stroop mentions Germans taking rifle fire "from outside the ghetto." Within the ghetto, Polish snipers, positioned on rooftops, picked off his men. The general called them "bandits" and "terrorists." When captured, they faced firing squads. As the executioners leveled their rifles, they shouted, "Long live Poland!"[67]

Day by day, battle losses, lack of ammunition, and exhaustion wore down the ZOB. As the pace of fighting slackened, Stroop began a massive search-and-destroy operation called the "Battle of the Bunkers." It was not really a battle but a manhunt, with police dogs and sound detectors. When troops found a bunker, they called for the inhabitants' surrender or, failing that, set off dynamite charges. Any survivors were tortured to reveal the location of other bunkers, shot at once, or sent to the boxcars. Several photos taken by German cameramen show terrified families with small children leaving bunkers with their hands raised or walking under armed guard along streets lined with burning buildings on either side.

For those in hiding, silence was a matter of life and death. With hunters just feet away, crying children endangered everyone. To keep their little ones quiet, parents drugged them. Sometimes people had to make decisions unthinkable in normal times. Deliberately, they put crying children to death. Survivors recalled mothers smothering their babies to save the rest of the group, and people poisoning babies to silence them. The consequences of not acting could be fatal. When, for instance, a baby began crying

SS troops pull Jews from bunkers during the suppression of the Warsaw ghetto uprising. (1943)

during a search, a rabbi ordered that no one harm the child. As a result, Nazis found and killed all twenty people in the bunker. "Where was God," a man asked when he learned about a similar tragedy. "Didn't He see what was happening here?"[68]

Steadily, SS search details uncovered hundreds of bunkers—631 by Stroop's count. Survivor Hillel Seidman recalled that the Nazis used Jewish traitors to coax people out of their bunkers. "We suddenly heard loud voices in the courtyard. Everyone held their breath. Eventually we realized it was somebody addressing us in Polish: 'These are fellow Jews speaking. Leave your hiding places and the Germans promise you that you will be sent to work.

Nothing will happen to you if you leave now. Otherwise they will pump gas into your cellar!'" When they left, the Germans marched them to the boxcars, but Seidman escaped.[69]

The end came on May 8, when Mordechai Anielewicz, his girl-friend Mira Fuchrer, and 118 other fighters were cornered in the "thieves' bunker," which they were using as a hideout. The thieves surrendered, but the fighters refused to give up. Nearly all died, either by German bullets or by their own hands. Thanks to the Home Army, a handful of other fighters—eighty or so—and a few hundred bunker people found safety on the Aryan side. Without their writings, it would be impossible to understand the revolt from the Jewish standpoint.

With resistance crumbling, the Home Army declared, "Helping the Jews escaping from the burning ghetto is a Christian obligation." Because the only way out by then was through the sewers, the Home Army sent sewer workers to guide them; a few charged for their services, but most did not. Warsaw's sewers go on for miles, forming a maze under the city. To enter them without knowledge of underground geography meant almost certain death. Those who ventured into this bleak underworld without a guide might wander for days before succumbing to starvation, thirst, disease, or poison gas pumped in by the Germans.[70]

Even with help, navigating the sewers was every bit as danger-ous as hiding in a bunker. A survivor told what it was like:

Refugees were huddling in the filth and the stink, in pipes so low and narrow that only one person could pass at a time, walking in a low crouch. They lay on the ground in the ex-

crement and other filth, pressed to each other. Some of the elderly people and children had fainted, with no one paying any attention. The stream of sewage washed away the bodies of the dead, making room for the living. The wounded lay there bleeding, their blood mixing with the sewage.[71]

Upon lifting a manhole cover, people could hardly recognize themselves. Zivia Lubetkin recalled: "Now when we saw each other in daylight—dirty, wrapped in rags, smeared with filth, faces thin and drawn, knees shaking with weariness—we were overcome with horror. Only our feverish eyes showed that we were still human beings." Some survivors went into hiding in Warsaw; others joined guerrilla bands operating in the forests near the capital. After the war, in 1946, Varsovians built a monument, their first, to the ghetto revolt. It was in the form of a sewer pipe topped by a manhole cover.[72]

Jürgen Stroop was pleased with himself. On May 16, he informed Berlin, "The former Jewish quarter in Warsaw is no more!" Later that day, he celebrated by dynamiting the Great Synagogue of Warsaw. Once the largest Jewish house of worship in the world, it had opened in 1878, the year of Janusz Korczak's birth. With his staff and troops proudly looking on, Stroop gave the Nazi salute, shouted *"Heil Hitler!"* and pressed the detonator button. He recalled: "With a thunderous, deafening bang and a rainbow burst of colors, the fiery explosion soared toward the clouds, an unforgettable tribute to our triumph over the Jews. . . . The will of Adolf Hitler and Heinrich Himmler has been done."[73]

As a final gesture of contempt for Jews, Himmler ordered the

ghetto leveled. Before assigning Stroop to a command outside Poland, he put him in charge of that project. For weeks, slave laborers tore down every building except the hospital and police barracks. When they finished, only heaps of rubble remained. It was as if a giant had picked up the ghetto, turned it upside down, and shaken everything out. The ghetto, a traveler later wrote, "is just a great plain of bricks, with twisted beds and bath tubs and sofas, pictures in frames, trunks, millions of things sticking out among the bricks." Afterward, the Gestapo used the wasteland as an execution ground for Poles seized for various "crimes," including aiding Jews.[74]

Reckoned in lives, the cost of the Warsaw ghetto revolt was high. Roughly 6,000 Jews died in the fighting or in the fires. Stroop reported seizing about 50,000 people from the bunkers in the wild

The Great Synagogue of Warsaw lies in rubble. (Date unknown)

Captured Jews being led away from bunkers in the burning Warsaw ghetto. (1943)

ghetto and the factories, which the SS closed. Of these, nearly all died in Treblinka or in slave-labor camps. Stroop reported 16 Germans killed and 85 wounded in the fighting, an underestimate, likely because he wanted to make himself look good. Historians today believe the Germans had 85 dead and 430 wounded.[75]

Numbers aside, the revolt was yet another blow to German prestige and morale. The Allies had already proved the absurdity of Nazi racial ideology. Germans were not "supermen." Like ordinary mortals, even Waffen-SS fanatics bled and died. Now a few hundred poorly armed civilians had shown that the Germans could not keep an oppressed people down. That realization heralded another tragedy, one that befell the city of Warsaw itself. An old saying was to prove all too true: "If you take a handful of Warsaw soil and squeeze it, the blood will run from it."[76]

Warsaw, Summer–Winter 1944

Though the Home Army had branches throughout Poland, its main efforts focused on Warsaw, Poland's capital and largest city. Several branches, each with a distinct role, prepared for the eventual uprising against the Nazis. The intelligence branch fed information to military planners and also radioed it to Allied intelligence services based in London. Combat units took their orders from the Home Army's high command, which coordinated their actions. Polish women served in every branch; without them, the resistance could not have functioned. As one-seventh of Home Army forces, women received regular military training. A special facility, the Women's Sabotage Officers' School, taught the "black arts" of derailing trains, torching warehouses, and doing general mischief.[77]

Home Army fighters during the Warsaw uprising. The white-and-red armband the woman wears indicates she is a member of the Polish resistance. (1944)

The Home Army could also call upon an extensive network of Girl Scouts and Boy Scouts. These youngsters swore to uphold the creed of the resistance: "Fight stubbornly for Poland's independence. . . . Serve your country honestly. . . . Be unyielding, cunning, and wise while dealing with the [Nazis]. . . . Be merciless to traitors. . . . Have faith."[78]

Teenage girls learned first aid; a select few became messengers, risky work requiring poise, daring, and the ability to make split-second decisions. Their teenage brothers did "small sabotage," acts meant to defy the enemy and boost Polish morale. Youngsters set off stink bombs in movie houses favored by off-duty German soldiers, and they mutilated German wall posters, defacing images of Hitler. They placed Polish flags in conspicuous places and painted patriotic graffiti on walls. A favorite design was an anchor formed by the letters *P* and *W*, for *Polska Walcząca* (Fighting Poland). "It used to drive the Germans crazy," a fighter recalled. On busy streets, ten-year-olds taunted soldiers. "When will Hitler go to hell?" they shouted, and then ran like hell. When questioned, onlookers had no idea who the little devils were or where they had gone.[79]

The logo of Fighting Poland.

If you were German, 1944 was a very bad year. Wherever you turned, you saw disaster. By then, fleets of American and British planes were bombing your cities, especially Berlin, around the clock, the Americans by day, the British by night.

Hitler never visited a bombed city, never saw what his war was doing to the German people. As usual, he blamed the Jews. The Nazi press howled, "The Jew is guilty," a slogan German teachers drilled into their pupils' heads. Meanwhile, having driven the German Army out of North Africa, Allied forces invaded Italy, ruled by Hitler's crony Benito Mussolini. On the night of June 5, the largest invasion fleet in history sailed from British ports. The next morning, D-Day, troops and supplies poured ashore in Normandy, a region in northwestern France along the English Channel coast. News of D-Day thrilled Poles. A Home Army man reported: "Warsaw breathed, smiled, cried and got drunk."[80]

Yet for Germany the worst was still to come. To support the Allies in Normandy, on June 22 the Red Army launched its biggest offensive of the war. A Soviet attack was a horrific ordeal for those on the receiving end. It began with ground-shaking barrages from thousands of cannons. At the same time, batteries of "Stalin organs," multiple rocket launchers, went into action, each firing scores of missiles at a time. The explosives burst above the enemy positions, showering metallic splinters that beheaded men or cut them in two. When the barrages lifted, what the Germans called the "tank terror" began. Under an umbrella of low-flying fighter planes, masses of Soviet T-34 tanks rolled toward them at top speed, followed by waves of infantry shouting *"Urrah! Urrah!"*

Nearly every Red Army man had a personal score to settle. "This is for my mother and sister," gunners chalked on their shells. "Kill," a leaflet distributed by the millions, best reflects their hatred:

The Germans are not human beings. . . . We shall not speak any more. We shall not get excited. We shall kill. Kill the German—that is what your children beseech you to do. Kill the German—this is the cry of your Russian earth. Do not waver. Do not let up. Kill.[81]

Called Ivan, the typical frontline soldier, the Soviet version of GI Joe, took no pity on anyone caught in an SS uniform. That summer, "Ivan" overran the sites of the Operation Reinhard death factories: Bełżec, Sobibór, Treblinka. The Red Army found no one alive. Because nearly all Polish Jews had been killed by the summer of 1943, there was less and less work for the slave laborers to do. Realizing they would soon be killed, at Treblinka they had stolen guns from a storeroom, torched several buildings, and broken through the barbed-wire fences. Though guards shot most of the escapees, about a hundred survived. Afterward, Himmler ordered all three camps demolished. The Treblinka campsite was leveled, plowed, and planted with trees. Yet, Soviet newsman Vasili Grossman reported, "the earth refuses to keep its awful secret." Grossman saw in the soil countless slivers of bone, teeth, "children's shoes with red pompoms," and clumps of human hair. The forest road leading to the campsite was pitch-black, gritty, paved with human ashes. "Pervading everything is the nauseating stench of corruption, a stench that neither fire, nor sunshine, rain, snow, or wind have been able to overcome."[82]

In five weeks, the Red Army advanced 450 miles, totally destroying nearly twenty German divisions and badly mauling

another fifty. By mid-July, its spearheads were thrusting toward the Vistula, driving the shattered Germans before them. In Warsaw, the dull rumble of artillery sounded in the distance. Amazed Varsovians watched as "a shapeless mass of beaten soldiers," filthy and exhausted, trudged through the heart of their city. "Aryan" Warsaw—German citizens, civil servants, and their families—hastily joined the exodus. For five years, they'd enjoyed the good life at Polish expense. Now they packed whatever belongings fit into their cars and headed west. Poles lined the streets, watching them pass. Young women waved handkerchiefs and called in mock sorrow, "Goodbye, goodbye, we will never see you again!"[83]

On July 29, Soviet forces halted on the east bank of the Vistula, within easy striking distance of Warsaw. That afternoon, Moscow Radio urged the Home Army to rise against the fleeing Germans, promising all-out Soviet help.

There was more to this request than met the eye. Stalin wanted to seize Poland in order to protect the Soviet Union from future invasions. The tyrant knew that the vast majority of Poles despised the Russians. Poles remembered the Soviet invasion of 1919 and how, twenty years later, the Russians divided their country with Hitler. Now the Home Army was standing in the way of an easy Soviet takeover. Rather than fight the Home Army, Stalin decided to spark an uprising in Warsaw and then sit back as the Nazis did his dirty work. Though distrusting Soviet promises and still poorly armed, Home Army leaders decided to strike anyway. They hoped for a quick victory against the weakened German

forces. Victory would allow them to install a government recognized by the Allied powers before the Red Army arrived.

August 1. Warsaw streets lay quiet, hardly a soul visible. At 4:30 p.m. sharp, flags of white and red, Poland's national colors, appeared in windows across the city. From all sides, concealed men and women wearing white-and-red armbands opened fire on the Germans. Almost immediately, Home Army fighters seized key points in the central city. Taken by surprise, the already-shaken enemy panicked, suffering five hundred killed and wounded. Varsovians celebrated late into the night. "We sang, we danced, we drank wine seized from German stores. Such delight!"[84]

Their delight was short-lived. When news of the uprising reached Berlin, Himmler sent reinforcements to halt the retreat and smash the uprising. The new arrivals consisted of Waffen-SS troops and two outfits made up of convicted German criminals and Red Army deserters—men who lived for violence. The SS chief's order left no doubt about their mission: "Destroy tens of thousands."[85]

What followed was a reign of terror unlike any in European history. Not even the religious wars of the sixteenth century saw such mayhem. SS men used women and children as shields, forcing them to ride on their tanks. Killers rampaged through hospitals, shooting bedridden patients, murdering everyone in operating rooms, and spraying maternity wards with machine-gun bullets. Patrols invaded churches and convents. In one church, they tortured the priest; in another, a German wrote, "they were pissing on a cross that was leaning against the wall." In the garden of the

convent on Wolska Street, they shot thirty-two hundred civilians and filled the well with their corpses. "Very small children and toddlers were lying there in the tight embrace of their mothers, the older ones were lying close holding the sleeves and parts of their mothers' coats," a Home Army man wrote. On a single day, August 5, Nazis killed an estimated forty thousand people. Warsaw remembers that day as "Black Saturday."[86]

At sundown on August 5, an SS officer with a long name and an evil reputation took command. General Erich von dem Bach-Zelewski of the Waffen-SS was a favorite of Hitler's. "Von dem Bach," the Führer used to say, "is so clever he can do anything, get around anything." A veteran of many killing fields, he'd overseen the shooting of more than 235,000 Jews in eastern Poland and the Ukraine. As a reward, Hitler had put him in charge of the campaign against Soviet partisans, bands of armed civilians who attacked isolated German outposts. In reprisal for attacks, he had troops surround villages and execute all their inhabitants.[87]

When he arrived in Warsaw, the murderous confusion offended the general's sense of *ordnung* (order). "Wild masses of policemen and soldiers were shooting civilians," Bach-Zelewski

Erich von dem Bach-Zelewski, an SS general who was one of Hitler's favorite officers. (1944)

recalled. "I saw [a] heap of bodies splashed with gasoline and set afire. Toward that fire a woman with a small child in her arms was led." The general called a halt to the murder spree, though not from kindness. Rather than waste their time killing harmless civilians, he ordered his men to concentrate on Home Army fighters. To restore discipline, he had several German officers shot for disobedience.[88]

Bach-Zelewski attacked the Home Army with everything he had. His airplanes, based at fields near Warsaw, pummeled its positions at fifteen-minute intervals. His artillery pulverized buildings at point-blank range. "Karl," a monster cannon, fired two-thousand-pound shells from the city's outskirts, turning entire blocks to rubble. Tanks prowled the streets, supporting infantry assaults with their cannons and machine guns. Rocket

A member of the Polish Home Army tries to escape through the Warsaw sewer system, but is captured by German troops. (1944)

launchers called "bellowing cows" gave spine-tingling moans as they fired multiple high-explosive bombs. As fires raged, the general destroyed the city's electrical plants and waterworks, leaving firefighters helpless. Across the Vistula, the Red Army waited, watching but not lifting a finger to stop the mayhem.

Polish casualties mounted and cemeteries filled, forcing burial details to dig graves in city parks. Women were in the thick of the action. They fired guns and threw Molotov cocktails; a fourteen-year-old destroyed two German tanks by herself. Because the Home Army lacked field radios, women carried messages to fighting units. Another teenage girl, a messenger, ran down a burning street waving a slip of paper and yelling at the top of her voice, "I am still a child, and I am frightened." Messengers might also see humor amid the madness. When a shell exploded nearby,

A German soldier sets buildings on fire, using a flamethrower, in the Warsaw ghetto. (1943)

two girls named Anna and Marysia kept running. Suddenly, Anna stopped, laughing excitedly. "What on earth's the matter?" Marysia asked crossly. "Your bottom's bare," Anna cried. Marysia replied, "That makes two of us!" The air pressure from the blast had torn off their clothes.[89]

Meanwhile, Yitzhak Zuckerman, a leader in the Warsaw ghetto revolt, appealed to Jews still hiding in the "secret city":

To the Jews Who Remain Alive!

This is our struggle too. . . . Hundreds of Jewish youth and members of the Jewish Fighting Organization stand shoulder to shoulder with their Polish comrades at the barricades. We . . . who have survived and all the Jewish youths capable of fighting are hereby called on to continue the struggle. No one should stay behind. Through war, we shall achieve victory, and a free, sovereign, strong and just Poland.[90]

Though we will never know the exact number, Jews joined the battle, chiefly in units of the Home Army. In what must have seemed sweet revenge, they helped storm the Umschlagplatz, now used as a supply hub for Bach-Zelewski's forces. Historians think it likely that more Jews fought in the 1944 uprising than in the ghetto revolt the previous year.[91]

As Bach-Zelewski tightened his grip, the Home Army pleaded for Allied aid. With everything—food, medicine, weapons, ammunition—running low, it could not hold out much longer. Stalin allowed American and British bombers to drop supplies, but the planes had to fly from distant bases in Italy. Warsaw was

not hard to find; airmen could see the pillars of smoke rising above it forty miles away. The problem for the Allied pilots was that the German and Polish lines were so close together that they had to fly low, and as a result, their cargoes often fell into enemy hands. Worse, the missions were very costly in Allied airmen's lives and aircraft. Commanders estimated that German antiaircraft guns downed one bomber for every ton of cargo delivered, forcing the cancellation of aid operations.[92]

Rather than fight to the last person, Bach-Zelewski made the Home Army a generous—for an SS man—surrender offer. According to his terms, which Home Army commander General Tadeusz Bór-Komorowski accepted on September 28, the civilian population could leave Warsaw immediately. Of these, 100,000 were free to shelter with relatives and friends or go as refugees to any Polish town able to receive them. Another 150,000 Varsovians, the healthiest and strongest, had to go to Germany as forced laborers in factories, on farms, and in bomb-damage repair crews. Working six days a week, for ten hours a day, they'd wear uniforms with the letter *P*, for "Pole," painted on the back.[93]

As for the Home Army fighters, Bach-Zelewski formally recognized them as prisoners of war with full rights under international law, a "privilege" the Nazis never granted Soviet soldiers. Their captors would no longer shoot them or starve them and would house them in POW camps, as they did American and British captives.

On October 4, some 19,300 Home Army members, including 3,000 women, marched out of Warsaw. Unbowed after two months of desperate fighting, they left singing patriotic songs.

Polish women also fought during the Warsaw uprising. (1944)

Even Bach-Zelewski, Nazi though he was, acknowledged their courage. He allowed them to carry their weapons, a traditional "courtesy of war," before handing them over at German checkpoints. Several Germans praised the Poles. A lieutenant wrote his mother: "Let us not deceive ourselves. Warsaw fell thanks to our heavy weapons, not to the courage of our units. . . . The insurgents deserved to be treated like soldiers. . . . They marched by in step, four abreast . . . without a sign of despair, heads held high with national pride. Exemplary!"[94]

The butcher's bill came high. The Home Army suffered 22,500 casualties: killed, wounded, and missing (meaning their remains were never recovered because they were blown to bits or buried under rubble). Anywhere from 150,000 to 250,000 Warsaw civilians died in mass executions, during the fighting, or from disease.

Bach-Zelewski put German casualties at 26,000, of whom at least 10,000 lost their lives.[95]

The general received the Knight's Cross with Oak Leaves, Swords, and Diamonds, the highest Nazi medal, equivalent to the United States' Medal of Honor—and another dreadful task. Adolf Hitler now vented his fury on the city he'd always hated. The hideous order arrived from Berlin: Nothing must remain of Warsaw! Everything of use or value must go to Germany! That done, the city must be *"glattraziert"*—totally razed, torn down, flattened to the ground. What followed has been called "the greatest urban catastrophe of mankind."[96]

Methodically, teams of looters went to work. Using lists prepared by SS economists, they filled 23,300 freight cars with items taken from apartments, shops, and warehouses. These included furniture, light fixtures, lamps, doors, window frames, ovens, faucets, electric generators, brass pipes, tools, scrap iron, rope, bolts of cloth, rolls of newsprint. Warsaw's cultural treasures went to Germany in thousands of individual wooden crates, each carefully labeled and stamped with the Nazi eagle and swastika. The city's art museums, galleries, and churches yielded paintings, statues, jewelry, rare-coin collections, antique vases, golden crosses, and musical instruments. Himmler's wife got two priceless violins and four accordions.[97]

As the last loot trains left, combat engineers reenacted the destruction of the Warsaw ghetto, but on a citywide scale. Using flamethrowers, Bach-Zelewski's arsonists burned block after block of apartment houses. Methodically, they drilled holes into

the walls of public buildings, inserted sticks of dynamite, and set them off. St. John's Cathedral, Opera House, Grand Theater, University of Warsaw, National Archives, National Museum: all were reduced to rubble. In 1933, just after Hitler came to power in Germany, Nazis had flung "anti-German" books into bonfires. In Warsaw, they burned entire libraries of precious books, manuscripts, and maps. Working systematically, they torched the Polish Library and the Załuski Library, the oldest public library in Poland, which held four hundred thousand printed items.[98]

It took three months to raze Warsaw. When the wreckers finished in early January 1945, 93 percent of the city lay in ruins, a desert of broken concrete and twisted metal. A Soviet pilot wrote: "We knew that Warsaw was once the most beautiful capital in Europe. Now, when we flew over it we saw huge palls of smoke, and even from the air we could smell burned flesh. My spine crawled, to see so much beauty transformed into ruins."[99]

Not all Varsovians left the doomed city. Dubbed the "Robinson Crusoes of Warsaw," after the hero of Daniel Defoe's novel about a man's survival after being marooned on a desert island, these people had marooned themselves. After the surrender, Jewish survivors left with Polish civilians and Home Army fighters. Some made it to safety; others did not. The Gestapo still hunted Jews. As Varsovians filed past the checkpoints, "Jew-spotters" pointed out fugitives, who were hustled away and shot. Knowing the danger, the "Robinsons" decided to take their chances amid the ruins. They hid, singly or in small groups, wherever they could. No doubt the majority starved or were buried under rubble

during the city's destruction. Their only hope lay with the Red Army. And, finally, Stalin ordered it to cross the Vistula.

Wednesday, January 17, 1945. The day dawned bright and cold. It had snowed during the night, and a light dusting of snow covered the ruins. Nothing moved in the streets. All lay quiet, until the "Robinsons" realized there were no Germans—anywhere. Like burglars, the last units had stolen away in the night. From the distance, the faint hum of male voices drifted over the rubble. The sound grew louder, until soldiers appeared, clad in padded jackets and fur caps with red stars.

It happened so quickly. Franciszka Grünberg, a dentist in peacetime, carried the image for the rest of her life. In her diary, she wrote, "The Soviet troops . . . were calling out to one another cheerfully, and after a moment we could hear a happy Russian song. Like a madwoman I pounced on my son and started kissing and hugging him, shouting, 'You survived the war, my son!' I let the hot tears stream slowly down my cheeks: tears of joy, that I had kept my son from the clutches of the bloody Nazi beast."[100]

❧ VI ❧

Reckonings

This is all as true as it is strange;
Nay, it is ten times true; for truth is truth
To the end of reckoning.

—William Shakespeare,
Measure for Measure (1604)

To the Bitter End

Crushing the Warsaw uprising was the Nazis' last important military success. The year 1945 would see the end of Adolf Hitler's Thousand-Year Reich. Signs of collapse were everywhere, as the tidal wave of war crashed upon Germany. To the east, by late January, Soviet tanks were forty miles from Berlin. To the west, Allied forces were advancing against flagging opposition. Though the Führer ordered his crumbling armies to fight to the last man, thousands of German soldiers surrendered each day. Fearing vengeance, as Red Army men committed atrocities against civilians, including sexual assaults on women, German troops who could rushed to give up to American and British forces.

During those final days, the Nazis mobilized German youth as never before. Members of the League of German Maidens took

on extra tasks. Girls and young women became aides in army hospitals, held office jobs, distributed food to bombed-out civilians, and delivered mail. Several thousand helped the "rubble ladies"— teams of women who cleared debris after air raids. Others had military duties, acting as air-raid wardens, switchboard operators, and messengers. At night, "searchlight girls" aimed powerful beams skyward, illuminating Allied planes for the antiaircraft gunners—work that exposed them to punishing attacks. When, for example, a British fighter plane struck her battery, a sixteen-year-old recalled, "I felt the blood on my face; it came from my left temple. My thigh was full of [iron] splinters." As if that weren't bad enough, "the corporal had his stomach ripped open so that his guts were hanging out. I stood in front of him, not being able to move. 'Lisa, take the pistol and kill me!' I could not do it." Another six million members of the League of German Maidens and the Hitler Youth were ordered to work sixty-hour weeks in industry, the majority in munitions factories. About 500,000 youngsters, including 125,000 teenage girls, dug trenches and tank traps, "really tough" work, a boy explained, "and there was no getting out of it."[1]

The Hitler Youth also saw battle as soldiers. Boys in their early teens helped adults in antiaircraft batteries, even firing the guns. Older boys volunteered for the Waffen-SS. Allied soldiers found them the most dangerous opponents they'd ever encountered. Born in the late 1920s and early 1930s, these young men had spent their entire conscious lives under Nazism. In the Führer's view, they embodied his racist ideal; they were the "fearless, cruel, domineering" youth he'd always wanted. "The Hitler Youth young-

sters are fanatical fighters," Hitler boasted. "These young German lads, some only sixteen years old, fight more fanatically than their older comrades."[2]

The 12th SS Hitler Youth Panzer Division best illustrates the Führer's youth ideal in action. Because it was composed of teenagers from sixteen to eighteen years old, regular German soldiers called it the "Baby Division." Yet its recklessness amazed

Hitler Youth members wounded while serving with an antiaircraft battery. (1943)

Canadian troops, veterans of ferocious battles in France. "They behaved like maniacs," a sergeant recalled. When surrounded, the boys of the 12th SS refused to give up, fighting literally to the last bullet. Allied battle reports also record instances of German boys becoming suicide bombers, tying explosives to their bodies and jumping onto Canadian tanks to destroy them; others lay down and let tanks roll over them as they detonated grenades. Youngsters who'd been taught that they were born to die for Germany had no respect for the enemy, living or dead. They routinely shot wounded prisoners and spitefully drove tanks over the corpses of Allied soldiers, mangling them beyond recognition.[3]

Americans faced fanatical youngsters, too. "The fourteen-year-

Hans-Georg Henke, a sixteen-year-old German soldier, cries as he's captured by Allied troops. (1945)

olds were very dangerous," an officer noted, "because they possessed no sense of adult behavior. They might produce a grenade they had hidden, and throw it after being taken prisoner." After-action reports tell of troops capturing gun-toting eight-year-olds and knocking out artillery units made up of boys age twelve and under. And when Nazi youths fired on patrols passing through villages, GIs called in air strikes, leveling the places and slaughtering their inhabitants. Yet elsewhere, when encountering little boys in baggy uniforms weeping and trembling with fear, GIs slapped them on the behind and said, "Go home to your mother."[4]

Other child-captives spewed defiance. Bernard Schmitt, an American medic, recalled the reaction of a boy he was treating for painful shrapnel wounds: "He was about fourteen, and looked like he was in a trance. I leaned over him and said in German, 'You dummy! Look at what this has gotten you!' Well, that boy suddenly heaved himself up, spat in my face, and shouted, 'Long live the Führer!'" A French Catholic priest told how a mortally wounded boy refused religious comfort; instead, he asked for a photo of his Führer to look upon as his life ebbed away.[5]

The Nazis also turned children into murderers. When British

Propaganda minister Joseph Goebbels shakes hands with Willi Hübner, a teenage member of the Hitler Youth. (1945)

planes bombed a stretch of railroad track outside a small town, a train taking inmates from one concentration camp to another came to a halt, and seventy people were able to break out of a boxcar. An SS patrol tracked them down, herded them into a ditch, and ordered the local Hitler Youth group to shoot them. Afterward, the father of one boy confronted the officer in charge: "Why was this asked of the children? Why them, of all people?" The reply echoed Hitler himself: "We want to educate the young to be tougher and not to shy away from any horror."[6]

As the Red Army encircled Berlin, Hitler fled to his bombproof bunker buried beneath the Reich Chancellery, his official residence and office complex. Though safely underground, everyone inside felt the tremors and saw the lights flicker whenever artillery shells struck the massive building above.

The Führer had become a physical wreck by then. After the war, Traudl Junge, who had been one of Hitler's private secretaries,

recalled that all "could see Hitler falling apart." His doctor injected him with stimulants to raise his energy level; cocaine drops in his right eye reduced violent twitching. "His ravaged face was a pale yellowish gray," and his breath stank. Seeing his "complete degeneration" upset a staff officer. "His body had collapsed in on itself, his hands and legs were trembling violently, and much of what he said sounded as if he was speaking in a state of feverish delirium." His appearance terrified a telephone operator. The young woman noted, "He looked broken, burnt-out, lost." Sometimes the tyrant sat alone, staring blankly, muttering to himself. "Saliva often trickled from the corners of his mouth—a picture of misery and of horror." At other times, he became manic, shouting orders to move army divisions from here to there—divisions that no longer existed.[7]

On April 20, 1945, his fifty-sixth birthday, Hitler made his last public appearance. During a lull in the shelling, he stepped into the Chancellery garden, pitted with craters, to give medals to members of the Hitler Youth wounded in the defense of Berlin. Most wore bandages or had their arms in slings. As he came down the row, "his trembling hands clasped at his back," he paused to pat each boy on the cheek. "Heil to you!" he said as he tottered back to his underground lair.[8]

That little ceremony was all a farce, because Hitler had no true regard for those children. As ever, the big idea—racist ideology—meant *everything* to the Führer; members of the Hitler Youth were merely tools, cannon fodder, not people precious in themselves. Günter Fraschka, a Hitler Youth group leader, finally realized this. With the nation disintegrating and further resistance

futile, he despised the Führer's sacrifice of German youth. Their godlike leader, Fraschka said, had betrayed them. The young "are to him no more than kindling for the furnace. . . . For those kids the dream of life vanishes like a soap bubble as the order to attack is given." He was right. Of the 5,000 members of the Hitler Youth who fought in the Battle of Berlin, 500 survived. In all, 125,000 Berliners lost their lives before the city's surrender.[9]

Ever the hater and "lunatic of one idea," the Führer followed his inhuman ideology to its logical conclusion. For Hitler, the eternal struggle of races was *the* law of existence, and only the superior race had the right to live. Germany's defeat, he told aides, had nothing to do with his ideas or actions. Defeat merely proved the German people unworthy of his genius. "Germany," he said as if in a trance, "was probably never mature and strong enough for the task I intended it to perform."[10]

Hitler did not regret the misery he'd brought to the German people. Having failed to live up to his demands—to nature's demands—they deserved to perish. Accordingly, on March 19, he had issued the Nero Decree (Nerobefehl), named for the mad emperor who'd ordered ancient Rome burned for his own amusement. Hitler wished Germany hurled back to the Stone Age. Railroads, bridges, tunnels, mines, factories, power plants, docks, dams, communications networks, hospitals, food stocks: all must be destroyed. Because the nation had proved itself weak, he declared, "whatever remains after this battle is in any case only the inadequates, because the good ones will be dead."[11]

As for the Jews, here, too, Hitler reaffirmed his ideology. Racial anti-Semitism was so ingrained in the man that he never doubted

the rightness of destroying them. During those last days, Hitler constantly returned to the subject, taking personal responsibility for the Holocaust. He boasted to Martin Bormann, his private secretary and most trusted lieutenant, "I exterminated the Jews in Germany and central Europe." Ordering mass murder gave him pride, not shame. To be sure, he claimed, humanity owed him "eternal gratitude" for what he'd done![12]

But time was running out. Hour by hour, Soviet troops pressed closer to the Chancellery. On April 29, at 4:00 a.m., Hitler dictated his "political testament," a final justification for his actions. In it, he denied ever having wanted war. A lie. The war was the Jews' fault, and he'd punished them by "humane means." More lies. The Nazi leader ended by urging Germany's future rulers to observe "the laws of race" and to resist without mercy "the universal poisoner of all peoples, International Jewry." That afternoon, he married Eva Braun.[13]

U.S. military newspaper *Stars and Stripes* headline the day after Hitler died. (1945)

On April 30, with Soviet troops less than a half mile from the Chancellery, the newlyweds committed suicide. Hitler shot himself in the right temple. Eva bit into a cyanide capsule. SS guards carried their bodies to the garden, doused them

with gasoline, set them on fire, and buried the charred remains in a shell hole. Soviet forensic experts later identified fragments of Hitler's skull through dental X-rays. They lie today in a cardboard box in the Russian State Archive in Moscow.

Justice Done, Delayed, Denied

Members of Hitler's inner circle, who had worshipped him since the early days of Nazism, came to violent ends. Joseph Goebbels and his wife, Magda, had been so infatuated with Hitler that they gave their six children, ages five to twelve, first names beginning with *H* in his honor: Helga, Hilde, Helmut, Holde, Hedda, Heide. To the parents, death was preferable to life without the Führer. "I would," said Magda, "rather have my children die than live in disgrace. . . . Our children have no place in Germany as it will be after the war." So after Hitler's suicide, an SS doctor injected the Goebbels children with a sedative and, as they slept, crushed a cyanide capsule between each

Hitler poses for a portrait with Joseph and Magda Goebbels, and three of their children. (1938)

child's teeth. Joseph Goebbels then ordered an SS guard to shoot him and his wife. Their bodies were also burned.[14]

Heinrich Himmler, ever the coward who cringed at the sight of blood, showed his true colors after his capture by British troops in May. By then, the war in Europe was over and Germany lay in ruins. When a British intelligence officer showed the former SS chief photos of corpses in concentration camps, he claimed innocence. "Am I responsible for the excesses of my subordinates?" he asked. Those were his last words. Suddenly, Himmler bit into a cyanide capsule hidden in his mouth, dying instantly. A sergeant bound the body in telegraph wire, drove it to a deserted marsh, then dug a grave and buried it. "Nobody," the British sergeant said, "will ever know where he is buried."[15]

Thousands of lower-ranking Nazis got rough justice. In the liberated countries, enraged mobs lynched captives and collaborators; women who'd been too friendly with German soldiers were humiliated by having their heads shaved. Former concentration camp prisoners beat guards to death with fists, sticks, and shovels. At Dachau, Germany's first concentration camp, GIs, crazed at finding piles of unburied bodies, shot SS guards. In one incident, a lieutenant machine-gunned 346 guards after they surrendered. No GI ever stood trial for violating the rights of German war prisoners at Dachau; evidently, army brass thought the laws of civilized warfare did not apply to SS men.[16]

Still other Nazis met their end legally. Among those we've already encountered was Ludwig Fischer, governor of the Warsaw district, who had hoped to make the Jews "disappear through hunger and want." A Polish court found Fischer guilty of murder

and sent him to the hangman.
Waffen-SS general Jürgen Stroop,
the butcher of the Warsaw ghetto,
swung on a gallows set up amid
the rubble. Varsovians agreed that
he'd placed the noose around his
own neck; Stroop's daily reports
and accompanying photos proved
his guilt beyond any doubt. SS
major Hermann Höfle hanged
himself while awaiting trial for his
role in the Great Action, the liqui-

SS general Jürgen Stroop's photo
after his capture in 1945.

dation of the Warsaw ghetto. Josef Blösche, a.k.a. "Frankenstein,"
the sadistic guard who'd shot child-smugglers, was recognized in
a photo from *The Stroop Report*. Blösche is shown pointing his
gun at Jewish prisoners, including children, being driven from
a bunker. In 1969, East Germany tried and executed him. Franz
Stangl, commandant of Treblinka, died of a heart attack while
serving a life sentence in West Germany. On the table in his prison
cell, guards found a book of fairy tales by Janusz Korczak. We do
not know how he came by it, or why it attracted him.[17]

Historic trials took place in the city of Nuremberg, where
the Nazis had staged annual rallies in the 1930s. Judges from the
United States, Great Britain, France, and the Soviet Union conducted these "Nuremberg Trials" fairly. Because the Nazis were
meticulous record-keepers, much of the evidence against them
came from captured documents, photos, films, and the testimony
of eyewitnesses. There were thirteen separate Nuremberg trials,

held from 1945 to 1949, of leading Nazis on charges of plotting aggressive war, war crimes, and crimes against humanity. The last, a broad charge, included the T4 euthanasia program and the murder of Jews during the Holocaust.

A group known as the International Military Tribunal held the first and most important trial, which lasted from November 1945 to October 1946. Twenty-one men sat in the dock as "major war criminals." Among them was Hans Frank, governor of the General Government region, and members of Hitler's inner circle. These included second-in-command Hermann Göring, armaments director Albert Speer, and foreign minister Joachim von Ribbentrop. The war planners were Admiral Karl Dönitz, General Alfred Jodl, and Field Marshal Wilhelm Keitel.

SS general Erich von dem Bach-Zelewski deserved to stand trial at Nuremberg, but he did not. An American judge described the destroyer of Warsaw as "a mild and rather serious accountant." Shrewdly, Bach-Zelewski cut a deal with the prosecution, agreeing to appear as an expert witness against the others in return for a lighter sentence. In his testimony, he admitted that the Nazis had committed atrocities, saying they were

Hans Frank, former Nazi governor of Poland's General Government region, in the witness box at Nuremberg in 1946, on trial for war crimes.

"the logical consequences of our ideology." However, he added, the guilt lay not with plain soldiers like himself, honorable men who'd followed superiors' orders. It lay with Himmler, a "soft and cowardly" creature, and with the military war planners. The general neglected to say that he was proud of having "cleansed" vast areas of Russia of Jews and "bandits." Nor did he mention that Himmler liked and trusted him, signing his letters to him "Your loyal Heinrich."[18]

Bach-Zelewski's testimony stunned the men in the dock. During a short break, he smirked when Göring shouted: "Why, that dirty, bloody, treacherous swine! . . . He was the bloodiest murderer in the whole goddamned setup!" The general, that *"Schweinhund,"* that filthy "pig-dog," was "selling his soul to save his stinking neck!" True enough, yet his testimony was devastating. Because of it and other evidence, the judges convicted Göring and sentenced him to death, but he cheated the gallows by taking cyanide. Afterward, the *Schweinhund* testified at war-crimes trials at least twenty-nine times. Bach-Zelewski eventually received a ten-year prison sentence but was let go; he never stood trial for war crimes. Arrested again in 1961, he was sentenced by a West German court to life in prison for the murder of six Communists in 1931. He died in a prison hospital, of natural causes, in 1972. A Nazi to the end, he declared, "I am still an absolute Hitler man."[19]

Hans Frank said he was not. After his arrest, GIs, enraged by the horrors they'd seen, formed a double line and beat Frank as he stumbled into prison. At Nuremberg, the rabid anti-Semite must have known the judges would condemn him, because every scrap

of evidence confirmed his guilt. The evidence included his diary, all forty-two volumes of it, in which he called Jews "malignant gluttons" and made statements such as this gem: "That we sentence 1,200,000 Jews to die of hunger should only be noted marginally." What happened next, however, shows that even the worst criminal may repent.[20]

Father Sixtus O'Connor, a U.S. Army chaplain, converted Frank to Catholicism—a conversion that he believed was genuine. However, others thought that Frank was faking and his "conversion" was a scam to save his neck. Whatever the reason, Frank confessed his sins and begged God's forgiveness. The man who'd once said "I belong to the Führer" now said "Hitler was the devil." He blamed his own stupidity for allowing Hitler to seduce him: "I have a great feeling of guilt—I have a feeling that I ran after Hitler like a wildfire without reason." On the witness stand, Frank said Hitler's guilt "is mine too, for we have fought Jewry for years and . . . my own diary bears witness against me. . . . A thousand years will pass and this guilt of Germany will not be erased." Sentenced to hang, he thanked the court for its fairness, adding, "I deserved it, and I expected it." On the fatal day, he approached the gallows with a smile on his face. Reporters invited by the court as witnesses thought he "gave the appearance of being relieved at the prospect of atoning for his evil deeds." Father O'Connor, who stood beside Frank as the trapdoor opened beneath him, claimed to have heard his last words: "Jesus, have mercy."[21]

Children of Monsters

Old Doctor Korczak understood that a family's history, no less than its present situation, shapes its children's image of themselves and their place in the world. Historians of the Holocaust are fortunate, for Jews recorded their reactions to events in diaries, memoirs, and poems. In this regard, we need only mention Anne Frank (1929–1945), a teenager whose *Diary of a Young Girl,* written while she was in hiding in Amsterdam, has become a literary classic. We should remember, however, that Nazi criminals were often family men, too. Amazingly, some of the worst seem to have been decent parents.

While Adolf Hitler never had children of his own, he was affectionate toward the children of others. His affection, often seen in photos, may have been an act to endear him to Germans as "father" of the nation. Yet men who knew Hitler said that their children "simply adored him" and that he was never so relaxed as when in

Hitler with Joseph Goebbels and his daughter Helga. (Date unknown)

their company. "It was one of the few moments," an aide recalled, "when a warm human feeling broke through." Alfred Nestor, the son of a high-ranking SS officer, always looked forward to visiting the Führer. "He loved children and used to dandle me on his knee," Nestor wrote about the man he called "Uncle Adolf." This raises an important question: If Hitler and other Nazi leaders were as described, how could they have murdered Jewish children? The likely answer attests to the evil power of racist ideology. Though they loved "racially pure" children, they could not imagine young "race enemies" as human beings.[22]

Ultimately, the children, grandchildren, nieces, and nephews of war criminals had to confront their elders' crimes. Being human, they did so in ways ranging from love to denial, shame, and hatred.

The Himmler family remains torn by Heinrich Himmler's legacy. Born in 1929, his daughter Gudrun, whom he nicknamed "Püppi" (Little Doll), was a fervent Nazi. According to a recent biography, Himmler and his daughter "had a close and loving relationship." Unable to believe her father could harm anyone, she thought the Allies framed him for others' crimes. Gudrun proudly gave the Hitler salute and led Silent Aid, a relief organization that helped aging SS veterans. In 2011, a London newspaper reported that Gudrun, who died in 2018, still worked "to keep the Nazi flame alive." But that was no easy task. After Germany's defeat, the victors uprooted the Nazi educational system. The Hitler Youth vanished, as did Nazi teachers and textbooks. In today's Germany, it is a crime to preach racism, deny the Holocaust, or fly the swastika flag.[23]

Katrin Himmler, the SS chief's great-niece, a freelance author by profession, is mortified to belong to "this terrible family." Born in 1967, Katrin utterly rejects racist ideology and anti-Semitism. Indeed, she married the Israeli son of a Holocaust survivor, with whom she had a son who knows all about his ancestry. Katrin's father-in-law lived in the Warsaw ghetto as a child. He escaped with his family, surviving on the Aryan side with forged papers provided by Żegota.[24]

Hermann Göring's daughter, Edda, was born in 1938. Like Heinrich Himmler, Göring was a doting father. Adolf Hitler was Edda's godfather. Edda, who died in December 2018, never spoke publicly about her father's service to the Führer. Nevertheless, she resented the Allies, particularly the Americans, for branding him a war criminal and indirectly killing him. "I love him very much, and cannot be expected to judge him any other way. He was a good father to me, and I have always missed him. That is all you need to know," she told an interviewer.[25]

Göring's great-niece Bettina and her brother have practiced their own version of eugenics. An expert in herbal medicine, Bettina lives in New Mexico because she wants to be as far away from her family's roots as possible. As a child, Bettina learned about her great-uncle and what he stood for. It disgusted her. But his ghost haunted her; she saw him every time she looked in the mirror. "The eyes, the cheekbones, the profile—I look just like him. I look more like him than his own daughter." She and her brother, burdened with their relative's guilt, decided they "didn't want any more Görings." Her brother had himself sterilized. "I cut the line," he explained. So did Bettina, who is married. "I had

myself sterilized so I would not pass on the blood of a monster," she said.[26]

Hans Frank's claim to religious conversion could not persuade his sons Norman (born 1928) and Niklas (born 1939) to forgive him. Norman, who died in 2010, said he "cried for his father often," and was puzzled about why "a man I love" had become corrupted by Nazi ideology. Yet he did, and that drove Norman to a sad but true conclusion: "Even being highly educated does not shield you from horrible crimes." Therefore, Norman, like Bettina Göring and her brother, decided not to have children. "I don't think the Franks should go on," he explained. "The son of a war criminal does not have permission to have children."[27]

Niklas Frank disagrees; he is married and has a daughter. To this day, he is haunted by a childhood memory. In 1942, his mother took him, at the age of three, on one of her shopping sprees in the Warsaw ghetto. He recalls driving slowly along crowded streets with his nose pressed against the limousine's window. They passed "skinny people in flapping clothes and children who stared at me with goggle eyes." Those skinny ones had "such beautiful stars on their arms, and the—the men over there, the ones with whips . . ." The gleaming black car stopped outside a shop, and while Mummy bought anything she wished at "special" prices, "I stayed in the car and stuck my tongue out at another child. He went away, and I was the winner." Later, a tall man with twin lightning bolts on his collar took Niklas for a walk. Pausing before a half-open door, the man picked Niklas up so he could see inside. " 'There's a wicked, wicked witch sitting in there!' says the man." Niklas saw the wreck of a woman staring blankly at the

floor. "I start to cry. 'She won't hurt you, she'll soon be dead,' the man comforts me."[28]

Of all the children of top Nazi criminals, Niklas is the most bitter. After his father's execution, he despised him for running "the largest slaughterhouse in history." Now a journalist, Niklas refers to his father as "that sweet-talking slimehole of a Hitler fanatic," spouting "cowardly crap." In his daydreams, the son travels back in time, pleading with his father to change before it is too late: When Heinrich Himmler visits, he should put "a bit of strychnine," a deadly poison, into his wine! He should quit shouting *"Ja, mein Führer"*—"Yes, my Führer"—to Adolf Hitler and be a man! Say "Kiss my ass, *mein Führer!*" Niklas still carries a photo of his father's corpse in his wallet "so I'm sure he's dead." Even so, "I can never distance myself from him. . . . With every passing year and every new detail I learn about him, I hate him more and more."[29]

Lower-level figures such as the leaders of the Einsatzgruppen paid for their crimes on the gallows, but most shooters escaped. Out of fear or shame, they hid their guilt from their children. Time, however, is a tattletale that reveals even the deepest secrets. A family might seem perfectly normal, until, in an unguarded moment, the truth slips out. Learning about a parent's crimes can be devastating. We know of cases where love and respect vanished in an instant, leaving only guilt for having been born to a killer.

Once, for instance, a young man identified only as Rudolf heard his father talk when drunk about his service in Russia. During a mass execution, he "had to shoot the children one by one

with a handgun," because the intoxicated SS men had aimed their machine guns too high. "Today," Rudolf says, "I am a German, a German bearing the identity of the son of a criminal. A life sentence. Reason: son of a murderer." When his father died, he attended the funeral, like a dutiful son. The next night, "I went back to the cemetery and pissed on his grave. I trampled on it, went crazy, cried. It was terrible. That was my farewell. I never went back there."[30]

Aftershocks

Poland was freed from Nazi tyranny, but it was not free. Joseph Stalin had no intention of withdrawing his forces, much less allowing Poles to choose their own government. Instead, he set up a puppet regime with a Polish face. Though Poles held every office, the real power lay with their Soviet "advisers" and the NKVD, Stalin's version of the Gestapo.

The NKVD set out to "decapitate" Poland, much as the Nazis had tried to do. It arrested anyone who might spark resistance to Soviet rule: teachers, journalists, priests, civic leaders, trade union officials. Astonishingly, it rounded up over sixty thousand people by the end of 1945. Of these, about half ended up in Siberian slave-labor camps or NKVD execution cells.[31]

Poland's Soviet "liberators" went even further, attacking patriots who'd resisted Nazi rule for six years. The NKVD, assisted by Polish Communists, dismantled the Polish underground, imprisoning or shooting nearly all its leaders. The Home Army, the mili-

tary arm of the underground, was as staunchly anti-Communist as it was anti-Nazi. "We want for Poland to be governed by the Poles who are faithful to her, and chosen by the entire nation," a spokesman declared. The Home Army waged a guerrilla war against the Communists. Striking swiftly, its detachments raided NKVD camps and prisons, freeing hundreds of patriots. Larger units fought pitched battles with Red Army troops, claiming hundreds of lives. Yet, as in the Warsaw uprising of 1944, the enemy was too strong. By 1947, the "Iron Curtain" had descended across Eastern Europe, and Poland was firmly in Communist hands. Up to twenty thousand Home Army veterans served long terms in Soviet prisons, and few of them returned to their families.[32]

The Communists barred patriotic Poles from public life. Żegota, the Polish resistance group that had aided Jews, was also linked to the underground and thus was a target. Zofia Kossak, known for her denunciations of both Nazism and Communism, became a marked woman. In June 1945, Jakub Berman, a Polish Jew and a loyal Communist, quietly called her to his office. Berman, as head of the Ministry of Public Security—the Polish secret police—was a top Stalin henchman. Knowing what she'd done to help his people, he advised her to escape while she still had the chance. Kossak fled to London, returning home when it seemed safe in 1957. She died in 1968 at the age of seventy-eight.

By then, most of Poland's surviving Jews had left the country. As the American journalist Janet Flanner observed during a visit, at the end of the war Jews felt as if they were "walking around in a cemetery. . . . Many would go anywhere on earth if they could only leave the scene of the tortures and murder of their families."

Of the 3.3 million Jews alive in Poland in 1939, over 90 percent died in the Holocaust. Roughly 350,000 survived, chiefly those who'd fled to Soviet territory when the war began and returned afterward.[33]

During the Nazi years, many Poles took advantage of the Jews' plight. Once the Nazis drove a family from its home, neighbors, especially in small towns and villages, scrambled to take over their property. When survivors returned, they might be greeted with "What! Still alive?" Local people resisted the Jews' efforts to reclaim property that Poles had come to regard as their own. As a result, anti-Semitism, always present to a degree, intensified. Between the summer of 1945 and the summer of 1946, roughly fifteen hundred Jews were murdered by Poles. The deadliest episode occurred in the city of Kielce, during which Polish soldiers and police officers participated in the slaughter of more than forty Jews. These murders triggered a stampede, as a quarter of a million Jews fled to West Germany (of all places), where the Allies housed them in "displaced persons" camps. From the camps, Zionist organizations smuggled whomever they could into Palestine. Britain, hoping to placate the Arab majority there, seized immigrant ships and returned their passengers to the DP camps. Yet the war had finished Britain as a world power. Disheartened and broke, in February 1947, the London government decided to give up control of Palestine. The United Nations then voted to partition it into two independent nations, one Arab and one Jewish.

The Middle East Connection

On May 14, 1948, as the last British troops left Palestine, Zionist leaders announced the creation of the State of Israel. In the war that followed, the armies of Egypt, Syria, Lebanon, Transjordan (today's Jordan), and Iraq attacked. "This will be a war of extermination and a momentous massacre," declared General Azzam Pasha, head of the Arab League, vowing to finish what Hitler had begun. It was not to be; the Israelis routed the invading armies, and over 550,000 Palestinian Arabs fled their homes. Most went to refugee camps on the West Bank of the Jordan River and the Gaza Strip, which the UN had assigned to a future Palestinian state— areas today governed by the Palestinian Authority and the terrorist group Hamas (Islamic Resistance Movement). Jewish refugees went in the opposite direction. In 1948, around 870,000 Jews were living in Arab lands, where Jews had lived for centuries. Within seven years, roughly half a million Jews had fled to Israel.[34]

That the Arab-Israeli conflict continues is due in part to Nazi influence. During World War II, renegade Arabs broadcast to the Middle East from Berlin. "Kill the Jews," cried Muhammad Amin al-Husseini, an exiled Palestinian leader and friend of Heinrich Himmler. "Kill them wherever you find them. This pleases God, history, and religion. This serves your honor. God is with you!" After Germany's defeat, thousands of Nazis, including wanted war criminals, escaped from Europe. Many went to South America, chiefly Argentina, where President Juan Perón welcomed them. Many others made their way to Egypt, Syria, and Iraq. Stung by their 1948 defeat, Arab rulers in these countries hired

Nazis to upgrade their armed forces and intelligence services. Egypt led the way. Its army had a secret unit of four hundred SS and Gestapo veterans to train its commandos and Palestinian terrorists. In about 1953, the unit planned the initial terrorist attacks into Israel by way of the Gaza Strip.[35]

Specialists in anti-Semitic propaganda spread Nazi ideology, intensifying Arab resentments. As the enemy of their Jewish enemy, Hitler was admired by countless Arabs. (Yet Hitler despised Arabs, privately calling them "semi-apes who deserve to be flogged.") In 1953, Colonel Muhammad Anwar el-Sadat, a future Egyptian president, declared: "Dear Hitler. I welcome you with all my heart. . . . You are eternal." Hitler was given an Arabic name, Abu Ali (Real Manly Man), and linked to Allah—God in Arabic. As this ditty put it:

> *In heaven Allah is your master*
> *On earth it is Adolf Hitler.*

Hitler's *Mein Kampf* became a must-read; the Arabic translation sold 911,000 copies in 1956–1958 alone. Praising Hitler was such a fad that parents named their sons after him. Nazi anti-Semitic writings and cartoons continue to circulate in the Middle East. To this day, militants give the Nazi salute at anti-Israel rallies and carry signs reading "God Bless Hitler" and "Be Prepared for the *Real* Holocaust!" Broadcasters for the Palestinian National Authority, which governs the Gaza Strip and parts of the West Bank, the landlocked territory near the Mediterranean coast bordered by the Jordan River, exalt Hilter, he of "blessed memory,"

Hitler's *Mein Kampf* in Arabic. (1956)

for killing "the most vile criminals on the face of the earth." Palestinian Authority schools and mass media teach youngsters to hate the "Zionist vermin"; preachers proclaim the glory of dying for a Jew-free Palestine. And, yes, they portray Jews as the root of all evil.[36]

Newly sworn-in Hezbollah fighters give the Nazi salute. (2009)

Legacies

In 1948, as fighting raged in Palestine, the Polish secret police arrested Irena Sendler on suspicion of treason. She was married and pregnant. In Gestapo fashion, she was questioned so brutally that she miscarried, losing her baby. Released in 1949 for lack of evidence, Sendler lived in obscurity, employed in various social work positions. In 1965, Yad Vashem honored her with the title "Righteous Among the Nations." Yet the Communist government of Poland would not allow her to travel to Jerusalem to receive the award. Though she remained largely unknown outside Poland and Israel, in 1999 high school students in Kansas performed *Life in a Jar,* a play based on her life. Over the years, the play brought her increasing recognition. In 2007, she was nominated for the Nobel Peace Prize but lost out to former vice president Al Gore, for his campaign against global warming. She died in May 2008, at the age of ninety-eight, in a Warsaw nursing home.

Meanwhile, Sendler's city became a symbol of the evils of racism in all its forms. In 1949, African American scholar and civil rights activist W. E. B. DuBois visited Warsaw. The 1940s were a bleak time for black people. The "color bar," as DuBois called racial segregation, prevailed, especially in the South, where state legislatures were enacting so-called Jim Crow laws. Owing to the alleged "inferiority" of African Americans, these laws locked black people into wretched housing, education, and employment. In Northern cities, blacks had been living in ghettos since the late 1800s. Though America's urban ghettos lacked walls, gates, and armed guards, they were in fact centers of oppression.

What DuBois saw prompted him to write "The Negro and the Warsaw Ghetto," an essay in which he linked "the Jewish problem" and "the Negro problem." Both reflected a mind-set that placed people in rigid categories based on so-called racial traits. Yet traits like morality, character, creativity, and work ethic had nothing to do with "blood," DuBois insisted, and everything to do with upbringing. "The race problem in which I was interested," he wrote, "cut across lines of color and physique and belief and status and was a matter of cultural patterns, perverted teaching and human hate and prejudice, which reached all sorts of people and caused endless evil to all men." The Warsaw ghetto was, in DuBois's opinion, the worst-ever expression of race-hatred. He added, "I have seen something of human upheaval in this world: the screams and shots of a race riot in Atlanta; the marching of the Ku Klux Klan; the threat of courts and police; the neglect and destruction of human habitation; but nothing in my wildest imagination was equal to what I saw in Warsaw in 1949."[37]

Reconstruction began within weeks of the German withdrawal. Usually, it went slowly, due to the scarcity of building materials and government inefficiency. With the collapse of Communism in Eastern Europe beginning in 1989, the Soviet Union began to withdraw its troops, stationed there since the end of World War II. Also in 1989, the pace of rebuilding increased as Poland held its first free elections in half a century.

Janusz Korczak's Warsaw is gone. A modern city of steel, concrete, and glass has arisen in its place. Nevertheless, it is a history-aware city like none other. Reminders of tragedy and heroism—memorial plaques and monuments—are everywhere.

The Little Insurgent
statue in Warsaw. (2008)

The Warsaw Uprising Monument, which honors the heroes of 1944, depicts insurgents, some wearing captured German helmets, going into action. *The Little Insurgent,* a statue of a boy holding a submachine gun, commemorates the youngsters who gave their lives in the struggle.

Of the Warsaw ghetto itself, little more than street names remain. Blocks of modern apartment houses dominate the space, but there are traces of the past. A fragment of redbrick wall survives at 62 Złota Street as a memorial to those it once imprisoned. At the site of the Umschlagplatz, a white stone monument resembling open boxcars marks the Jews' departure point for Treblinka. Since their full names are unknown, and there would have been no room for so many names anyhow, the designers inscribed a list of all known Polish Jewish first names. A monument called the Anielewicz Mound stands on the site of 18 Miła Street, where Mordechai Anielewicz and his fighters made their last stand. Their remains lie beneath the rubble mound. On April 19, 2013, the seventieth anniversary of the Warsaw ghetto revolt, the Museum of the History of the Polish Jews opened on the site of the former ghetto. A massive structure, the museum tells the thousand-year history of Poland's Jewish community through exhibits and educational and cultural programs.

Janusz Korczak is a beloved figure in today's Poland. For

The Dom Sierot orphanage today. (Date unknown)

reasons we cannot explain, General Bach-Zelewski's wreckers spared the Dom Sierot building at 92 Krochmalna Street. Now called Children's Home No. 2, it is dedicated to Korczak's memory. A bronze bust of him watches over the place from a pedestal near the entrance, and a memorial plaque to Madame Stefa is set into the building's wall. Indoors, whimsical moldings of animals and Winnie-the-Pooh look down, as they did when the Old Doctor and his children left for the ghetto. The *Janusz Korczak Monument* in the city center portrays the educator embracing six children and standing in front of the trunk of a massive tree whose branches are arranged as a *menorah*, the candelabra lit in celebration of Hanukkah, the Jewish Festival of Lights. A monument at the Jewish Cemetery depicts Korczak's last walk. He is carrying

The *Janusz Korczak Monument* in Warsaw. (2010)

one child, whose arms are wrapped around his neck, and he holds the hand of another, who is followed by three more children.[38]

Korczak's work for children is acclaimed worldwide. In 1971, Soviet astronomers named a newly discovered asteroid "2163 Korczak" in his memory. In 1978, UNESCO recognized the centennial of his birth as "a memorable date in the history of humanity." The 1990 film *Korczak* dramatized his ghetto years, as did Jeffrey Hatcher's play *Korczak's Children* (2006) and Adam B. Silverman's opera *Korczak's Orphans* (2009). The Polish government declared 2012 "the Year of Janusz Korczak." A Janusz Korczak International Association promotes the study of his writings and spreads his message. Outside Poland, schools bear his name, and postage stamps his image. He received, posthumously, the German Peace Prize. German teachers read his works, above all *How to Love a Child,* and apply his theories in their classrooms.

The Old Doctor's ideas are also reflected in the first human

rights document ever issued by a world body. In 1924, the League of Nations, established after World War I to keep the peace, issued the Declaration of the Rights of the Child. This document bears the signatures of leading educators, among them Janusz Korczak, who helped to draft it. The declaration recognizes that every child is entitled to "normal development, both materially and spiritually": not only proper food, clothing, and shelter, but "protect[ion] against every form of exploitation."[39]

The United Nations, the League's successor, reissued and updated the Declaration of the Rights of the Child in 1959 and again in 1989. The revised versions reject eugenics, the idea of breeding "superior" and eliminating "inferior" races. As Korczak taught, they hold every child precious. Moreover, "the child who is physically, mentally and socially handicapped" is entitled by his very humanity to "special treatment, education and care." Likewise, the child must not be brainwashed, enslaved to an ideology, but educated "on the basis of equal opportunity to develop his abilities, his individual judgment, and his sense of moral and social responsibility." Most important, children are to be valued for themselves, "for their own good," not as tools for realizing adult goals.[40]

Children's Rights in the Age of Terrorism

Toward the end of her life, in an interview with ABC News, Irena Sendler voiced her frustration with how little the world had learned. "After the Second World War, it seemed that humanity understood something and that nothing similar would happen

again," she said, then added sadly, "Humanity has understood nothing. Religious, tribal, national wars continue. The world continues to be in a sea of blood."[41]

Her lament would have gladdened Adolf Hitler. He had believed that nature requires the extermination of the "racially inferior." But there were (and are) those who believe that killing for political or religious ends is morally justified. And some have not hesitated to use children to achieve their goals. There are many modern instances of adults sacrificing children—enough to fill a separate book. Let these suffice.

During America's active participation in the Vietnam War (1965–1973), the North Vietnamese and their Vietcong partners enlisted boys and girls as young as thirteen as fighters, spies, and suicide bombers. In one case, a Vietcong fighter gave a little girl an unpinned hand grenade and told her to give it to her teacher. An eyewitness related: "At the classroom door the child drops the grenade, killing herself and injuring nine children." Recruiters preferred children, a scholar explained, "because they are more easily influenced in their thinking, are willing to run risks . . . and are less likely to question the arrangements for an operation"— precisely the thinking of Hitler Youth leaders. Many Vietnamese children received awards and titles such as "Valiant Destroyer of the Yanks." An uncounted number, however, were killed, maimed, or psychologically damaged for life.[42]

More recently, a civil war in South Sudan has been flickering on and off since 2013. It is a struggle for political power between the central government and breakaway groups. Both sides

have forced children to become, in effect, military slaves. Human Rights Watch has detailed accounts of villages being raided by opposing forces, and boys and girls kidnapped and made to fight or work for their keep. A seventeen-year-old told interviewers how his unit was ordered to commit atrocities: "The order was to kill anything we found. . . . There were also those who took the children—some of them infants—by their ankles to crush their heads against the trees or any hard thing. And then civilians were taken into a house and the soldiers set it on fire. I saw it." Again history repeated itself: Hitler's Einsatzgruppen committed exactly the same crimes.[43]

Others sacrifice children in order to destroy unbelievers and convert the world to their view of the one "true" religion. Like Judaism and Christianity, Islam teaches compassion and the sanctity of human life as a creation of Allah. The Prophet Muhammad preached that for anyone to take another's life "would be as if he slew the whole people. And if any saved a life, it would be as if he saved the life of the whole people"—that is, the human race. Islam also condemns suicide as the destruction of Allah's creation, a sin punishable by everlasting torment in hell. Islam has been a great civilizing force; even in war, its laws ban deliberate attacks on women, children, the elderly, the clergy, and the infirm. Nevertheless, a tiny fraction of the world's 1.6 billion Muslims embrace violence. Though done in the name of Islam, their actions are blatantly contrary to its teachings. Whereas Hitler acted because of "natural law," these violent extremists see their cause as so holy that they may do anything to achieve their goals.[44]

During the Iran-Iraq War (1980–1988), tens of thousands of Iranian boys as young as twelve were pulled out of school, indoctrinated in the glory of dying for the faith, and sent to the front with a plastic "key to Paradise" tied around their necks. Upon the wearer's death, the key was supposed to open the heavenly gates for his spirit. Chanting *"Allahu akbar"*—"Allah is the greatest"— the boys ran into minefields, detonating the explosives with their bodies to clear paths for the assault troops that followed. Like Allied soldiers facing fanatical members of the Hitler Youth, Iraqis were appalled by the slaughter. "You can shoot down the first wave and then the second," an officer said. "But at some point the corpses are piling up in front of you, and all you want to do is scream and throw away your weapon. Those are human beings, after all!"[45]

One hundred thousand Iranian boys are thought to have died in "human wave" attacks. Each boy's family received a "certificate of martyrdom," entitling its members to discounts on food and other things. As Ayatollah Ruholla Khomeini, Iran's supreme leader, said, "The Tree of Islam can only grow if it's constantly fed with the blood of martyrs." So when the Iraqis wanted to return boy-captives as part of a prisoner exchange, Khomeini would not hear of it. Like Hitler saying that all good Germans had already died by 1945, the ayatollah refused to accept those youngsters. "They are not Iranians," he declared with certainty. "Ours have gone to paradise and we shall see them there."[46]

Likewise, early in the twenty-first century, in Afghanistan and Pakistan, the Taliban, a fundamentalist Islamic militia, see chil-

dren as expendable, as objects to use and use up as needed. Qari Abdullah, a Taliban commander in charge of recruiting children, was brutally clear. "If you're fighting, then God provides you with means [to win]," he said. "Kids themselves are tools to achieve God's will. And whatever comes your way, you sacrifice." A fellow recruiter further explained, "Children are innocent, so they are the best tools." Notice: The Taliban openly acknowledge that they regard children as instruments, not as people.[47]

Many groups similar to the Taliban run schools to brainwash children into becoming suicide bombers. The groups' aim is to create anxiety, terrorizing those under threat to the point where they fear even leaving their homes to shop or go to work. In Syria and Iraq, ISIS (Islamic State) trained preteens as terrorists, desensitizing them to violence by having them shoot prisoners or slit their throats. ISIS also uses children as remote-controlled bombs. Echoing the Nazi euthanasia program, ISIS issued a *fatwa* (religious decree) in 2015 urging the faithful to "kill newborn babies with Down's syndrome and congenital deformities and disabled children." ISIS, too, enslaved girls and young women. An official pamphlet did not mince words: "It is permissible to buy, sell, or give as a gift female captives and slaves, for they are mere property."[48]

Shocking as such fanaticism is, it need not be the last word. For if being human means anything, it means there is no inevitable fate that we must meekly accept. Other than our mortality, the inevitable death of every living being, there is no preset "destiny" in human affairs. Like the children of a few of the Nazi

war criminals, we can learn from the past, grow, and become better people. Irena Sendler understood this, and she ended her interview on an upbeat note. The Polish Angel admired the Old Doctor. As if his spirit spoke from her heart, she said, "The world can be better if there's love, tolerance, and humility."[49]

Notes

PROLOGUE: THE TWO SADDEST NATIONS ON EARTH

1. Martin Gilbert, "Churchill and the Holocaust: The Possible and Impossible," www.winstonchurchill.org/thelifeofchurchill/war-leader/churchill -and-the-holocaust-the-possible-and-impossible.

2. David Cesarani, *Final Solution: The Fate of the Jews, 1933–1949* (New York: St. Martin's Press, 2016), 508.

3. Lucy S. Dawidowicz, *The War Against the Jews, 1933–1945* (New York: Holt, Rinehart and Winston, 1975), 197–198; Alexandra Richie, *Warsaw 1944: Hitler, Himmler, and the Warsaw Uprising* (New York: Farrar, Straus & Giroux, 2013), 131.

4. Sandra Joseph, "Janusz Korczak," www.korczak.org.uk/korczak.html.

5. Janusz Korczak, *The Children's Home*, in *Selected Works of Janusz Korczak*, ed. Igor Newerly, np.

6. "The Legend of the Thirty-Six," neveshalom.org/html/arts/art_gallery _legend36.htm; "Janusz Korczak: Sculptor of Children's Souls," jewish bookworld.org/2016/02/janusz-korczak-sculptor-of-childrens-souls-by -marcia-talmage-schneider.

7. Fritz Redlich, *Hitler: Diagnosis of a Destructive Prophet* (New York: Oxford University Press, 1998), 326. The personal physician was Karl Brandt.

8. "Man of the Century," *Time*, September 21, 1999; Redlich, *Hitler*, 338–339.

9. Ashley Montagu, *Man's Most Dangerous Myth: The Fallacy of Race* (1942; repr., Cleveland: World Publishing, 1964), 23.

10. Adolf Hitler, *Mein Kampf*, trans. Ralph Manheim (Boston: Houghton Mifflin, 1999), 339.

11. Martin Luther King Jr., "The Other America" (speech, Stanford University, 1967), vimeo.com/117362753.

12. Jonathan C. Friedman, ed., *The Routledge History of the Holocaust* (London: Routledge, 2011), 53.

13. Debórah Dwork, *Children with a Star: Jewish Youth in Nazi Europe* (New Haven, CT: Yale University Press, 1991), xxxiii; Samuel D. Kassow, *Who*

Will Write Our History? Emanuel Ringelblum, the Warsaw Ghetto, and the Oyneg Shabes Archive (Bloomington: University of Indiana Press, 2007), 308; Charles G. Roland, *Courage Under Siege: Starvation, Disease, and Death in the Warsaw Ghetto* (New York: Oxford University Press, 1992), 171.

14. Pope John Paul II, "We Remember: A Reflection on the Shoah," www
.vatican.va/roman_curia/pontifical_councils/christuni/documents_/rc_pc
_christuni_doc_16031998_shoah_en.html.

I: THE OLD DOCTOR

1. Betty Jean Lifton, *The King of Children: A Biography of Janusz Korczak* (New York: Farrar, Straus & Giroux, 1988), 13.

2. Ibid., 15.

3. Marek Jaworski, *Janusz Korczak,* trans. Karol Jakubowicz (Warsaw: Interpress, 1978), 18; Janusz Korczak, *The Ghetto Years: 1939–1942,* ed. Yitzhak Perlis (Tel Aviv: Ghetto Fighters' House & Hakibbutz Hameuchad Publishing House, 1980), 110.

4. George Z. F. Bereday, "Janusz Korczak: In Memory of the Hero of Polish Children's Literature," *The Polish Review* 24, no. 1 (1979), 29; Lifton, *The King of Children,* 25.

5. Mark Bernheim, *Father of the Orphans: The Story of Janusz Korczak* (New York: Dutton, 1989), 18–19.

6. Jaworski, *Janusz Korczak,* 128.

7. Bernheim, *Father of the Orphans,* 35.

8. Jaworski, *Janusz Korczak,* 20.

9. Lifton, *The King of Children,* 32–33.

10. Ibid., 33.

11. Ibid., 82.

12. Ibid., 33–34, 83.

13. Ibid., 40, 41.

14. Ibid., 44, 45.

15. Ibid., 122.

16. Ibid., 60.

17. Bernheim, *Father of the Orphans,* 71.

18. Elzbieta Mazur and Graznya Pawlak, "Stefania Wilczyńska: A Companion in Janusz Korczak's Struggle," www.lcm.unige.it/ricerca/pub/24/7PAWLAK-MAZUR.pdf, 131.

19. Lifton, *The King of Children*, 114.

20. Ibid., 78–79.

21. Philip E. Veerman, "In the Shadow of Janusz Korczak: The Story of Stefania Wilczyńska," *The Melton Journal*, no. 23 (Spring 1990), 15; Mazur and Pawlak, "Stefania Wilczyńska," 128; Bernheim, *Father of the Orphans*, 78.

22. Lifton, *The King of Children*, 98–99.

23. Richie, *Warsaw 1944*, 107.

24. Lifton, *The King of Children*, 105.

25. Ibid., 115.

26. Dina Kraft, "In Orphans' Twilight, Memories of a Doomed Utopia," *New York Times*, January 23, 2008; Veerman, "In the Shadow of Janusz Korczak," 14.

27. Kraft, "In Orphans' Twilight"; Joseph Steinhart, "I Remember Janusz Korczak," www.korczak.org.uk/i-remember-janusz.html.

28. Lifton, *The King of Children*, 126.

29. Ibid., 128; Bernheim, *Father of the Orphans*, 111; Jaworski, *Janusz Korczak*, 97–98.

30. Bernheim, *Father of the Orphans*, 82; Gabriel Eichsteller, "Janusz Korczak: His Legacy and Its Relevance for Children's Rights Today," *International Journal of Children's Rights* 17, no. 3 (July 2009), 386–387; Janusz Korczak, *How to Love a Child*, in *Selected Works of Janusz Korczak*, ed. Martin Wolins, trans. Jerzy Bachrach (Washington, DC: National Science Foundation, 1967), 129–130, available at Janusz Korczak Association of Canada, januszkorczak.ca/publications.

31. Jaworski, *Janusz Korczak*, 86.

32. Joop W. A. Berding, "Janusz Korczak: What It Means to Become an Educator," *Encounter: Education for Meaning and Social Justice* 17, no. 4 (Winter 2004), 15.

33. Bernheim, *Father of the Orphans*, 80; Korczak, *How to Love a Child*, 351–352; Newerly 351–352.

34. Korczak, *How to Love a Child*, 313.

35. Berding, "Janusz Korczak," 14.

36. Bruno Bettelheim, "Janusz Korczak: A Tale for Our Time," in *Freud's Vienna and Other Essays* (New York: Vintage Books, 1991), 8.

37. Jaworski, *Janusz Korczak*, 30–31.

38. Lifton, *The King of Children*, 140; Bernheim, *Father of the Orphans*, 75.

39. Joseph, "Janusz Korczak,"; Steinhart, "I Remember Janusz Korczak"; Lifton, *The King of Children*, 119; Arnon, "The Passion of Janusz Korczak," 44.

40. Lifton, *The King of Children*, 207–208; Joseph, "Janusz Korczak."

41. Joseph, "Janusz Korczak."

42. Ronald E. Modras, "The Interwar Polish Catholic Press on the Jewish Question," *Annals of the American Academy of Political and Social Science* 548 (November 1996), 171; Stewart Steven, *The Poles* (New York: Macmillan, 1982), 311.

43. Celia S. Heller, *On the Edge of Destruction: Jews of Poland Between the Two World Wars* (New York: Columbia University Press, 1977), 15–16; Isaac Bashevis Singer, *The King of the Fields* (New York: Farrar, Straus & Giroux, 1988), 172; Bernard Lewis, *Semites and Anti-Semites: An Inquiry into Conflict and Prejudice* (New York: Norton, 1986), 101.

44. Richard C. Lukas, *The Forgotten Holocaust: The Poles Under German Occupation, 1939–1945* (1986; repr., New York: Hippocrene Books, 1997), 123; Leon Weliczker Wells, "Life in the Shtetl," info-poland.icm.edu.pl /web/pop_people/jews/jewish_heritage/shtetls/Wells.shtml.

45. Irving Howe, *World of Our Fathers* (1968; repr., New York: Harcourt Brace Jovanovich, 1976), 10.

46. Heller, *On the Edge of Destruction*, 65, 145–146.

47. Chone Shmeruk, "Isaac Bashevis Singer on Bruno Schulz," *The Polish Review* 36, no. 2 (1991), 162.

48. Theodore S. Hamerow, *Remembering a Vanished World: A Jewish Childhood in Interwar Poland* (New York: Berghahn Books, 2001), 135–137; Alina Cala, "The Social Consciousness of Young Jews in Interwar Poland," *Polin: Studies in Polish Jewry* 8 (1994), 45; Rafael F. Scharf, *Poland, What Have I to Do with Thee? Essays Without Prejudice* (London: Vallentine, Mitchell, 1998), 197.

49. Elie Wiesel, *A Jew Today* (New York: Random House, 1978), 4–5.

50. Joshua D. Zimmerman, *The Polish Underground and the Jews, 1939–1945* (New York: Cambridge University Press, 2015), 275.

51. Byron L. Sherwin, *Sparks Amidst the Ashes: The Spiritual Legacy of Polish Jewry* (New York: Oxford University Press, 1997), 131.

52. Friedman, *The Routledge History of the Holocaust*, 12; William F. Hagen, "Before the 'Final Solution': Toward a Comparative Analysis of Political

Anti-Semitism in Interwar Germany and Poland," *Journal of Modern History* 68, no. 2 (June 1996), 359.

53. Samuel Chiel, "Janusz Korczak: Assimilationist or Positive Jew?" *Judaism* (Summer 1975), 320.

54. Ibid.

55. Itzchak Belfer, *White House in a Gray City* (Toronto: Janusz Korczak Association of Canada, 2016), 17, 21, 22.

56. Anna Landau-Czajka, "The Jewish Question in Poland: Views Expressed in the Catholic Press Between the Two World Wars," *Polin: Studies in Polish Jewry* 11 (1998), 26; Michael Phayer, *The Catholic Church and the Holocaust, 1930–1965* (Bloomington: Indiana University Press, 2000), 7–8; Abraham Brumberg, "Anti-Semitism and the Treatment of the Holocaust in Postcommunist Poland," www.timeandspace.lviv.ua/files/sessionBrumberg_152pdf.

57. Anna Landau-Czajka, "The Image of the Jew in the Catholic Press During the Second Republic," *Polin: Studies in Polish Jewry* 8 (1994), 170; Landau-Czajka, "The Jewish Question in Poland," 266.

58. Joel Cang, "Opposition Parties in Poland and Their Attitudes Towards the Jews and the Jewish Problem," *Jewish Social Studies* 1, no. 2 (April 1939), 242, 243.

59. Heller, *On the Edge of Destruction*, 122, 123; Roland, *Courage Under Siege*, 9.

60. Heller, *On the Edge of Destruction*, 143; Hagen, "Before the 'Final Solution,'" 354.

61. Arnon, "The Passion of Janusz Korczak," 49.

62. Stephen Bonsal, *Suitors and Suppliants: The Little Nations at Versailles* (New York: Prentice-Hall, 1946), 65–66.

63. Benny Morris, *Righteous Victims: A History of the Zionist-Arab Conflict, 1881–2001* (New York: Vintage Books, 2001), 91, 94; Heller, *On the Edge of Destruction*, 280.

64. Lifton, *The King of Children*, 196–197.

65. Chiel, "Janusz Korczak," 324; Lifton, *The King of Children*, 198.

66. Lifton, *The King of Children*, 201.

67. Ibid., 202, 203.

68. Ibid., 205.

69. Korczak, *The Ghetto Years*, 19; Belfer, *White House in a Gray City*, 26, 41; Lifton, *The King of Children*, 231.

70. Lifton, *The King of Children*, 218.

71. Ibid., 212–213.

72. Arnon, "The Passion of Janusz Korczak," 42; Efrat Efron, "Moral Education Between Hope and Hopelessness: The Legacy of Janusz Korczak," *Curriculum Inquiry*, January 2008, 51; Bernheim, *Father of the Orphans*, 124; Janusz Korczak, "The Senate of Madmen," www.religiouseducation.net /papers/rea2015-silverman.pdf.

73. Arnon, "The Passion of Janusz Korczak," 48.

II: THE HATER

1. Michael Burleigh, "National Socialism as a Political Religion," *Totalitarian Movements and Political Religions* 1, no. 2 (Autumn 2000), 7.

2. Laurence Rees, *Hitler's Charisma: Leading Millions into the Abyss* (New York: Pantheon Books, 2012), 12; Robert G. L. Waite, *The Psychopathic God: Adolf Hitler* (New York: Basic Books, 1977), 201; Hitler, *Mein Kampf*, 202.

3. Hitler, *Mein Kampf*, 206.

4. Ibid., 214–215.

5. Mukti Jain Campion, "How the World Loved the Swastika—Until Hitler Stole It," BBC News, October 23, 2014, www.bbc.com/news/magazine -29644591.

6. Dorothy Thompson, "I Saw Hitler," *Cosmopolitan*, March 1932, 13–14.

7. William L. Shirer, *The Nightmare Years, 1930–1940* (Boston: Little, Brown, 1984), 127.

8. David Redles, *Hitler's Millennial Reich: Apocalyptic Belief and the Search for Salvation* (New York: New York University Press, 2005), 151.

9. Waite, *The Psychopathic God*, 9, 19; Hermann Rauschning, *The Voice of Destruction* (New York: Putnam, 1940), 82.

10. Redles, *Hitler's Millennial Reich*, 113. The First German Empire had existed during the Middle Ages; it came to an end in 1806. The Second German Empire, created in 1871, lasted to the end of World War I.

11. Waite, *The Psychopathic God*, 371; Klaus P. Fischer, *The History of an Obsession: German Judeophobia and the Holocaust* (New York: Continuum, 1998), 362; Rees, *Hitler's Charisma*, 97.

12. Heinz Höhne, *The Order of the Death's Head: The Story of Hitler's SS*, trans. Richard Barry (New York: Coward-McCann, 1970), 43; Redles, *Hitler's Millennial Reich*, 70, 83; Alexandra Richie, *Faust's Metropolis: A History of Berlin* (New York: Carroll & Graf, 1998), 521.

13. Waite, *The Psychopathic God*, 376; Viktor Reimann, *Goebbels: The Man Who Created Hitler* (Garden City, NY: Doubleday, 1976), 58, 60.

14. Hitler, *Mein Kampf*, 107; Michael Burleigh, *The Third Reich: A New History* (London: Macmillan, 2000), 113.

15. Louis P. Lochner, *What About Germany?* (New York: Dodd, Mead, 1942), 98; "Nazi Songs," en/wikipedia.org/wiki/Nazi_songs.

16. Lochner, *What About Germany?*, 99.

17. Otto Strasser, *Hitler and I*, trans. Gwenda David and Eric Mosbacher (Boston: Houghton Mifflin, 1940), 64, 65.

18. Waite, *The Psychopathic God*, 208; Richard Rhodes, *Masters of Death: The SS-Einsatzgruppen and the Invention of the Holocaust* (New York: Knopf, 2002), 143; Adolf Hitler, *Hitler's Table Talk, 1941–1944*, trans. Norman Cameron and R. H. Stevens (New York: Enigma Books, 2000), 572.

19. Gerald Fleming, *Hitler and the Final Solution* (Berkeley: University of California Press, 1984), 15; Claudia Schmölders, *Hitler's Face: The Biography of an Image*, trans. Adrian Daub (Philadelphia: University of Pennsylvania Press, 2006), 1.

20. Redles, *Hitler's Millennial Reich*, 155; Melita Maschmann, *Account Rendered: A Dossier on My Former Self* (London: Abelard-Schuman, 1965), 61.

21. Charles Darwin, *On the Origin of Species by Means of Natural Selection, or the Preservation of Favoured Races in the Struggle for Life* (1859; repr., London: Penguin Books, 1968), 459.

22. Waite, *The Psychopathic God*, 77; Rauschning, *The Voice of Destruction*, 6; Hitler, *Mein Kampf*, 289.

23. Jayson Whitehead, "From Darwin to Hitler: An Interview with Richard Weikart," May 19, 2005, www.rutherford.org/publications_resources/old speak/from_darwin_to_hitler_an_interview_with_richard-weikart; Montagu, *Man's Most Dangerous Myth*, 31. Aryan languages include German, Greek, Russian, Hindi, and Persian, to name a few.

24. Hitler, *Mein Kampf*, 327.

25. Rauschning, *The Voice of Destruction*, 242; Gitta Sereny, *Albert Speer: His Battle with Truth* (New York: Knopf, 1995), 362.

26. Rauschning, *The Voice of Destruction*, 241; Hitler, *Hitler's Table Talk*, 118.

27. Dawidowicz, *The War Against the Jews*, 19.

28. Pope Benedict XVI quoting Pope John Paul II, w2.vatican.va/content/benedict-xvi/en/speeches/2005/august/documents_hf_benxvi_spe_20050819.colognesynagogue.hmtl.

29. Hitler, *Hitler's Table Talk*, 75–76, 114, 145, 343–344.

30. *Cross into Swastika?* (London: Hodder and Stoughton, 1940), 43, at digital
.kenyon.edu/rarebooks/5. Circumcision is a religious rite involving the surgical removal of the foreskin that covers the head of the penis on the eighth
day after a boy's birth.

31. Rauschning, *The Voice of Destruction*, 49; Hitler, *Hitler's Table Talk*, 51;
Hitler, *Mein Kampf*, 65, 290.

32. Adolf Hitler to Adolf Gemlich, September 16, 1919, in Jeremy Noakes and
Geoffrey Pridham, eds., *Nazism, 1919–1945: A History in Documents and
Eyewitness Accounts* (New York: Schocken Books, 1990), 12–14.

33. Fleming, *Hitler and the Final Solution*, 17.

34. Edward Delman, "Understanding Hitler's Anti-Semitism," review of *Black
Earth: The Holocaust as History and Warning*, by Timothy Snyder, *The
Atlantic*, December 9, 2015.

35. Bernt Engelmann, *In Hitler's Germany: Everyday Life in the Third Reich*,
trans. Krishna Winston (New York: Schocken Books, 1988), 9, 21.

36. Fischer, *The History of an Obsession*, 229; "The Edelweiss Pirates,"
libcom.org/forums/thought/the-edelweiss-pirates.

37. Carl Lamson Carmer, *The War Against God* (New York: Henry Holt,
1943), 3.

38. Redles, *Hitler's Millennial Reich*, 36; Thompson, "I Saw Hitler," 20; Scott
Christianson, *The Last Gasp: The Rise and Fall of the American Gas
Chamber* (Berkeley: University of California Press, 2010), 87.

39. Friedman, *The Routledge History of the Holocaust*, 343.

40. Detlev J. K. Peukert, *Inside Nazi Germany: Conformity, Opposition, and
Racism in Everyday Life*, trans. Richard Deveson (New Haven, CT: Yale
University Press, 1987), 238, 239.

41. Joachim C. Fest, *The Face of the Third Reich: Portraits of the Nazi Leadership* (New York: Pantheon Books, 1970), 98–100. For an overview of the
Gestapo, see Robert Gellately, *The Gestapo and German Society: Enforc-
ing Racial Policy, 1933–1945* (New York: Oxford University Press, 1990).

42. "Hitler's Willing Executioners," cbmiller.com/mpl/re-hitlers-willing
-executioners; Claudia Koonz, *The Nazi Conscience* (Cambridge, MA:
Belknap Press, 2003), 41.

43. Dawidowicz, *The War Against the Jews*, 169.

44. Daniel Jonah Goldhagen, *Hitler's Willing Executioners: Ordinary Germans and the Holocaust* (New York: Knopf, 1996), 138; Henry Friedlander, "From Euthanasia to the Final Solution," www.lbihs.at/Friedlander
FromEuthanasia.pdf.

45. Goldhagen, *Hitler's Willing Executioners,* 72; Koonz, *The Nazi Conscience,* 177; Fischer, *The History of an Obsession,* 279; Saul Friedländer, *Nazi Germany and the Jews: The Years of Persecution, 1933–1939* (New York: HarperPerennial, 1998), 285; "Anti-Jewish Laws," alphahistory.com /holocaust/anti-jewish-laws.

46. Fischer, *The History of an Obsession,* 281–282; Martin Gilbert, *The Holocaust: A History of the Jews of Europe During the Second World War* (New York: Holt, Rinehart and Winston, 1985), 71.

47. Marion A. Kaplan, *Between Dignity and Despair: Jewish Life in Nazi Germany* (New York: Oxford University Press, 1998), 122.

48. Christabel Bielenberg, *Christabel* (New York: Penguin Books, 1989), 39; Martin Gilbert, *Kristallnacht: Prelude to Destruction* (New York: HarperCollins, 2006), 95, 117.

49. Phayer, *The Catholic Church and the Holocaust, 1930–1965,* 16; Milton Mayer, *They Thought They Were Free: The Germans, 1933–45* (Chicago: University of Chicago Press, 1955), 49–50.

50. Kaplan, *Between Dignity and Despair,* 72–73; Daniel A. Gross, "The U.S. Government Turned Away Thousands of Jewish Refugees, Fearing That They Were Nazi Spies," *Smithsonian,* November 18, 2015, www .smithsonianmag.com/history-us-government-turned-away-thousands -jewish-refugees-fearing-they-were-nazi-spies-180957324; Gilbert, *Kristallnacht,* 115.

51. Robert N. Rosen, *Saving the Jews: Franklin D. Roosevelt and the Holocaust* (New York: Thunder's Mouth Press, 2006), 85.

52. Mark Jonathan Harris and Deborah Oppenheimer, eds., *Into the Arms of Strangers: Stories of the Kindertransport* (New York: Bloomsbury, 2000), 111.

53. Debórah Dwork and Robert Jan Van Pelt, *Flight from the Reich: Refugee Jews, 1933–1946* (New York: Norton, 2009), 180.

54. Sandra Joseph, ed., *A Voice for the Child: The Inspirational Words of Janusz Korczak* (London: Thorsons, 1999), 55.

55. P. S. Stachura, "The Ideology of the Hitler Youth in the Kampfzeit," *Journal of Contemporary History* 8, no. 3 (July 1973), 158.

56. Koonz, *The Nazi Conscience,* 131; Lynn H. Nicholas, *Cruel World: The Children of Europe in the Nazi Web* (New York: Knopf, 2005), 97.

57. Rauschning, *The Voice of Destruction,* 252.

58. Erika Mann, *School for Barbarians: Education Under the Nazis* (1938; repr., Mineola, NY: Dover, 2014), 21.

59. George L. Mosse, *Nazi Culture: Intellectual, Cultural, and Social Life in the Third Reich* (New York: Schocken Books, 1984), 291.

60. Gregor A. Ziemer, *Education for Death: The Making of the Nazi* (New York: Oxford University Press, 1941), 48.

61. Koonz, *The Nazi Conscience,* 137, 147.

62. Mann, *School for Barbarians,* 66–67.

63. Nicholas, *Cruel World,* 86; Louis L. Snyder, *Encyclopedia of the Third Reich* (New York: McGraw-Hill, 1976), 281.

64. Mary Mills, "Propaganda and Children During the Hitler Years," www.nizkor.org/hweb/people/m/mills-mary/mills-00.html.

65. Mann, *School for Barbarians,* 16–17, 116.

66. Eric A. Johnson and Karl-Heinz Reuband, eds., *What We Knew: Terror, Mass Murder, and Everyday Life in Nazi Germany; An Oral History* (New York: Basic Books, 2005), 47; Friedländer, *Nazi Germany and the Jews,* 38.

67. Wendy Lower, *Hitler's Furies: German Women in the Killing Fields* (Boston: Houghton Mifflin, 2013), 39; Koonz, *The Nazi Conscience,* 150; Fischer, *The History of an Obsession,* 250; Mann, *School for Barbarians,* 103.

68. *Cross into Swastika?,* 21.

69. Mann, *School for Barbarians,* 147; *Cross into Swastika?,* 17.

70. Guido Knopp, *Hitler's Children,* trans. Angus McGoech (Stroud, UK: Sutton, 2002), viii–ix.

71. Ibid., 58–59.

72. Louis Hagen, *Ein Volk, Ein Reich: Nine Lives Under the Nazis* (Stroud, UK: Spellmount, 2011), 198; Frederic C. Tubach, *German Voices: Memories of Life During Hitler's Third Reich* (Berkeley: University of California Press, 2011), 43; Nicholas, *Cruel World,* 101.

73. Richie, *Faust's Metropolis,* 462; Peter Kurth, *American Cassandra: The Life of Dorothy Thompson* (Boston: Little, Brown, 1990), 200–201.

74. Tom Segev, *Soldiers of Evil: The Commandants of the Nazi Concentration Camps,* trans. Haim Watzman (New York: McGraw-Hill, 1987), 86.

75. Peter Neumann, *The Black March: The Personal Story of an SS Man,* trans. Constantine Fitzgibbon (1959; repr., New York: Bantam Books, 1967), 51, 63.

76. Friedrich Reck-Malleczewen, quoted in Burleigh, "National Socialism as a Political Religion," 18.

77. Garland E. Allen, "Science Misapplied: The Eugenics Age Revisited," *Technology Review* 99, no. 6 (August/September 1996), 22–31, behrenttech .weebly.com/uploads/9/1/0/5/9105268/eugenics.pdf.

78. Rauschning, *The Voice of Destruction*, 246.

79. Hans Peter Bleuel, *Sex and Society in Nazi Germany*, trans. J. Maxwell Brownjohn (Philadelphia: Lippincott, 1973), 18; Waite, *The Psychopathic God*, 39; Heike B. Görtemaker, *Eva Braun: Life with Hitler*, trans. Damien Searls (New York: Knopf, 2011), 61, 62; Traudl Junge, *Until the Final Hour: Hitler's Last Secretary*, trans. Anthea Bell (New York: Arcade, 2004), 75.

80. Bleuel, *Sex and Society in Nazi Germany*, 120–121; Richard Grunberger, *The 12-Year Reich: A Social History of Nazi Germany, 1933–1945* (New York: Holt, Rinehart and Winston, 1971), 238–239; Nicholas, *Cruel World*, 57.

81. Marc Hillel and Clarissa Henry, *Of Pure Blood*, trans. Eric Mossbacher (New York: McGraw-Hill, 1976), 16; Nicholas, *Cruel World*, 57–58.

82. Leila J. Rupp, "Mother of the 'Volk': The Image of Women in Nazi Ideology," *Signs* 3, no. 2 (Winter 1977), 363–364, 371; Grunberger, *The 12-Year Reich*, 236.

83. Richard Breitman, *The Architect of Genocide: Himmler and the Final Solution* (New York: Knopf, 1991), 108–109.

84. Bleuel, *Sex and Society in Nazi Germany*, 169; Grunberger, *The 12-Year Reich*, 246.

85. Hagen, *Ein Volk, Ein Reich*, 202.

86. Ibid., 202–203; Catrine Clay and Michael Leapman, *Master Race: The Lebensborn Experiment in Nazi Germany* (London: Hodder & Stoughton, 1995), 34; "The Woman Who Gave Birth for Hitler," www.history extra.com/article/feature/woman-who-gave-birth-hitler.

87. Koonz, *The Nazi Conscience*, 273.

88. Theodore Roosevelt to Charles B. Davenport, January 3, 1913, www .lettersofnote.com/2011/03/society-has-no-business-to-permit.html; "History of Eugenics," Christian Medical and Dental Associations, cmda.org /resources/publication/history-of-eugenics.

89. Edwin Black, *War Against the Weak: Eugenics and America's Campaign to Create a Master Race* (New York: Four Walls Eight Windows, 2003), 121.

90. Edwin Black, "The Horrifying American Roots of Nazi Eugenics," history newsnetwork.org/article/1796.

91. Gisela Bock, "Racism and Sexism in Nazi Germany: Motherhood, Compulsory Sterilization, and the State," *Signs* 8, no. 4 (Spring 1983), 409.

92. Geoffrey J. Giles, " 'The Most Unkindest Cut of All': Castration, Homosexuality and Nazi Justice," *Journal of Contemporary History* 27, no. 1 (January 1992), 49; Felix Kersten, *The Kersten Memoirs, 1940–1945,* trans. Constantine Fitzgibbon and James Oliver (New York: Macmillan, 1956), 57; Grunberger, *The 12-Year Reich,* 238; Georgetown University, High School Bioethics Curriculum Project, "Chapter 5: The Nazi Eugenics Programs," highschoolbioethics.georgetown.edu/units/cases/unit4_5 .html; Karl Kessler, "Physicians and the Nazi Euthanasia Program," *International Journal of Mental Health* 36, no. 1 (Spring 2007), 7.

93. Christianson, *The Last Gasp,* 22.

94. Ibid., 25–26, 32; Janet Lyon, "On the Asylum Road with Woolf and Mew," www.english.upenn.edu/sites/www.english.upenn.edu/files/Lyon-Janet _On-Asylum-Road-with-Wolfe-Mew.pdf; Victoria Brignell, "The Eugenics Movement Britain Wants to Forget," *New Statesman,* December 9, 2010.

95. Kessler, "Physicians and the Nazi Euthanasia Program," 4; Robert Jay Lifton, *The Nazi Doctors: Medical Killing and the Psychology of Genocide* (New York: Basic Books, 1986), 3.

96. Friedman, *The Routledge History of the Holocaust,* 141; Sally M. Rogow, "Hitler's Unwanted Children: Children with Disabilities, Orphans, Juvenile Delinquents, and Non-Conformist Young People in Nazi Germany," www.holocaust-trc.org/wp-content/uploads/2013/02/unwanted.pdf.

97. Stephanie Jarrett and Bernadette Moorhead, "Social Eugenics Practices with Children in Hitler's Nazi Germany and the Role of Social Work: Lessons for Current Practice," *Journal of Social Work Values and Ethics* 8, no. 1 (2011), 1–10; Rogow, "Hitler's Unwanted Children"; Fischer, *The History of an Obsession,* 294; "Introduction to Nazi Euthanasia," www .holocaustresearchproject.org/euthan; Jeremiah A. Barondess, "Medicine Against Society: Lessons from the Third Reich," *JAMA* 276, no. 20 (November 27, 1996), 1659.

98. Lifton, *The Nazi Doctors,* 95; Gitta Sereny, *Into That Darkness: An Examination of Conscience* (1974; repr., New York: Vintage Books, 1983), 59.

99. "Cardinal Clemens von Galen Against Nazi Euthanasia," www.history place.com/speeches/galen.htm; "Euthanasia Program," www.ushmm.org /wlc/en/article.php?Moduled=10005200.

III: THE HEART OF THE TRAGEDY

1. E. L. Woodward and Rohan Butler, eds., *Documents on British Foreign Policy, 1919–1939,* 3rd series, vol. 7 (London: HMSO, 1954), 258–260.

2. Ibid.

3. Gilbert, *The Holocaust*, 87; Martin Gilbert, *A History of the Twentieth Century*, vol. 2, *1933–1951* (New York: Morrow, 1999), 259.

4. William L. Shirer, *Berlin Diary: The Journal of a Foreign Correspondent, 1934–1941* (New York: Knopf, 1941), 201; Tubach, *German Voices*, 66.

5. Władysław Szpilman, *The Pianist: The Extraordinary Story of One Man's Survival in Warsaw, 1939–45* (Toronto: McArthur, 2003); Ruth Altbeker Cyprys, *A Jump for Life: A Survivor's Journal from Nazi-Occupied Poland* (New York: Continuum, 1997), 15–16.

6. Mary Berg, *The Diary of Mary Berg: Growing Up in the Warsaw Ghetto*, trans. Norbert Guterman and Sylvia Glass (1945; repr., Oxford: One-World, 2007), 3.

7. Richie, *Warsaw 1944*, 15, 629; Rees, *Hitler's Charisma*, 183.

8. Waite, *The Psychopathic God*, 34.

9. Israel Gutman, *Resistance: The Warsaw Ghetto Uprising* (Boston: Houghton Mifflin, 1994), 11.

10. Adolf Berman, "The Fate of the Children in the Warsaw Ghetto," in *The Catastrophe of European Jewry*, ed. Yisrael Gutman and Livia Roth-kirchen (Jerusalem: Yad Vashem, 1976), 400.

11. Lifton, *The King of Children*, 247.

12. Mazur and Pawlak, "Stefania Wilczyńska," 136; Lifton, *The King of Children*, 249–250.

13. Lifton, *The King of Children*, 250–251.

14. Otto D. Tolischus, "Poles Unprepared for Blow So Hard," *New York Times*, September 12, 1939.

15. Ben H. Shepherd, *Hitler's Soldiers: The German Army in the Third Reich* (New Haven, CT: Yale University Press, 2016), 49; Halik Kochanski, *The Eagle Unbowed: Poland and the Poles in the Second World War* (Cambridge, MA: Harvard University Press, 2012), 82, 94; Jadwiga M. Biskupska, "Extermination and the Elite: Warsaw Under the Nazi Occupation, 1939–1944" (PhD diss., Yale University, 2013), 104.

16. Chaim Aron Kaplan, *Scroll of Agony: The Warsaw Diary of Chaim A. Kaplan*, trans. Abraham I. Katsh (1965; repr., New York: Collier Books, 1981), 37, 41; Maria Szubert, *Between Black Death and Red Plague: A Personal Snapshot; The Second World War and Life Under Communism in Poland Through the Eyes of a Survivor* (2014), at lulu.com, 14.

17. Niklas Frank, *In the Shadow of the Reich*, trans. Arthur S. Wensinger (New York: Knopf, 1991), 109.

18. Rees, *Hitler's Charisma*, 183; Rhodes, *Masters of Death*, 100.

19. Fischer, *The History of an Obsession*, 220.

20. Richie, *Warsaw 1944*, 126; Michael Burleigh, *Moral Combat: Good and Evil in World War II* (New York: Harper, 2011), 142; Kochanski, *The Eagle Unbowed*, 115; Noakes and Pridham, *Nazism*, 988; Phayer, *The Catholic Church and the Holocaust*, 21.

21. "Diary of a Polish Physician," www.eyewitnesstohistory.com/pfpoland .htm.

22. Nicholas, *Cruel World*, 242; Kochanski, *The Eagle Unbowed*, 99.

23. Fischer, *The History of an Obsession*, 310; Lifton, *The Nazi Doctors*, 43.

24. Friedman, *The Routledge History of the Holocaust*, 125; Gitta Sereny, "Stolen Children: Interview with Gitta Sereny," jewishvirtuallibrary.org /jsource/Holocaust/children.html.

25. Richard C. Lukas, *Did the Children Cry? Hitler's War Against Jewish and Polish Children, 1939–1945* (New York: Hippocrene Books, 1994), 108; Clay and Leapman, *Master Race*, 99–100.

26. Clay and Leapman, *Master Race*, 102; Sereny, "Stolen Children."

27. Lukas, *Did the Children Cry?*, 117; Sereny, "Stolen Children."

28. Gilbert, *The Holocaust*, 105–106, 132; Alexander Donat, *The Holocaust Kingdom* (New York: Holt, Rinehart and Winston, 1965), 17; Kassow, *Who Will Write Our History?*, 296.

29. Belfer, *White House in a Gray City*, 43.

30. Kaplan, *Scroll of Agony*, 87; Berg, *The Diary of Mary Berg*, 37.

31. Noakes and Pridham, *Nazism*, 1051–1052.

32. Dawidowicz, *The War Against the Jews*, 219.

33. Gutman, *Resistance*, 58; Isaiah Trunk, *Judenrat: The Jewish Councils in Eastern Europe Under Nazi Occupation* (New York: Macmillan, 1972), 302.

34. Richie, *Warsaw 1944*, 132; Kaplan, *Scroll of Agony*, 162.

35. Eugene Davidson, comp., *The Trial of the Germans: An Account of the Twenty-Two Defendants Before the International Military Tribunal at Nuremberg* (New York: Macmillan, 1966), 438.

36. Berg, *The Diary of Mary Berg*, 79; Ringelblum, *Notes from the Warsaw Ghetto*, 22; Kaplan, *Scroll of Agony*, 150.

37. Kaplan, *Scroll of Agony*, 234; Berg, *The Diary of Mary Berg*, 34, 36.

38. Noakes and Pridham, *Nazism*, 1052.

39. Burleigh, *Moral Combat*, 419.

40. Susan D. Glazer, "Ghettos Under the Nazis," www.myjewishlearning.com /article/ghettos-under-the nazis.

41. Michal Grynberg, ed., *Words to Outlive Us: Voices from the Warsaw Ghetto*, trans. Philip Boehm (New York: Henry Holt, 2002), 8–10; Gutman, *Resistance*, 82.

42. Gutman, *Resistance*, 77–78.

43. Bernard Goldstein, *Five Years in the Warsaw Ghetto (The Stars Bear Witness)* (Edinburgh: AK Press/Nabat, 2005), 54.

44. Ibid., 55.

45. Berman, "The Fate of the Children in the Warsaw Ghetto," 403–404; Barbara Engelking and Jacek Leociak, *The Warsaw Ghetto: A Guide to the Perished City*, trans. Emily Harris (New Haven, CT: Yale University Press, 2009), 321.

46. Lifton, *The King of Children*, 262–263.

47. Korczak, *The Ghetto Years*, 24, 25.

48. Lifton, *The King of Children*, 29, 364–365; Korczak, *The Ghetto Years*, 49; Michael Zylberberg, *A Warsaw Diary, 1939–1945* (London: Vallentine, Mitchell, 1969), 38.

49. Szpilman, *The Pianist*, 59; Kaplan, *Scroll of Agony*, 225.

50. Kaplan, *Scroll of Agony*, 57–58.

51. Snyder, *Black Earth*, 221.

52. "List of Cities by Population Density," en.wikipedia.org/wiki/List_of_cities _by_population_density; Kaplan, *Scroll of Agony*, 209.

53. Szpilman, *The Pianist*, 68–69; Kaplan, *Scroll of Agony*, 276.

54. Kassow, *Who Will Write Our History?*, 267.

55. Isaiah Trunk, "Epidemics and Mortality in the Warsaw Ghetto, 1939–1942," *YIVO Annual of Jewish Social Science* 8 (1953), 88.

56. Gutman, *Resistance*, 86; Roland, *Courage Under Siege*, 102.

57. Dawidowicz, *The War Against the Jews*, 209.

58. Roger Manvell and Heinrich Fraenkel, *The Incomparable Crime: Mass Extermination in the Twentieth Century; The Legacy of Guilt* (New York: Putnam, 1967), 102; Jacob Apenszlak, ed., *The Black Book of Polish Jewry: An Account of the Martyrdom of Polish Jewry Under the Nazi Occupation* (New York: American Federation for Polish Jews, 1943), 55.

59. Szpilman, *The Pianist*, 12.

60. Cyprys, *A Jump for Life,* 37–38; Lewin, *A Cup of Tears,* 123.

61. Kaplan, *Scroll of Agony,* 328.

62. Lewin, *A Cup of Tears,* 23; Patricia Heberer, *Children During the Holocaust* (Lanham, MD: AltaMira Press in association with the United States Holocaust Memorial Museum, 2011), 343.

63. Lukas, *Did the Children Cry?,* 33; Gunnar S. Paulsson, *Secret City: The Hidden Jews of Warsaw, 1940–1945* (New Haven, CT: Yale University Press, 2002), 69; Donat, *The Holocaust Kingdom,* 31; Ringelblum, *Notes from the Warsaw Ghetto,* 283; Irene Tomaszewski and Tecia Werbowski, *Zegota: The Rescue of Jews in Wartime Poland* (Montreal: Price-Patterson, 1994), 25; Marek Edelman, "The Warsaw Ghetto Uprising," in *The Warsaw Ghetto: The 45th Anniversary of the Uprising* (Warsaw: Interpress, 1987), 17–39, www.writing.upenn.edu/~afilreis/Holocaust/warsaw-uprising.html.

64. Lukas, *Did the Children Cry?,* 32; Jaworski, *Janusz Korczak,* 159; Berg, *The Diary of Mary Berg,* 64–65.

65. Philip Friedman, ed., *Martyrs and Fighters: The Epic of the Warsaw Ghetto* (New York: Praeger, 1954), 54; Peretz Opoczynski, "Smuggling in the Warsaw Ghetto, 1941," in *A Holocaust Reader,* ed. Lucy S. Dawidowicz (West Orange, NJ: Behrman House, 1976), 201, 202; Ringelblum, *Polish-Jewish Relations During the Second World War,* 86.

66. Lukas, *Did the Children Cry?,* 34.

67. Friedman, *Martyrs and Fighters,* 53; Ringelblum, *Polish-Jewish Relations During the Second World War,* 85.

68. Donat, *The Holocaust Kingdom,* 37.

69. Ringelblum, *Polish-Jewish Relations During the Second World War,* 64–66; Gerald L. Posner, *Hitler's Children: Sons and Daughters of Leaders of the Third Reich Talk About Their Fathers and Themselves* (New York: Random House, 1991), 21; Peter Fritzsche, *An Iron Wind: Europe Under Hitler* (New York: Basic Books, 2016), 147.

70. Ringelblum, *Notes from the Warsaw Ghetto,* 109, 222; Berg, *The Diary of Mary Berg,* 5, 52; Janina Bauman, *Winter in the Morning: A Young Girl's Life in the Warsaw Ghetto and Beyond, 1939–1945* (New York: Free Press, 1986), 67; Roland, *Courage Under Siege,* 50.

71. Katarzyna Person, "Sexual Violence During the Holocaust: The Case of Forced Prostitution in the Warsaw Ghetto," *Shofar* 33, no. 2 (Winter 2015), 109; Szpilman, *The Pianist,* 13–14; Yisrael Gutman, *The Jews of Warsaw, 1939–1943: Ghetto, Underground, Revolt* (Bloomington: Indiana University Press, 1982), 108; Berg, *The Diary of Mary Berg,* 81.

72. Jacob Celemenski, *Elegy for My People: Memoirs of an Underground Courier of the Jewish Labor Bund in Nazi-Occupied Poland, 1939–45* (Melbourne: Jacob Celemenski Memorial Trust, 2000), 49–50.

73. Lukas, *Did the Children Cry?*, 29; Friedman, *Martyrs and Fighters*, 90.

74. Ringelblum, *Notes from the Warsaw Ghetto*, 39; Jaworski, *Janusz Korczak*, 161.

75. Azriel Eisenberg, ed., *Witness to the Holocaust* (New York: Pilgrim Press, 1981), 306.

76. On the role of poetry in the Warsaw ghetto, see Frieda W. Aaron, "Yiddish and Polish Poetry in the Ghettos and Camps," *Modern Language Studies* 19, no. 1 (Winter 1989), 72–87; and Adam Gillon et al., " 'Here Too as in Jerusalem': Selected Poems of the Ghetto," *The Polish Review* 10, no. 3 (Summer 1965), 22–42.

77. Itzhak Katzenelson, "The Song of the Murdered Jewish People," trans. Noah H. Rosenbloom, motlc.wiesenthal.com/site/pp.asp?c=ivKVLcMVIsG&b =476157.

78. Lukas, *Did the Children Cry?*, 29.

79. Ringelblum, *Notes from the Warsaw Ghetto*, 52.

80. Zylberberg, *A Warsaw Diary*, 27.

81. I. L. Peretz, "All Men Are Brothers," opensiddur.org.

82. Bernheim, *Father of the Orphans*, 134; John Morreall, "Humor in the Holocaust: Its Critical, Cohesive, and Coping Functions," www.holocaust-trc .org/humor-in-the-holocaust.

83. [Betty Jean Lifton], "Who Was Janusz Korczak?," www.korczak.com /Biography/kap-1who.htm; Lifton, *The King of Children*, 270, 271.

84. Grynberg, *Words to Outlive Us*, 30; Engelking and Leociak, *The Warsaw Ghetto*, 592–593; Adam Kirsch, "Atrocious Normalcy," *The New Republic*, September 16, 2009, newrepublic.com/article/69188/atrocious-normalcy; Donat, *The Holocaust Kingdom*, 44.

85. Nora Levin, *The Holocaust: The Destruction of European Jewry, 1933– 1945* (New York: T. Y. Crowell, 1968), 712; Korczak, *The Ghetto Years*, 147, 155.

86. Lifton, *The King of Children*, 254, 255; Adir Cohen, *The Gate of Light: Janusz Korczak, the Educator and Writer Who Overcame the Holocaust* (Rutherford, NJ: Fairleigh Dickinson University Press, 1994), 57.

87. Jaworski, *Janusz Korczak*, 165; Korczak, *The Ghetto Years*, 109, 113.

88. Korczak, *The Ghetto Years*, 141, 148, 171.

89. Zylberberg, *A Warsaw Diary*, 154.

IV: A DREAM SO TERRIBLE

1. Fleming, *Hitler and the Final Solution*, 26; Peter Fritzsche, *Life and Death in the Third Reich* (Cambridge, MA: Belknap Press of Harvard University Press, 2008), 148.

2. Antony Beevor, *The Second World War* (Boston: Little, Brown, 2012), 189.

3. Robert Leckie, *Delivered from Evil: The Saga of World War II* (New York: Harper & Row, 1987), 247.

4. Max Hastings, *Armageddon: The Battle for Germany, 1944–45* (New York: Knopf, 2004), 287; Allan Hall, " 'They Seized Three-Year-Old Children and Shot Them': Darkest Atrocities of the Nazis Laid Bare in the Secretly Recorded Conversations of German Prisoners of War," *Daily Mail*, September 16, 2012, www.dailymail.co.uk/news/article-2204160 /Darkest-atrocities-Nazis-laid-bare-secretly-recorded-conversations -German-prisoners-war.html.

5. Richard J. Evans, *The Third Reich at War: How the Nazis Led Germany from Conquest to Disaster* (New York: Penguin Press, 2009), 183–184; Jonathan North, "Soviet Prisoners of War: Forgotten Nazi Victims of World War II," *World War II* magazine, January 12, 2006, www.historynet/com /soviet-prisoners-of-war-forgotten-nazi-victims-of-world-war-ii.html; Hitler, *Hitler's Table Talk*, 236; Mark Mazower, *Hitler's Empire: How the Nazis Ruled Europe* (New York: Penguin Press, 2008), 163.

6. Andreas Hillgruber, "War in the East and the Extermination of the Jews," www.yadvashem.org/untoldstories/documents/studies/Andreas _Hillgruber.pdf.

7. Adam Cohen, *Imbeciles: The Supreme Court, American Eugenics, and the Sterilization of Carrie Buck* (New York: Penguin Press, 2016), 192; Ian Kershaw, "Hitler's Role in the 'Final Solution,' " www.genocideeducation.ca /kershaw.pdf; Hillgruber, "War in the East and the Extermination of the Jews"; Timothy Snyder, *Bloodlands: Europe Between Hitler and Stalin* (New York: Basic Books, 2010), 188.

8. Redlich, *Hitler*, 173; Sereny, *Albert Speer*, 248, 262; Joachim C. Fest, *Hitler* (New York: Harcourt Brace Jovanovich, 1973), 392.

9. Sereny, *Albert Speer*, 248–249.

10. Hillgruber, "War in the East and the Extermination of the Jews."

11. Robert S. Wistrich, *Hitler's Apocalypse: Jews and the Nazi Legacy* (New York: St. Martin's Press, 1985), 121.

12. Fischer, *The History of an Obsession,* 336–337; Levin, *The Holocaust,* 245; Hillgruber, "War in the East and the Extermination of the Jews"; David Kitterman, "Germans Who Said 'No!': Germans Who Refused to Execute Civilians During World War II," *German Studies Review* 11, no. 2 (May 1988), 252. The leaders of the four killer groups were Otto Rasch, who held two doctoral degrees; Otto Ohlendorf and Franz Walter Stahlecker, who each had a doctorate; and Arthur Nebe.

13. Gail Harwood Nelson, "The Molding of Personality: SS Indoctrination and Training Techniques" (master's thesis, University of Colorado, 1972), 150.

14. "Hitler and Nazis: The Best Way to See What Anti-Semites Really Hate Is to Examine Their Own Rhetoric," www.aish.com/print/?contentID=8468 3857&section=/sem/wtj; Rhodes, *Masters of Death,* 145.

15. Ernst Klee, ed., *"The Good Old Days": The Holocaust as Seen by Its Perpetrators and Bystanders,* trans. Deborah Burnstone (New York: Free Press, 1991), 163; Fritzsche, *Life and Death in the Third Reich,* 275; Cesarani, *Final Solution,* 399.

16. Richie, *Faust's Metropolis,* 510.

17. Bielenberg, *Christabel,* 251–252.

18. Albert Speer, *Spandau: The Secret Diaries,* trans. Richard and Clara Winston (New York: Macmillan, 1976), 80.

19. "Minutes of the Wannsee Conference, January 20, 1942," prorev.com /wannsee.htm; Christopher R. Browning, *Origins of the Final Solution: The Evolution of Nazi Jewish Policy, September 1939–March 1942* (Lincoln: University of Nebraska Press, 2004), 410–414; Friedländer, *Nazi Germany and the Jews,* 339–345.

20. Gilbert, *The Holocaust,* 209.

21. Yitzhak Arad, *Belzec, Sobibor, Treblinka: The Operation Reinhard Death Camps* (Bloomington: Indiana University Press, 1999). This is the best account of the death factories.

22. Berg, *The Diary of Mary Berg,* 111.

23. Gilbert, *A History of the Twentieth Century,* 414; Lower, *Hitler's Furies,* 122–123.

24. Donat, *The Holocaust Kingdom,* 46; Ringelblum, *Notes from the Warsaw Ghetto,* 301; Fritzsche, *An Iron Wind,* 8.

25. "Minutes of the Wannsee Conference, January 20, 1942."

26. Berg, *The Diary of Mary Berg*, 135.

27. Ibid., 144–145; Friedman, *Martyrs and Fighters*, 143–144.

28. Kaplan, *Scroll of Agony*, 314–315.

29. Szpilman, *The Pianist*, 79–80.

30. Edelman, "The Warsaw Ghetto Uprising."

31. Berman, "The Fate of the Children in the Warsaw Ghetto," 406–407; Nicholas Stargardt, *Witnesses to War: Children's Lives Under the Nazis* (New York: Knopf, 2006), 179–180; Zylberberg, *A Warsaw Diary*, 52–53; Korczak, *The Ghetto Years*, 85.

32. Korczak, *The Ghetto Years*, 86.

33. Engelking and Leociak, *The Warsaw Ghetto*, 704.

34. Ibid.; Gilbert, *The Holocaust*, 388; "Hermann Julius Höfle," www.holocaustresearchproject.org/ar/hofle.html.

35. Noakes and Pridham, *Nazism*, 1157–1158; Michel Mazor, *The Vanished City: Everyday Life in the Warsaw Ghetto* (New York: Marsilio, 1994), 144, 145.

36. Berman, "The Fate of the Children in the Warsaw Ghetto," 308.

37. Engelking and Leociak, *The Warsaw Ghetto*, 164; Stargardt, *Witnesses to War*, 181.

38. Engelking and Leociak, *The Warsaw Ghetto*, 164.

39. Levin, *The Holocaust*, 320; Joseph L. Lichten, "Adam Czerniaków and His Times," *The Polish Review* 29, no. 1/2 (1984), 89.

40. Talmud, judaism.stackexchange.com/questions/74049/anyone-who-saves-a-life-is-as-if-he-saved-an-entire-world-jewish-life-or-any/74050. The Quran, the holy book of the Muslims, has almost exactly the same words: "If any one saved a life, it would be as if he saved the life of the whole of mankind" (5:32).

41. Engelking and Leociak, *The Warsaw Ghetto*, 699; Edelman, "The Warsaw Ghetto Uprising."

42. Levin, *The Holocaust*, 322.

43. Engelking and Leociak, *The Warsaw Ghetto*, 701–702; Grynberg, *Words to Outlive Us*, 152.

44. Matthew Brzezinski, *Isaac's Army: A Story of Courage and Survival in Nazi-Occupied Poland* (New York: Random House, 2012), 180; Grynberg, *Words to Outlive Us*, 161.

45. Friedman, *Martyrs and Fighters*, 157–158.

46. Engelking and Leociak, *The Warsaw Ghetto*, 594.

47. Arad, *Belzec, Sobibor, Treblinka*, 64.

48. "Gas Chambers at Belzec, Sobibor and Treblinka," www.holocaust researchproject.org/ar/argaschambers.html.

49. Sereny, *Into That Darkness*, 155; Snyder, *Bloodlands*, 268.

50. Jankel Wiernik, *A Year in Treblinka* (New York: American Representation of the General Jewish Workers' Union of Poland, 1945), 23.

51. Samuel Rajzman, "Treblinka Death Camp: An Account Before the American House Committee on Foreign Affairs in 1945," www.holocaust researchproject.org/trials/rajzmantestimony.html; Sereny, *Into That Darkness*, 157.

52. Arad, *Belzec, Sobibor, Treblinka*, 241.

53. "Treblinka Extermination Process," Historpedia, Fall 2012, sites.google .com/a/umn.edu/historpedia/home/politics-and-government/treblinka -extermination-process-fall-2012.

54. Alexander Donat, ed. *The Death Camp Treblinka: A Documentary* (New York: Schocken Books, 1979), 3, 4. "Treblinka Eyewitness Accounts in Aktion Reinhard Forum," 6.

55. Sereny, *Into That Darkness*, 189.

56. Jean-François Steiner, *Treblinka*, trans. Helen Weaver (New York: Simon and Schuster, 1967), 212; Gord McFee, "The Operation Reinhard Extermination Camps," archive.org/stream/TheOperationReinhard ExterminationCamps/MicrosoftWord-Document1_djvu.txt.

57. Arad, *Belzec, Sobibor, Treblinka*, 86; Steiner, *Treblinka*, 215.

58. Arad, *Belzec, Sobibor, Treblinka*, 120; "The 'Final Solution': Operation Reinhard—the Death Camps of Belzec, Sobibor and Treblinka," jewish virtuallibrary/org/jsource/Holocaust/reinhard.html.

59. "Treblinka Eyewitness Accounts in Aktion Reinhard Forum," 31.

60. McFee, "The Operation Reinhard Extermination Camps."

61. Arad, *Belzec, Sobibor, Treblinka*, 154–155, 158.

62. Ibid., 158.

63. Wiernik, *A Year in Treblinka*, 27; McFee; "The Operation Reinhard Extermination Camps."

64. Sereny, *Into That Darkness*, 201.

65. Kershaw, "Hitler's Role in the 'Final Solution,'"; Fischer, *The History of an Obsession*, 145.

66. Junge, *Until the Final Hour,* 88; "Henriette von Schirach," en.wikipedia .org.wiki/Henriette_von_Schirach. Henriette's husband, Baldur von Schirach, headed Hitler Youth from 1931 to 1940.

67. On village Jew-hunts, see Cesarani, *Final Solution,* 647–648; Menachem Begin, quoted in Steven, *The Poles,* 317; Elie Wiesel, *Legends of Our Time* (New York: Holt, Rinehart and Winston, 1968), 164.

68. Noakes and Pridham, *Nazism,* 939.

69. Goldhagen, *Hitler's Willing Executioners,* 157.

70. Yitzhak ("Antek") Zuckerman, *A Surplus of Memory: Chronicle of the Warsaw Ghetto Uprising,* trans. Barbara Harshav (Berkeley: University of California Press, 1993), 421, 461; "The Righteous Among the Nations," www.yadvashem.org/righteous/statistics.html; Kochanski, *The Eagle Unbowed,* 318; Hans G. Furth, "One Million Polish Rescuers of Hunted Jews?," *Journal of Genocide Research* 1, no. 2 (1999), 229.

71. Bauman, *Winter in the Morning,* 57; Grynberg, *Words to Outlive Us,* 309–310.

72. Richard C. Lukas, ed., *Out of the Inferno: Poles Remember the Holocaust* (Lexington: University Press of Kentucky, 1989), 123.

73. Paulsson, *Secret City: The Hidden Jews of Warsaw, 1940–1945* (New Haven, CT: Yale University Press, 2002).

74. Zuckerman, *A Surplus of Memory,* 421, 461.

75. Paulsson, *Secret City,* 5; Ringelblum, *Notes from the Warsaw Ghetto,* 153; Cyprys, *A Jump for Life,* 26.

76. Noakes and Pridham, *Nazism,* 1070–1071; Lukas, *The Forgotten Holocaust,* 143; Lukas, *Out of the Inferno,* 13; "Paying the Ultimate Price: Józef and Wiktoria Ulma," www.yadvashem.org/yv/en/exhibitions/righteous /ulma.asp; Tomaszewski and Werbowski, *Zegota,* 37.

77. Gillon et al., " 'Here Too as in Jerusalem,' " 26.

78. Mordecai Paldiel, *Churches and the Holocaust: Unholy Teaching, Good Samaritans, and Reconciliation* (Jersey City, NJ: KTAV Publishing House, 2006), 402, note 13; Nechama Tec, *When Light Pierced Darkness: Christian Rescue of Jews in Nazi-Occupied Poland* (New York: Oxford University Press, 1986), 111; Adam Michnik, "Poles and the Jews: How Deep the Guilt?," *New York Times,* March 17, 2001.

79. Tec, *When Light Pierced Darkness,* 111–112.

80. Lukas, *The Forgotten Holocaust,* 146; Tomaszewski and Werbowski, *Zegota,* 59.

81. Lukas, *Did the Children Cry?,* 34; Marjorie Wall Bingham, "Women and the Warsaw Ghetto: A Moment to Decide," *World History Connected* 6,

no. 1, worldhistoryconnected.press.illinois.edu/6.2/bingham.html; Vera Laska, ed., *Women in the Resistance and in the Holocaust: The Voices of Eyewitnesses* (Westport, CT: Greenwood Press, 1983), 255.

82. Zofia Kossak, "Protest!," www.jhi.pl/en/blog/2013-08-09-protest.

83. Chana Kroll, "Irena Sendler: Rescuer of the Children of Warsaw," www.chabad.org/theJewishWoman/article_cdo/aid/939081/jewish /Irena-Sendler.htm; Richard C. Lukas, "Irena Sendler: World War II's Polish Angel," www.franciscanmedia.org/irena-sendler-world-war-iis-polish angel.

84. Tilar J. Mazzeo, *Irena Sendler's Children: The Extraordinary Story of the Woman Who Saved 2,500 Children from the Warsaw Ghetto* (New York: Gallery Books, 2017), 22–23.

85. Steven J. DuBord, "Irena Sendler: Humble Holocaust Heroine," www.thenewamerican.com/culture/history/item/14540-irena-sendler -humble-holocaust-heroine.

86. Mazzeo, *Irena Sendler's Children*, 69.

87. Richard Pendlebury, "The 'Female Schindler' Who Saved 2,500 Jewish Children but Died Wishing She'd Rescued More," *Daily Mail*, May 22, 2008, www.dailymail.co.uk/femail/article-1021048/Female-Schindler-Irena -Sendler-saved-2-500-Jewish-children-died-aged-98.html; Marek Halter, *Stories of Deliverance: Speaking with Men and Women Who Rescued Jews from the Holocaust,* trans. Michael Bernard (Chicago: Open Court, 1998), 9–11.

88. Nahum Bogner, "The Convent Children: The Rescue of Jewish Children in Polish Convents During the Holocaust," www.yadvashem.org/righteous /resources/rescue-of-jewish-children-in-polish-convents.html.

89. Ringelblum, *Notes from the Warsaw Ghetto*, 136–137.

90. Mazzeo, *Irena Sendler's Children*, 106–108.

91. David M. Dastych, "Irena Sendler: Compassion and Courage," canadafreepress.com/article/3230; Dennis Hevesi, "Irena Sendler, Lifeline to Young Jews, Is Dead at 98," *New York Times,* May 13, 2008; Lukas, *Did the Children Cry?,* 161.

92. Hevesi, "Irena Sendler"; Mazzeo, *Irena Sendler's Children*, 233–234; "Irena Sendler (1910–2008)," www.jewishvirtuallibrary.org/jsource/biography /irenasendler.html.

93. Irena Sendler, "How I Rescued Children from the Warsaw Ghetto," www .dzieciholocaustu.org.pl/szab58.php?s=en_sendlerowa.php; *Irena Sendler: In the Name of the Mothers,* www.pbs/program/irena-sendler; Lukas, *Did the Children Cry?,* 164.

94. Ewa Kurek, *Your Life Is Worth Mine: How Polish Nuns in World War II Saved Hundred of Jewish Lives in German-Occupied Poland, 1939–1945* (New York: Hippocrene Books, 1997), 53, 54, 91, 94; Nicholas, *Cruel World*, 376.

95. Kurek, *Your Life Is Worth Mine*, 48–49.

96. Bogner, "The Convent Children," 35.

97. Kurek, *Your Life Is Worth Mine*, 96, 190.

98. Anna Clarke, "Sister Wanda," *Polin: Studies in Polish Jewry* 7 (1992), 258.

99. Cyprys, *A Jump for Life*, 170.

100. Kurek, *Your Life Is Worth Mine*, 33.

V: WRITTEN IN SMOKE AND ASHES

1. Lifton, *The King of Children*, 323.

2. Korczak, *The Ghetto Years*, 189, 190.

3. Ibid., 91–92; Grynberg, *Words to Outlive Us*, 43; Roland, *Courage Under Siege*, 182.

4. Korczak, *The Ghetto Years*, 98–99.

5. Ibid.; Lifton, *The King of Children*, 324; Korczak, *The Ghetto Years*, 99.

6. Korczak, *The Ghetto Years*, 191.

7. Ibid., 66–67.

8. Ibid., 65–66.

9. Ibid., 79.

10. Rabindranath Tagore, *The Post Office*, trans. Devabrata Mukherjee (1914), available at www.gutenberg.org/files/6523/6523-h/6523-h.htm.

11. Bernheim, *Father of the Orphans*, 142; Jaworski, *Janusz Korczak*, 178.

12. Korczak, *The Ghetto Years*, 81.

13. Ibid., 211–212.

14. Berg, *The Diary of Mary Berg*, 169; Lifton, *The King of Children*, 339.

15. Wladyslaw Szlengel, "A Page from the Deportation Diary," available at "Janusz Korczak Poems and Translations," Cameron, Esther, trans. thehypertexts.com/Janusz_Korczak_Poetry_Poems_Translations_%20by_Esther_Cameron.htm.

16. Hillel Seidman, *The Warsaw Ghetto Diaries*, trans. Yosef Israel (Southfield, MI: Targum Press, 1997), 77.

17. Szpilman, *The Pianist*, 96; Mazzeo, *Irena Sendler's Children*, 122–125.

18. Marek Rudnicki, "My Recollections of the Deportation of Janusz Korczak," *Polin: Studies in Polish Jewry* 7 (1992), 220–221.

19. "Nachum Remba," www.holocaustresearchproject.org/revolt/remba.html.

20. Korczak, *The Ghetto Years*, 97.

21. Ibid., 97–98.

22. Jaworski, *Janusz Korczak*, 189–190; Republic of Poland, Ministry of Foreign Affairs, *The Mass Extermination of Jews in German Occupied Poland* (London: Hutchinson, 1942), 9.

23. Levin, *The Holocaust*, 321.

24. Donat, *The Holocaust Kingdom*, 92.

25. Adina Blady Szwajger, *I Remember Nothing More: The Warsaw Children's Hospital and the Jewish Resistance* (New York: Pantheon Books, 1990), 57, 58.

26. Engelking and Leociak, *The Warsaw Ghetto*, 729; Reuben Ainsztein, *The Warsaw Ghetto Revolt* (New York: Holocaust Library, 1979), 55.

27. Lewin, *A Cup of Tears*, 46–47; Donat, *The Holocaust Kingdom*, 95.

28. Itzhak Katzenelson, "The Day of My Great Disaster," poetryinhell.org /ghetto-hunger-struggle-2/yitzkhok-katzenelson-the-great-day-of-my -disaster.

29. Engelking and Leociak, *The Warsaw Ghetto*, 751; Joseph L. Lichten, "The Warsaw Ghetto Uprising: Legend and Reality," *The Polish Review* 8, no. 3 (Summer 1963), 66–67.

30. Itzhak Katzenelson, "I Had a Dream," info-poland.icm.edu.pl/exhib /ghetto2/dream.html.

31. Jennifer Lassley, "A Defective Covenant: Abandonment of Faith Among Jewish Survivors of the Holocaust," *International Social Science Review* 20, no. 2 (2015), digitalcommons.northgeorgia.edu/issr/vol90/iss2/3; Wladyslaw Szlengel, "It's High Time," in Aaron, "Yiddish and Polish Poetry in the Ghettos and Camps," 78.

32. Kochanski, *The Eagle Unbowed*, 315; Engelking and Leociak, *The Warsaw Ghetto*, 645; Dawidowicz, *The War Against the Jews*, 249–250; Zylberberg, *A Warsaw Diary*, 57.

33. Nehemia Polen, "Cultural and Religious Life in the Warsaw Ghetto," motlc.wiesenthal.com/site/pp.asp?c=ivKVLcMVIsG&b=476145; Friedman, *Martyrs and Fighters*, 103–104; Dawidowicz, *The War Against the Jews*, 308; Cyprys, *A Jump for Life*, 93–94.

34. Ringelblum, *Notes from the Warsaw Ghetto*, 310, 326.

35. Gutman, *Resistance*, 150.

36. Friedman, *Martyrs and Fighters*, 194.

37. Ibid., 199. ZOB is short for Zydowska Organizacja Bojowa.

38. Goldstein, *Five Years in the Warsaw Ghetto*, 101–102; Levin, *The Holocaust*, 326–327; Martin Winstone, *The Dark Heart of Hitler's Europe: Nazi Rule in Poland Under the General Government* (London: I.B. Tauris, 2014), 165–166.

39. Goldstein, *Five Years in the Warsaw Ghetto*, 101–102; Donat, *The Holocaust Kingdom*, 228.

40. Brzezinski, *Isaac's Army*, 145, 146; Engelking and Leociak, *The Warsaw Ghetto*, 750.

41. Szpilman, *The Pianist*, 101; Lukas, *The Forgotten Holocaust*, 176.

42. Zivia Lubetkin, *In the Days of Destruction and Revolt*, trans. Ishai Tubbin (Tel Aviv: Ghetto Fighters' House & Hakibbutz Hameuchad Publishing House, 1981), 91.

43. Dan Kurzman, *The Bravest Battle: The Twenty-Eight Days of the Warsaw Ghetto Uprising* (New York: Putnam, 1976), 31–32.

44. Ibid., 196–197; Israel Shahak, "The 'Life of Death': An Exchange," *New York Review of Books,* January 29, 1987, www.nybooks.com/articles /1987/01/29/the-life-of-death-an-exchange; Gutman, *Resistance*, 170; Levin, *The Holocaust*, 344.

45. Engelking and Leociak, *The Warsaw Ghetto*, 99–100.

46. Levin, *The Holocaust*, 344.

47. Wladyslaw Szlengel, "Counterattack," info-poland.icm.edu.pl/exhib/ghetto2 /bunt.html.

48. Friedman, *Martyrs and Fighters*, 221–222.

49. Gutman, *The Jews of Warsaw*, 343–344, 363; Hanna Krall, *Shielding the Flame: An Intimate Conversation with Dr. Marek Edelman, the Last Surviving Leader of the Warsaw Ghetto Uprising,* trans. Joanna Stasinska and Lawrence Wechsler (New York: Henry Holt, 1986), 262.

50. Zuckerman, *A Surplus of Memory*, 475.

51. Gutman, *Resistance*, 345.

52. Ringelblum, *Notes from the Warsaw Ghetto*, 343; Donat, *The Holocaust Kingdom*, 112; Gutman, *Resistance*, 197.

53. Fritzsche, *Life and Death in the Third Reich*, 297.

54. Lukas, *The Forgotten Holocaust,* 178; Gutman, *Resistance,* 204.

55. Kurzman, *The Bravest Battle,* 30, 129.

56. Gutman, *Resistance,* 207; Kurzman, *The Bravest Battle,* 98, 99.

57. Gilbert, *The Holocaust,* 558.

58. Kurzman, *The Bravest Battle,* 124; Cesarani, *Final Solution,* 614.

59. Gutman, *Resistance,* 203, 209.

60. Jürgen Stroop, *The Stroop Report: The Jewish Quarter of Warsaw Is No More!,* trans. Sybil Milton (New York: Pantheon Books, 1979).

61. Ziviah Lubetkin, "The Last Days of the Warsaw Ghetto: A Survivor's Account of a Heroic Chapter in Jewish History," *Commentary Magazine,* May 1, 1947, www.commentarymagazine.com/articles/the-last-days-of-the-warsaw-ghettoa-survivors-account-of-a-heroic-chapter-in-jewish-history.

62. Edelman, "The Warsaw Ghetto Uprising."

63. Barbara Engelking, *Holocaust and Memory: The Experience of the Holocaust and Its Consequences,* trans. Emma Harris (London: Leicester University Press, 2001), 55; Shahak, "The 'Life of Death'"; Calel Perechodnik, "The Attitudes of the Poles Toward the Jews," www.jewishvirtuallibrary.org/the-attitudes-of-the-poles-toward-the-jews.

64. Gutman, *Resistance,* 229; Zuckerman, *A Surplus of Memory,* 493; Helena Elbaum Dorembus, "Through Helpless Eyes: A Survivor's Diary of the Warsaw Ghetto Uprising," *Moment,* April 1993, 58.

65. Cyprys, *A Jump for Life,* 132; Gutman, *Resistance,* 229; Kurzman, *The Bravest Battle,* 102.

66. Kasimierz Moczarski, *Conversations with an Executioner* (Englewood Cliffs, NJ: Prentice-Hall, 1981), 148–149, 153; Stroop, *The Stroop Report.*

67. David J. Landau, *Caged: A Story of Jewish Resistance* (Sydney: Pan Macmillan Australia, 2000), 97; Stroop, *The Stroop Report.*

68. Engelking and Leociak, *The Warsaw Ghetto,* 784–785; Michael Nevins, "Jewish Medical Ethics: Moral Dilemmas Faced by Jewish Doctors During the Holocaust," www.jewishvirtuallibrary.org/moral-dilemmas-faced-by-jewish-doctors-during-the-holocaust; Cesarani, *Final Solution,* 609.

69. Seidman, *The Warsaw Ghetto Diaries,* 277.

70. Gutman, *Resistance,* 231; Lukas, *The Forgotten Holocaust,* 180; Goldstein, *Five Years in the Warsaw Ghetto,* 171; Engelking and Leociak, *The Warsaw Ghetto,* 787.

71. Kurzman, *The Bravest Battle,* 214.

72. Lubetkin, "The Last Days of the Warsaw Ghetto"; "The Warsaw Ghetto, 1940–3," www.johndclare.net/Nazi_Germany3_WarsawGhetto.html.

73. Stroop, *The Stroop Report*; Moczarski, *Conversations with an Executioner*, 164.

74. Keith Lowe, *Savage Continent: Europe in the Aftermath of World War II* (New York: St. Martin's Press, 2012), 5.

75. Stroop, *The Stroop Report*; Engelking and Leociak, *The Warsaw Ghetto*, 787.

76. Heather Kirk, *Warsaw Spring* (Toronto: Napoleon Publishing, 2001), 244.

77. J. K. Zawodny, *Nothing but Honour: The Story of the Warsaw Uprising, 1944* (Stanford, CA: Hoover Institution Press, 1978), 44, 46.

78. Lukas, *The Forgotten Holocaust*, 97.

79. Ibid., 98; Tadeusz Bor-Komorowski, *The Secret Army: Memoirs of General Bor-Komorowski* (Barnsley, UK: Frontline Books, 2011), 84; Cyprys, *A Jump for Life*, 172–173; Witold Gorski, "I Was 16 at the Time," Warsaw Uprising 1944, www.warsawuprising.com/witness/gorski1.htm.

80. Stargardt, *Witnesses to War*, 250; Lukas, *The Forgotten Holocaust*, 100.

81. Hastings, *Armageddon*, 129; "Ilya Ehrenburg Hate Statement Regarding Germans," forum.axishistory.com/viewtopic.php?t=4243.

82. Vasili Grossman, "The Treblinka Hell," in *The Years of War (1941–1945)*, trans. Elizabeth Donnelly and Rose Prokofiev (Moscow: Foreign Languages Publishing House, 1946), 406–407.

83. Richie, *Warsaw 1944*, 132, 133.

84. Kochanski, *The Eagle Unbowed*, 405; Bernadeta Tendyra, "The Warsaw Women Who Took on Hitler," *The Telegraph*, July 27, 2004, www.telegraph.co.uk/culture/3621391/The-Warsaw-women-who-took-on-Hitler.html.

85. Zawodny, *Nothing but Honour*, 55.

86. Cyprys, *A Jump for Life*, 195; Richie, *Warsaw 1944*, 287, 288; Kochanski, *The Eagle Unbowed*, 406; Lieutenant Peter Stölten, "Letters to the Family," Warsaw Uprising 1944, www.warsawuprising.com/witness/stolten.htm.

87. Thomas D. Parrish, ed., *The Simon and Schuster Encyclopedia of World War II* (New York: Simon and Schuster, 1978), 45.

88. Kochanski, *The Eagle Unbowed*, 406.

89. Zawodny, *Nothing but Honour*, 46, 47; Tendyra, "The Warsaw Women Who Took on Hitler."

90. Levin, *The Holocaust*, 360–361.

91. Timothy Snyder, "Jews, Poles and Nazis: The Terrible History," *New York Review of Books,* June 24, 2010, www.nybooks.com/articles/2010/06/24 /jews-poles-nazis-terrible-history.

92. Lukas, *The Forgotten Holocaust,* 216; Kochanski, *The Eagle Unbowed,* 411.

93. Richie, *Warsaw 1944,* 606–609.

94. Stölten, "Letters to the Family."

95. Gregor Dallas, *Poisoned Peace: 1945—the War That Never Ended* (New Haven, CT: Yale University Press, 2005), 164, 169.

96. Kochanski, *The Eagle Unbowed,* 424.

97. Richie, *Warsaw 1944,* 626–627.

98. Ibid.

99. Lowe, *Savage Continent,* 4.

100. Grynberg, *Words to Outlive Us,* 430.

VI: RECKONINGS

1. Knopp, *Hitler's Children,* 229; Michael H. Kater, *Hitler Youth* (Cambridge, MA: Harvard University Press, 2004), 236; Richard Ernst Schroeder, "The Hitler Youth as a Paramilitary Organization" (PhD diss., University of Illinois–Chicago, 1975), 211–214.

2. Schroeder, "The Hitler Youth as a Paramilitary Organization," 255.

3. Michael E. Sullivan, "Hitler's Teenaged Zealots: Fanatics, Combat Motivation, and the 12th SS Panzer Division Hitlerjugend" (PhD diss., University of New Brunswick, 1999), 23–24, 29; Gerhard Rempel, "The Misguided Generation: Hitler Youth and the S.S., 1933–1945" (PhD diss., University of Wisconsin–Madison, 1971), 697; Knopp, *Hitler's Children,* 227; Kater, *Hitler Youth,* 214.

4. Hastings, *Armageddon,* 557; Rempel, "The Misguided Generation," 248; "Hitler's Boy Soldiers," www.historyplace.com/worldwar2/hitleryouth/hj -boy-soldiers.htm; Nicholas, *Cruel World,* 523.

5. Johannes Steinhoff, Peter Pecher, and Dennis Showalter, eds., *Voices from the Third Reich: An Oral History* (New York: Da Capo Press, 1994), 426; Albert Salomon, "The Spirit of the Soldier and Nazi Militarism," *Social Research* 9, no. 1 (February 1942), 92.

6. Knopp, *Hitler's Children,* 231.

7. Sereny, *Albert Speer,* 533; Walter Kempowski, *Swansong 1945: A Collective Diary of the Last Days of the Third Reich,* trans. Shaun Whiteside (New

York: Norton, 2015), 46, 146, 210, 214; Richard Bessel, *Germany 1945: From War to Peace* (New York: HarperCollins, 2009), 99.

8. Kempowski, *Swansong 1945*, 68.

9. Rempel, "The Misguided Generation," 242, 243; Hastings, *Armageddon*, 548.

10. Junge, *Until the Final Hour*, 175.

11. Hastings, *Armageddon*, 515; Richie, *Faust's Metropolis*, 575. The full text of the Nero Decree is in Louis L. Snyder, ed., *Hitler's Third Reich: A Documentary History* (Chicago: Nelson-Hall, 1981), 503–505.

12. Hillgruber, "War in the East and the Extermination of the Jews."

13. The full text of the "political testament" is in Snyder, *Hitler's Third Reich*, 518–521.

14. Junge, *Until the Final Hour*, 175.

15. Peter Padfield, *Himmler: A Full-Scale Biography of One of Hitler's Most Ruthless Executioners* (New York: MJF Books, 1990), 610, 611.

16. Martin Gilbert, *The Day the War Ended: May 8, 1945—Victory in Europe* (New York: Henry Holt, 1995), 38.

17. Kurzman, *The Bravest Battle*, 347; Sereny, *Into That Darkness*, 365.

18. Norman Davies, *Rising '44: The Battle for Warsaw* (New York: Viking, 2004), 543; Leon Goldenshon, *The Nuremberg Interviews: An American Psychiatrist's Conversations with the Defendants and Witnesses* (New York: Knopf, 2004), 271; Ann Tusa and John Tusa, *The Nuremberg Trial* (New York: Atheneum, 1984), 172; Philip W. Blood, *Hitler's Bandit Hunters: The SS and the Nazi Occupation of Europe* (Washington, DC: Potomac Books, 2008), 278.

19. Giles MacDonogh, *After the Reich: The Brutal History of the Allied Occupation* (New York: Basic Books, 2007), 445; "Erich von dem Bach-Zelewski, SS Leader in Warsaw Razing," obituary, *New York Times*, March 21, 1972, 44. The judges convicted nineteen of the twenty-two defendants at Nuremberg. Twelve, among them Bormann, Göring, von Ribbentrop, Jodl, and Keitel, received death sentences. Because Bormann had evaded capture—historians now think he died while trying to escape from Berlin—he was tried and sentenced in absentia (that is, while absent). Dönitz, Speer, and five others received prison sentences of ten years to life. Three of the accused were acquitted and freed.

20. Posner, *Hitler's Children*, 31; Garry O'Connor, *The Butcher of Poland: Hitler's Lawyer Hans Frank* (Stroud, UK: Spellmount, 2014), 220, 221.

21. Father Brian Jordan, "Chaplain at Nuremberg," www.osv.com/OSV Newsweekly/ByIssue/Article/Tabld/735/ArtMID/13636/ArticleID/10747

/Chaplain-at-Nuremberg.aspx; Goldenshon, *The Nuremberg Interviews,* 24; Frank, *In the Shadow of the Reich,* 47; G. M. Gilbert, *Nuremberg Diary* (New York: Farrar, Straus, 1947), 24, 25, 136, 253, 394; MacDonogh, *After the Reich,* 447–448; Kingsbury Smith, "The Execution of the Nazi War Criminals," law2.umkc.edu/faculty/projects/ftrials/nuremberg/Nuremberg News10_16_46.html.

22. Waite, *The Psychopathic God,* 40–41; Alfred Nestor, *Uncle Hitler: A Child's Traumatic Journey Through Nazi Hell to the Safety of Britain* (London: Mirage, 2011), 50.

23. Peter Longerich, *Heinrich Himmler* (New York: Oxford University Press, 2012), 468; Allan Hall, "Himmler's Daughter Aged 81: She Still Works with Neo-Nazis and Helps SS Officers Evade Justice," *Daily Mail,* June 17, 2011; John Simkin, "Gudrun Himmler," spartacus-educational.com /Gudrun_Himmler.htm.

24. "Famous Nazi Descendants: Reich Ancestry," hitlernews.cloudworth.com /famous-descendants-offspring-children-relatives.php; Belinda Luscombe, "10 Questions for Katrin Himmler," *Time,* November 26, 2012.

25. Posner, *Hitler's Children,* 201.

26. Aron Heller, "Nazi Leader's Grandniece, Jewish Woman Find [*sic*] Peace," *Times Herald,* October 31, 2008; Frances Cronin, "Nazi Legacy: The Troubled Descendants," BBC News, May 23, 2012, www.bbc.com/news /magazine-18120890; Allan Hall, "Hermann Goering's Great-Niece: 'I Had Myself Sterilized So I Would Not Pass On the Blood of a Monster,'" *Daily Mail,* January 20, 2010.

27. Posner, *Hitler's Children,* 13, 31, 40; Warren Manger, "Meet Hitler's Godson," *Daily Mirror,* November 21, 2015, 30.

28. Stephan Lebert and Norbert Lebert, *My Father's Keeper: Children of Nazi Leaders; An Intimate History of Damage and Denial,* trans. Julian Evans (Boston: Little, Brown, 2001), 148; Frank, *In the Shadow of the Reich,* 136–137.

29. Elisabeth Wehrmann, "The Sins of the Fathers," a review of *In the Shadow of the Reich,* by Niklas Frank, *Los Angeles Times,* September 22, 1991, articles.latimes.com/1991–09-22/books/bk-3761_1_niklas-frank; O'Connor, *The Butcher of Poland,* 231, 239–240.

30. Peter Sichrovsky, *Born Guilty: Children of Nazi Families,* trans. Jean Steinberg (New York: Basic Books, 1988), 41–42.

31. Jan T. Gross, *Fear: Anti-Semitism in Poland After Auschwitz* (New York: Random House, 2006), 13.

32. "Anti-Communist Armed Underground in Poland After 1944: An Introduction," The Doomed Soldiers, www.doomedsoldiers.com/introduction .html; Gross, *Fear,* 14–15.

33. Janet Flanner, *Janet Flanner's World: Uncollected Writings, 1932–1975*, ed. Irving Drutman (New York: Harcourt Brace Jovanovich, 1979), 136; Gross, *Fear,* 28; Lowe, *Savage Continent,* 208. By 2011, a mere seventy-five hundred Jews were living in Poland.

34. Morris, *Righteous Victims,* 219.

35. Edwin Black, *The Farhud: Roots of the Arab-Nazi Alliance in the Holocaust* (Washington, DC: Dialog Press, 2010), 324; Glenn B. Infield, *Skorzeny: Hitler's Commando* (New York: St. Martin's Press, 1981), 209.

36. Lochner, *What About Germany?,* 3; Andrey S. Kulikov, "The Sickness Bequeathed: Islamic Anti-Semitism, Nazi Fascism, and Ethno-Centric Nationalism Continuity in the Muslim Middle East" (master's thesis, University of Kansas, 2008), 50, 52, 70; Serge Trifkovic, "Islam's Nazi Connections," archive/frontpagemag.com/Printable.aspx?Artld=20831; Black, *The Farhud,* 324.

37. Michael Rothberg, "W. E. B. DuBois in Warsaw: Holocaust Memory and the Color Line, 1949–1952," *Yale Journal of Criticism* 14, no. 1 (Spring 2001), 172, 177; Michael Rothberg, "From Gaza to Warsaw: Mapping Multidirectional Memory," *Criterion* 53, no. 4 (Fall 2011), 527.

38. Martin Gilbert, *Holocaust Journey: Traveling in Search of the Past* (New York: Columbia University Press, 1997), 315.

39. Geneva Declaration of the Rights of the Child (1924), www.un-documents.net/gdrc1924.htm.

40. U.N. Declaration of the Rights of the Child (1959) and U.N. Convention on the Rights of the Child (1989), Canadian Children's Rights Council, canadiancrc.com/UN_CRC/UN_convention_on_the_Rights_of_the_Child-Overview.aspx.

41. DuBord, "Irena Sendler."

42. Robert Tynes, "Child Soldier Use: The Diffusion of a Tactical Innovation," www.usma.edu/nsc/SiteAssets/SitePages/5th%20Annual%20Network%20Science%20Workshop/The%20Diffusion%20of%20a%20Tactical%20Innovation.pdf?Mobile=1; "The Vietnam War: Children at War," blogs.bl.uk/asian-and-african/2016/02/the-vietnam-war-children-at-war.html.

43. "South Sudan: Warring Parties Break Promises on Child Soldiers," www.hrw.org/print/314321.

44. Quran, 5:32.

45. Matthias Küntzel, "Ahmadinejad's Demons: A Child of the Revolution Takes Over," *The New Republic,* April 24, 2006, www.matthiaskuentzel.de/contents/ahmadinejads-demons.

46. P. W. Singer, *Children at War* (New York: Pantheon Books, 2005), 22; Christoph Reuter, *My Life Is a Weapon: A Modern History of Suicide Bombing*, trans. Helena Ragg-Kirkby (Princeton, NJ: Princeton University Press, 2004), 45, 48, 49.

47. Sharmeen Obaid-Chinoy, "'Children Are Tools to Achieve God's Will,' the Taliban Commander Told Me," Independent, July 29, 2009, www .independent.co.uk/voices/commentators/sharmeen-obaid-chinoy -children-are-tools-to-achieve-gods-will-the-taliban-commander-told-me -1764029; Singer, *Children at War,* 26.

48. Kalsoom Lakhani, "Indoctrinating Children: The Making of Pakistan's Suicide Bombers," *CTC Sentinel* 3, no. 6 (June 2010), 11–13; Combating Terrorism Center at West Point, www.ctc.usma.edu/posts/indoctrinating- children-the-making-of-pakistan%E2%80%99s-suicide-bombers; Wesley J. Smith, "'Kill Down Babies!' ISIS and in the West," www.national review.com/corner/infanticide-down-babies-pushed-isis-and-peter-singer; Dionne Searcey, "Boko Haram Using More Children as Suicide Bomb- ers, UNICEF Says," *New York Times,* April 13, 2016; "Islamic State (ISIS) Releases Pamphlet on Female Slaves," Middle East Research Institute: Jihad and Terrorism Threat Monitor, www.memrijttm.org/islamic-state -releases-pamphlet-on-female-slaves.html.

49. DuBord, "Irena Sendler."

Selected Sources

SOURCES RELATED TO JANUSZ KORCZAK

Arnon, Joseph. "The Passion of Janusz Korczak." *Midstream* 19, no. 5 (May 1973), 32–53.

Bereday, George Z. F. "Janusz Korczak: In Memory of the Hero of Polish Children's Literature." *The Polish Review* 24, no. 1 (1979), 27–32.

Bernheim, Mark. *Father of the Orphans: The Story of Janusz Korczak.* New York: Dutton, 1989.

Bettelheim, Bruno. "Janusz Korczak: A Tale for Our Time." In *Freud's Vienna and Other Essays.* New York: Vintage Books, 1991.

Cameron, Esther, trans. "Janusz Korczak Poems and Translations." thehyper texts.com/Janusz_Korczak_Poetry_Poems_Translations_%20by_Esther _Cameron.htm. A collection of poems about Janusz Korczak.

Cohen, Adir. *The Gate of Light: Janusz Korczak, the Educator and Writer Who Overcame the Holocaust.* Rutherford, NJ: Fairleigh Dickinson University Press, 1994.

Czerwinski, Edward J. "All the Faces of Janusz Korczak." *The Polish Review* 24, no. 1 (1979), 33–38.

Efron, Sara Efrat. "Moral Education Between Hope and Hopelessness: The Legacy of Janusz Korczak." *Curriculum Inquiry* 38, no. 1 (January 2008), 39–62.

Eichsteller, Gabriel. "Janusz Korczak: His Legacy and Its Relevance for Children's Rights Today." *International Journal of Children's Rights* 17, no. 3 (July 2009), 377–391.

Jaworski, Marek. *Janusz Korczak.* Translated by Karol Jakubowicz. Warsaw: Interpress, 1978.

Joseph, Sandra, ed. *A Voice for the Child: The Inspirational Words of Janusz Korczak.* London: Thorsons, 1999.

Korczak, Janusz. *The Ghetto Years: 1939–1942.* Edited by Yitzhak Perlis. Tel Aviv: Ghetto Fighters' House & Hakibbutz Hameuchad Publishing House, 1980. This edition contains an important essay by the editor, "Final Chapter: Korczak in the Warsaw Ghetto."

————. *King Matt the First*. Translated by Richard Lourie. New York: Farrar, Straus & Giroux, 1986. First published in Polish in 1923.

————. *Selected Works of Janusz Korczak*. Edited by Martin Wolins. Translated by Jerzy Bachrach. Washington, DC: National Science Foundation, 1967. Available at Janusz Korczak Association of Canada, januszkorczak.ca/publications.

Lewinski, Jerzy. "The Death of Adam Czerniaków and Janusz Korczak's Last Journey." *Polin: Studies in Polish Jewry* 7 (1992), 224–252.

Lifton, Betty Jean. *The King of Children: A Biography of Janusz Korczak*. New York: Farrar, Straus & Giroux, 1988.

Merzan, Ida. "Ms. Stefania—Janusz Korczak's Closest Associate." Jewish Historical Institute. www.jhi.pl/en/blog/2015-05-25-ms-stefania-janusz-korczak-s-closest-associate.

Rudnicki, Marek. "My Recollections of the Deportation of Janusz Korczak." *Polin: Studies in Polish Jewry* 7 (1992), 219–223.

Stambler, Moses. "Janusz Korczak: His Perspectives on the Child." *The Polish Review* 25, no. 1 (1980), 3–33.

Sterling, Eric. "Janusz Korczak: Scholar-Artist." *The Polish Review* 43, no. 1 (1998), 13–21.

Veerman, Philip E. "In the Shadow of Janusz Korczak: The Story of Stefania Wilczyńska." *The Melton Journal*, no. 3 (Spring 1990), 14–15.

GENERAL SOURCES

Aaron, Frieda W. *Bearing the Unbearable: Yiddish and Polish Poetry in the Ghettos and Concentration Camps*. Albany: State University of New York Press, 1990.

Ainsztein, Reuben. *The Warsaw Ghetto Revolt*. New York: Holocaust Library, 1979.

Allen, Garland E. "Science Misapplied: The Eugenics Age Revisited." *Technology Review* 99, no. 6 (August/September 1996), 22–31. behrenttech.weebly.com/uploads/9/1/0/5/9105268/eugenics.pdf.

Aly, Götz, Peter Chroust, and Christian Pross. *Cleansing the Fatherland: Nazi Medicine and Racial Hygiene*. Translated by Belinda Cooper. Baltimore: Johns Hopkins University Press, 1994.

Arad, Yitzhak. *Belzec, Sobibor, Treblinka: The Operation Reinhard Death Camps*. Bloomington: Indiana University Press, 1999.

Bachrach, Susan. "In the Name of Public Health—Nazi Racial Hygiene." *New England Journal of Medicine* 351 (July 29, 2004), 417–420.

Barondess, Jeremiah A. "Medicine Against Society: Lessons from the Third Reich." *JAMA* 276, no. 20 (November 27, 1996), 1657–1661.

Bauer, Yehuda. *A History of the Holocaust*. New York: Franklin Watts, 1982.

Bauman, Janina. *Beyond These Walls: Escaping the Warsaw Ghetto; A Young Girl's Story*. London: Virago Press, 2006.

———. *Winter in the Morning: A Young Girl's Life in the Warsaw Ghetto and Beyond, 1939–1945*. New York: Free Press, 1986.

Beevor, Antony. *The Fall of Berlin, 1945*. New York: Viking, 2002.

Berding, Joop W. A., "Janusz Korczak—An Introduction," korczak.info/pdf/nl /joop-berding_korczak.introduction.pdf.

———. "Janusz Korczak: What It Means to Become an Educator," *Encounter: Education for Meaning and Social Justice*, Winter 2004, 11–16.

Berg, Mary. *The Diary of Mary Berg: Growing Up in the Warsaw Ghetto*. Translated by Norbert Guterman and Sylvia Glass. Oxford: OneWorld, 2007. First published in 1945 as *Warsaw Ghetto, a Diary by Mary Berg*.

Berman, Adolf. "The Fate of the Children in the Warsaw Ghetto." In *The Catastrophe of European Jewry*, edited by Yisrael Gutman and Livia Rothkirchen, 400–421. Jerusalem: Yad Vashem, 1976.

Bernheim, Mark. *Father of the Orphans: The Story of Janusz Korczak* (New York: Dutton, 1989).

Bingham, Marjorie Wall. "Women and the Warsaw Ghetto: A Moment to Decide." *World History Connected* 6, no. 1. worldhistoryconnected.press.illinois .edu/6.2/bingham.html.

Biskupska, Jadwiga M. "Extermination and the Elite: Warsaw Under the Nazi Occupation, 1939–1944." PhD diss., Yale University, 2013.

Black, Edwin. *War Against the Weak: Eugenics and America's Campaign to Create a Master Race*. New York: Four Walls Eight Windows, 2003.

Blackburn, Gilmer W. *Education in the Third Reich: A Study of Race and History in Nazi Textbooks*. Albany: State University of New York Press, 1985.

Bleuel, Hans Peter. *Sex and Society in Nazi Germany*. Translated by J. Maxwell Brownjohn. Philadelphia: Lippincott, 1973.

Block, Gay, and Malka Drucker. *Rescuers: Portraits of Moral Courage in the Holocaust*. New York: Holmes & Meier, 1992.

Bock, Gisela. "Racism and Sexism in Nazi Germany: Motherhood, Compulsory Sterilization, and the State." *Signs* 8, no. 4 (Spring 1983), 400–421.

Bogner, Nahum. "The Convent Children: The Rescue of Jewish Children in Polish Convents During the Holocaust." www.yadvashem.org/righteous/resources /rescue-of-jewish-children-in-polish-convents.html.

Breitman, Richard. *The Architect of Genocide: Himmler and the Final Solution.* New York: Knopf, 1991.

———. "Himmler and the 'Terrible Secret' Among the Executioners." *Journal of Contemporary History* 26, no. 3/4 (September 1991), 431–451.

Browning, Christopher R. *Ordinary Men: Reserve Police Battalion 101 and the Final Solution in Poland.* New York: Harper Perennial, 1993.

Brzezinski, Matthew. *Isaac's Army: A Story of Courage and Survival in Nazi-Occupied Poland.* New York: Random House, 2012.

Burleigh, Michael. *Death and Deliverance: "Euthanasia" in Germany, c. 1900–1945.* New York: Cambridge University Press, 1994.

———. *The Third Reich: A New History.* London: Macmillan, 2000.

Burleigh, Michael, and Wolfgang Wippermann. *The Racial State: Germany, 1933–1945.* New York: Cambridge University Press, 1991.

Carpenter, John, and Bogdana Carpenter. "Władysław Szlengel." *Chicago Review* 52, no. 2/4 (Autumn 2006), 287–291.

Cesarani, David. *Final Solution: The Fate of the Jews, 1933–1949.* New York: St. Martin's Press, 2016.

Clarke, Anna. "Sister Wanda." *Polin: Studies in Polish Jewry* 7 (1992), 253–259.

Clay, Catrine, and Michael Leapman. *Master Race: The* Lebensborn *Experiment in Nazi Germany.* London: Hodder & Stoughton, 1995.

Corelli, Marie. "Poisoning Young Minds in Nazi Germany: Children and Propaganda in the Third Reich." *Social Education* 66, no. 4 (May–June 2002), 228–233.

Cyprys, Ruth Altbeker. *A Jump for Life: A Survivor's Journal from Nazi-Occupied Poland.* New York: Continuum, 1997.

Czerniaków, Adam. *The Warsaw Diary of Adam Czerniaków: Prelude to Doom.* Edited by Raul Hilberg et al. Translated by Stanislaw Staron et al. New York: Stein and Day, 1979.

David, Janina. *A Square of Sky and a Touch of Earth: A Wartime Childhood in Poland.* New York: Penguin Books, 1981.

Davidson, Eugene, comp. *The Trial of the Germans: An Account of the Twenty-Two Defendants Before the International Military Tribunal at Nuremberg.* New York: Macmillan, 1966.

Dawidowicz, Lucy S. *The War Against the Jews, 1933–1945.* New York: Holt, Rinehart and Winston, 1975.

Donat, Alexander, ed. *The Death Camp Treblinka: A Documentary.* New York: Holocaust Library, 1979. Long excerpts can be found at "Treblinka: Eye-

witness Accounts," holocaustcontroversies.yuku.com/topic/1916/Re-Treblinka
-Eyewitness-Accounts#.V9614_krJD9.

———. *The Holocaust Kingdom: A Memoir*. New York: Holt, Rinehart and Winston, 1965.

Dwork, Debórah, and Robert Jan Van Pelt. *Flight from the Reich: Refugee Jews, 1933–1946*. New York: Norton, 2009.

Edelman, Marek. "The Warsaw Ghetto Uprising." In *The Warsaw Ghetto: The 45th Anniversary of the Uprising*, 17–39. Warsaw: Interpress, 1987. www.writing.upenn.edu/~afilreis/Holocaust/warsaw-uprising.html.

Eisenberg, Azriel, ed. *Witness to the Holocaust*. New York: Pilgrim Press, 1981.

Engelking, Barbara, and Jacek Leociak. *The Warsaw Ghetto: A Guide to the Perished City*. Translated by Emily Harris. New Haven, CT: Yale University Press, 2009.

Engelmann, Bernt. *In Hitler's Germany: Everyday Life in the Third Reich*. Translated by Krishna Winston. New York: Schocken Books, 1988.

Evans, Richard J. *The Third Reich at War: How the Nazis Led Germany from Conquest to Disaster*. New York: Penguin Press, 2009.

Evans, Suzanne E. *Forgotten Crimes: The Holocaust and People with Disabilities*. Chicago: Ivan R. Dee, 2004.

Fleming, Gerald. *Hitler and the Final Solution*. Berkeley: University of California Press, 1984.

Frank, Niklas. *In the Shadow of the Reich*. Translated by Arthur S. Wensinger. New York: Knopf, 1991.

Friedlander, Henry. *The Origins of Nazi Genocide: From Euthanasia to the Final Solution*. Chapel Hill: University of North Carolina Press, 1995.

Friedländer, Saul. *Nazi Germany and the Jews: The Years of Extermination, 1939–1945*. New York: HarperCollins, 2007.

———. *Nazi Germany and the Jews: The Years of Persecution, 1933–1939*. New York: Harper Perennial, 1998.

Friedman, Philip, ed. *Martyrs and Fighters: The Epic of the Warsaw Ghetto*. New York: Praeger, 1954.

Fritzsche, Peter. *An Iron Wind: Europe Under Hitler*. New York: Basic Books, 2016.

Furth, Hans G. "One Million Polish Rescuers of Hunted Jews?" *Journal of Genocide Research* 1, no. 2 (1999), 227–232.

Gallagher, Hugh Gregory. *By Trust Betrayed: Patients, Physicians, and the License to Kill in the Third Reich*. New York: Henry Holt, 1990.

Garlinski, Józef. "The Polish Underground State (1939–45)." *Journal of Contemporary History* 10, no. 2 (April 1975), 219–259.

Gerwarth, Robert. *Hitler's Hangman: The Life of Heydrich*. New Haven, CT: Yale University Press, 2011.

Gessner, Peter K. "Irena Sendler: WWII Rescuer and Hero." info-poland.icm .edu.pl/classroom/sendler/index.html.

Gilbert, G. M. *Nuremberg Diary*. New York: Farrar, Straus, 1947.

Gilbert, Martin. *A History of the Twentieth Century*. Vol. 2, *1933–1951*. New York: Morrow, 1999.

———. *The Holocaust: A History of the Jews of Europe During the Second World War*. New York: Holt, Rinehart and Winston, 1985.

———. *Holocaust Journey: Traveling in Search of the Past*. New York: Columbia University Press, 1997.

———. *Kristallnacht: Prelude to Destruction*. New York: HarperCollins, 2006.

Gillon, Adam, et al. " 'Here Too as in Jerusalem': Selected Poems of the Ghetto." *The Polish Review* 10, no. 3 (Summer 1965), 22–42.

Glass, James M. *"Life Unworthy of Life": Racial Phobia and Mass Murder in Hitler's Germany*. New York: Basic Books, 1997.

Goldenshon, Leon. *The Nuremberg Interviews: An American Psychiatrist's Conversations with Defendants and Witnesses*. New York: Knopf, 2004.

Goldhagen, Daniel Jonah. *Hitler's Willing Executioners: Ordinary Germans and the Holocaust*. New York: Knopf, 1996.

Goldstein, Bernard. *Five Years in the Warsaw Ghetto (The Stars Bear Witness)*. Edinburgh: AK Press/Nabat, 2005.

Gross, Jan T. *Fear: Anti-Semitism in Poland After Auschwitz*. New York: Random House, 2006.

Grunberger, Richard. *The 12-Year Reich: A Social History of Nazi Germany, 1933–1945*. New York: Holt, Rinehart and Winston, 1971.

Grynberg, Michal, ed. *Words to Outlive Us: Voices from the Warsaw Ghetto*. Translated by Philip Boehm. New York: Henry Holt, 2002.

Gutman, Israel. *The Jews of Warsaw, 1939–1943: Ghetto, Underground, Revolt*. Bloomington: Indiana University Press, 1982.

———. *Resistance: The Warsaw Ghetto Uprising*. Boston: Houghton Mifflin, 1994.

Hagen, Louis. *Ein Volk, Ein Reich: Nine Lives Under the Nazis*. Stroud, UK: Spellmount, 2011.

Halter, Marek. *Stories of Deliverance: Speaking with Men and Women Who Rescued Jews from the Holocaust.* Translated by Michael Bernard. Chicago: Open Court, 1998.

Hayes, Peter. *Why? Explaining the Holocaust.* New York: Norton, 2017.

Heller, Celia S. *On the Edge of Destruction: Jews of Poland Between the Two World Wars.* New York: Columbia University Press, 1977.

Hillel, Marc, and Clarissa Henry. *Of Pure Blood.* Translated by Eric Mossbacher. New York: McGraw-Hill, 1976.

Hitler, Adolf. *Hitler's Table Talk, 1941–1944.* Translated by Norman Cameron and R. H. Stevens. New York: Enigma Books, 2000.

———. *Mein Kampf.* Translated by Ralph Manheim. Boston: Houghton Mifflin, 1999. First published in German in 1925.

Höhne, Heinz. *The Order of the Death's Head: The Story of Hitler's SS.* Translated by Richard Barry. New York: Coward-McCann, 1970.

Housden, Martyn. *Hans Frank,* Lebensraum *and the Holocaust.* New York: Palgrave Macmillan, 2003.

Jäckel, Eberhard. *Hitler's World View: A Blueprint for Power.* Translated by Herbert Arnold. Cambridge, MA: Harvard University Press, 1981.

Johnson, Eric A., and Karl-Heinz Reuband, eds. *What We Knew: Terror, Mass Murder, and Everyday Life in Nazi Germany; An Oral History.* New York: Basic Books, 2005.

Junge, Traudl. *Until the Final Hour: Hitler's Last Secretary.* Translated by Anthea Bell. New York: Arcade, 2004.

Kaplan, Chaim Aron. *Scroll of Agony: The Warsaw Diary of Chaim A. Kaplan.* Translated by Abraham I. Katsh. New York: Macmillan, 1965. Reprint, New York: Collier Books, 1981.

Kaplan, Marion A. *Between Dignity and Despair: Jewish Life in Nazi Germany.* New York: Oxford University Press, 1998.

Kassow, Samuel D. *Who Will Write Our History? Emanuel Ringelblum, the Warsaw Ghetto, and the Oyneg Shabes Archive.* Bloomington: University of Indiana Press, 2007.

Kater, Michael H. *Hitler Youth.* Cambridge, MA: Harvard University Press, 2004.

Kershaw, Ian. *The End: The Defiance and Destruction of Hitler's Germany, 1944–1945.* New York: Penguin Press, 2011.

———. "Hitler's Role in the 'Final Solution.'" www.genocideeducation.ca /kershaw.pdf.

Kessler, Karl. "Physicians and the Nazi Euthanasia Program." *International Journal of Mental Health* 36, no. 1 (Spring 2007), 4–16.

Klee, Ernst, ed. *"The Good Old Days": The Holocaust as Seen by Its Perpetrators and Bystanders.* Translated by Deborah Burnstone. New York: Free Press, 1991.

Kloczowski, Jerzy. "The Religious Orders and the Jews in Nazi-Occupied Poland." *Polin: Studies in Polish Jewry* 3 (1988), 238–243.

Knopp, Guido. *Hitler's Children.* Translated by Angus McGeoch. Stroud, UK: Sutton, 2002.

Koch, H. W. *The Hitler Youth: Origins and Development, 1922–1945.* New York: Stein and Day, 1975.

Kochanski, Halik. *The Eagle Unbowed: Poland and the Poles in the Second World War.* Cambridge, MA: Harvard University Press, 2012.

Koonz, Claudia. *The Nazi Conscience.* Cambridge, MA: Belknap Press, 2003.

Korbonski, Stefan. *The Jews and the Poles in World War II.* New York: Hippocrene Books, 1989.

Krynski, Magnus J., and Robert A. Maguire. "Anna Swirszczynska: Thirty-Four Poems on the Warsaw Uprising." *The Polish Review* 22, no. 3 (1977), 77–100.

Kurek, Ewa. *Your Life Is Worth Mine: How Polish Nuns in World War II Saved Hundreds of Jewish Lives in German-Occupied Poland, 1939–1945.* New York: Hippocrene Books, 1997.

Kurzman, Dan. *The Bravest Battle: The Twenty-Eight Days of the Warsaw Ghetto Uprising.* New York: Putnam, 1976.

Landau, David J. *Caged: A Story of Jewish Resistance.* Sydney: Pan Macmillan Australia, 2000.

Langer, Walter C. *The Mind of Adolf Hitler: The Secret Wartime Report.* New York: Basic Books, 1972.

Lebert, Stephan, and Norbert Lebert. *My Father's Keeper: Children of Nazi Leaders; An Intimate History of Damage and Denial.* Translated by Julian Evans. Boston: Little, Brown, 2001.

Levin, Nora. *The Holocaust: The Destruction of European Jewry, 1933–1945.* New York: Thomas Y. Crowell, 1968.

Lewin, Abraham. *A Cup of Tears: A Diary of the Warsaw Ghetto.* Translated by Christopher Hutton. Oxford: Basil Blackwell, 1988.

Lifton, Robert Jay. *The Nazi Doctors: Medical Killing and the Psychology of Genocide.* New York: Basic Books, 1986.

Longerich, Peter. *Heinrich Himmler.* New York: Oxford University Press, 2012.

Lower, Wendy. *Hitler's Furies: German Women in the Killing Fields.* Boston: Houghton Mifflin, 2013.

Lubetkin, Zivia. *In the Days of Destruction and Revolt.* Translated by Ishai Tubbin. Tel Aviv: Ghetto Fighters' House & Hakibbutz Hameuchad Publishing House, 1981.

Lukas, Richard C. *Did the Children Cry? Hitler's War Against Jewish and Polish Children, 1939–1945.* New York: Hippocrene Books, 1994.

———. *The Forgotten Holocaust: The Poles Under German Occupation, 1939–1944.* Lexington: University Press of Kentucky, 1986. Reprint, New York: Hippocrene Books, 1997.

———. "Irena Sendler: World War II's Polish Angel." www.franciscamedia.org /irena-sendler-world-war-iis-polish-angel.

———, ed. *Out of the Inferno: Poles Remember the Holocaust.* Lexington: University Press of Kentucky, 1989.

Mazor, Michel. *The Vanished City: Everyday Life in the Warsaw Ghetto.* New York: Marsilio, 1994.

Mazower, Mark. *Hitler's Empire: How the Nazis Ruled Europe.* New York: Penguin Press, 2008.

Mazzeo, Tilar J. *Irena Sendler's Children: The Extraordinary Story of the Woman Who Saved 2,500 Children from the Warsaw Ghetto.* New York: Gallery Books, 2017.

Meed, Vladka. *On Both Sides of the Wall: Memoirs from the Warsaw Ghetto.* Translated by Steven Meed. New York: Holocaust Library, 1979.

Mehler, Barry. "Eliminating the Inferior: American and Nazi Sterilization Programs." *Science for the People* 19, no. 6 (November/December 1987), 14–18. ferris-pages.org/ISHR/archives2/mehler/eliminating.htm.

Michlic, Joanna Beata. *Poland's Threatening Other: The Image of the Jew from 1880 to the Present.* Lincoln: University of Nebraska Press, 2006.

Mills, Mary. "Propaganda and Children During the Hitler Years." www.nizkor .org/hweb/people/m/mills-mary/mills-00.html.

Montagu, Ashley. *Man's Most Dangerous Myth: The Fallacy of Race.* New York: Columbia University Press, 1942. Reprint, Cleveland: World Publishing, 1964.

Moskovitz, Sarah Traister, trans. "Poetry in Hell: Yiddish Poetry in the Ringelblum Archives." poetryinhell.org.

Nicholas, Lynn H. *Cruel World: The Children of Europe in the Nazi Web.* New York: Knopf, 2005.

Noakes, Jeremy, and Geoffrey Pridham, eds. *Nazism, 1919–1945: A History in Documents and Eyewitness Accounts.* New York: Schocken Books, 1990.

O'Connor, Garry. *The Butcher of Poland: Hitler's Lawyer Hans Frank.* Stroud, UK: Spellmount, 2014.

Padfield, Peter. *Himmler.* New York: MJF Books, 1997.

Paldiel, Mordecai. *Churches and the Holocaust: Unholy Teaching, Good Samaritans, and Reconciliation.* Jersey City, NJ: KTAV Publishing House, 2006.

Paulsson, Gunnar S. *Secret City: The Hidden Jews of Warsaw, 1940–1945.* New Haven, CT: Yale University Press, 2002.

Peukert, Detlev J. K. *Inside Nazi Germany: Conformity, Opposition, and Racism in Everyday Life.* Translated by Richard Deveson. New Haven, CT: Yale University Press, 1987.

Phayer, Michael. *The Catholic Church and the Holocaust, 1930–1965.* Bloomington: Indiana University Press, 2000.

Posner, Gerald L. *Hitler's Children: Sons and Daughters of Leaders of the Third Reich Talk About Their Fathers and Themselves.* New York: Random House, 1991.

Redlich, Fritz. *Hitler: Diagnosis of a Destructive Prophet.* New York: Oxford University Press, 1998.

Reimann, Viktor: *Goebbels: The Man Who Created Hitler.* Garden City, NY: Doubleday, 1976.

Rempel, Gerhard. *Hitler's Children: The Hitler Youth and the SS.* Chapel Hill: University of North Carolina Press, 1989.

Rhodes, Richard. *Masters of Death: The SS-Einsatzgruppen and the Invention of the Holocaust.* New York: Knopf, 2002.

Richie, Alexandra. *Warsaw 1944: Hitler, Himmler, and the Warsaw Uprising.* New York: Farrar, Straus & Giroux, 2013.

Ringelblum, Emanuel. *Notes from the Warsaw Ghetto: The Journal of Emanuel Ringelblum.* Translated by Jacob Sloan. New York: McGraw-Hill, 1958. Reprint, New York: Schocken Books, 1974.

———. *Polish-Jewish Relations During the Second World War.* Translated by Dafna Allen et al. Jerusalem: Yad Vashem, 1974.

Rogow, Sally M. "Hitler's Unwanted Children: Children with Disabilities, Orphans, Juvenile Deliquents, and Non-Conformist Young People in Nazi Germany." www.holocaust-trc.org/wp-content/uploads/2013/02/unwanted.pdf.

Roland, Charles G. *Courage Under Siege: Starvation, Disease, and Death in the Warsaw Ghetto.* New York: Oxford University Press, 1992.

Rupp, Leila J. "Mother of the 'Volk': The Image of Women in Nazi Ideology." *Signs* 3, no. 2 (Winter 1977), 362–379.

Segev, Tom. *Soldiers of Evil: The Commandants of the Nazi Concentration Camps.* Translated by Haim Watzman. New York: McGraw-Hill, 1987.

Seidman, Hillel. *The Warsaw Ghetto Diaries*. Translated by Yosef Israel. Southfield, MI: Targum Press, 1997.

Sendler, Irena. "How I Rescued Children from the Warsaw Ghetto." www .dzieciholocaustu.org.pl/szab58.php?s=en_sendlerowa.php.

Sherwin, Byron L. *Sparks Amidst the Ashes: The Spiritual Legacy of Polish Jewry*. New York: Oxford University Press, 1997.

Shmeruk, Chone. "Isaac Bashevis Singer on Bruno Schulz." *The Polish Review* 36, no. 2 (1991), 161–167.

———. "Polish-Jewish Relations in the Historical Fiction of Isaac Bashevis Singer." *The Polish Review* 32, no. 4 (1987), 401–413.

Sichrovsky, Peter. *Born Guilty: Children of Nazi Families*. Translated by Jean Steinberg. New York: Basic Books, 1988.

Snyder, Timothy. *Bloodlands: Europe Between Hitler and Stalin*. New York: Basic Books, 2010.

Stargardt, Nicholas. *Witnesses to War: Children's Lives Under the Nazis*. New York: Knopf, 2006.

Steiner, Jean-François. *Treblinka*. Translated by Helen Weaver. New York: Simon and Schuster, 1967.

Steinhoff, Johannes, Peter Pecher, and Dennis Showalter, eds. *Voices from the Third Reich: An Oral History*. New York: Da Capo Press, 1994.

Szpilman, Władysław. *The Pianist: The Extraordinary Story of One Man's Survival in Warsaw, 1939–45*. Toronto: McArthur, 2003. *The Pianist* was later made into a powerful film depicting courage and survival in the midst of horror.

Szubert, Maria. *Between Black Death and Red Plague: A Personal Snapshot; The Second World War and Life Under Communism in Poland Through the Eyes of a Survivor*. 2014. lulu.com.

Szwajger, Adina Blady. *I Remember Nothing More: The Warsaw Children's Hospital and the Jewish Resistance*. New York: Pantheon Books, 1990.

Tec, Nechama. *When Light Pierced Darkness: Christian Rescue of Jews in Nazi-Occupied Poland*. New York: Oxford University Press, 1986.

Tomaszewski, Irene, and Tecia Werbowski. *Zegota: The Rescue of Jews in Wartime Poland*. Montreal: Price-Patterson, 1994.

Trunk, Isaiah. *Judenrat: The Jewish Councils in Eastern Europe Under Nazi Occupation*. New York: Macmillan, 1972.

Tubach, Frederic C. *German Voices: Memories of Life During Hitler's Third Reich*. Berkeley: University of California Press, 2011.

Waite, Robert G. L. *The Psychopathic God: Adolf Hitler*. New York: Basic Books, 1977.

Wiernik, Jankel. *A Year in Treblinka.* New York: American Representation of the General Jewish Workers' Union of Poland, 1945.

Winstone, Martin. *The Dark Heart of Hitler's Europe: Nazi Rule in Poland Under the General Government.* London: I.B. Tauris, 2014.

Wistrich, Robert S. *Hitler's Apocalypse: Jews and the Nazi Legacy.* New York: St. Martin's Press, 1985.

Zawodny, J. K. *Nothing but Honour: The Story of the Warsaw Uprising, 1944.* Stanford, CA: Hoover Institution Press, 1978.

Zimmerman, Joshua D. *The Polish Underground and the Jews, 1939–1945.* New York: Cambridge University Press, 2015.

Zuckerman, Yitzhak, "Antek." *A Surplus of Memory: Chronicle of the Warsaw Ghetto Uprising.* Translated by Barbara Harshav. Berkeley: University of California Press, 1993.

Zylberberg, Michael. *A Warsaw Diary, 1939–1945.* London: Vallentine, Mitchell, 1969.

PHOTOGRAPH COLLECTIONS

Georg, Willy. *In the Warsaw Ghetto: Summer 1941.* New York: Aperture, 1993. Photographs taken by a German soldier inside the Warsaw ghetto in the summer of 1941.

Keller, Ulrich, ed. *The Warsaw Ghetto in Photographs: 206 Views Made in 1941.* New York: Dover, 1984. These photos were made by German propaganda teams to highlight Jewish "depravity."

Vishniac, Roman. *A Vanished World.* New York: Farrar, Straus & Giroux, 1983. A classic collection by a world-famous photographer of Jewish life in Eastern Europe from 1935 to 1938, before the Holocaust.

———. *Children of a Vanished World.* Edited by Mara Vishniac Kohn and Miriam Hartman Flacks. Berkeley: University of California Press, 1999. Photographs by Vishniac showing the daily life of Jewish children in Eastern Europe from 1935 to 1938.

DOCUMENTARIES

Knopp, Guido, dir. *Hitler's Children.* 2000. English version 2014. top documentaryfilms.com/hitlers-children. A five-part history of Hitler Youth as told in film footage and interviews with former members.

Ze'evi, Chanoch, dir. *Hitler's Children.* 2011. Distributed by Film Movement. Interviews with children and relatives of major Nazi war criminals, including Katrin Himmler, Niklas Frank, and Bettina Göring.

Picture Credits

Alamy: 5, 87
Alfred A. Knopf Books for Young Readers: 285
Austrian National Library: 93
Bettmann/Getty: 95
Cezary p: 326
Galerie Bilderwelt/Getty: 113
German Federal Archives: 58, 64, 66, 67, 69, 83, 86, 152, 169, 173, 290, 291, 292, 301, 303, 307, 313
Getty: 81, 217, 323 (bottom)
Ira Nowinski/Corbis/VCG: 2
Israel Images: 16
Joe LeMonnier: 150
John Florea/Getty: 302
Keystone-France/Getty: 100
Kirn Vintage Stock/Getty: 96
PD-Egypt: 323 (top)
PD-Poland: 147, 149, 163, 205, 229, 264, 272, 284, 295

PD-US: 6, 23, 35, 49, 73, 89, 90, 127, 130, 134, 207, 260, 274, 283, 306, 309, 310, 328
Roger-Viollet/Getty: 107
Roman Wroblewski: 25, 31, 170, 248
Samuel and Ada Willenberg: 212
Shutterstock: 13, 57, 123, 181, 239, 299
Simon Cygielski: 327
Stadtarchiv München: 144
Steven Heller: 61, 62
Ullstein Bild Dtl./Getty: 43, 97, 111
United States Holocaust Memorial Museum: 60, 235, 253, 275, 279
Universal History Archive/Getty: 104, 116
Universal Images Group/Getty: 114
woody1778a: 146
Yad Vashem: 141, 193, 282

Index

ALSO BY ALBERT MARRIN

Black Gold: The Story of Oil in Our Lives

FDR and the American Crisis

Flesh & Blood So Cheap: The Triangle Fire and Its Legacy
A National Book Award Finalist

Thomas Paine: Crusader for Liberty

Uprooted: The Japanese American Experience During World War II
A Sibert Honor Book

Very, Very, Very Dreadful: The Influenza Pandemic of 1918

A Volcano Beneath the Snow: John Brown's War Against Slavery

A Light in the Darkness